THE CONVICT GIRL

Published by

Librario Publishing Ltd

ISBN: 1-904440-77-0

Copies can be ordered via the Internet
www.librario.com

or from:

Brough House, Milton Brodie, Kinloss
Moray IV36 2UA
Tel /Fax No 00 44 (0)1343 850 617

Printed and bound by Digisource GB Ltd

MARY BRYANT
THE CONVICT GIRL
The Real Story

To Keith & Linda,
Thanks for everything.
Love,
Laurie Sheehan
13 August 2006

By

LAURIE SHEEHAN

Librario

Dedicated to the memory of my beloved mother,

ELSIE SHEEHAN

ACKNOWLEDGEMENTS

I am especially indebted to the writings of 'Bryant expert' C.H. Currey and those of Watkin Tench, John White, David Collins, Arthur Phillip, John Hunter, William Bradley, George B. Worgan, Ralph Clark, John Easty, James Scott, Arthur Bowes Smyth, Jon Nicol, William Bligh, Edward Edwards, James Boswell, Arthur Young, Mollie Gillen, John Keast, Sir Arthur Quiller-Couch, Geoffrey C. Ingleton, Frederick A. Pottle, John Cobley, Geoffrey Rawson, Portia Robinson, John Beattie, Peter King, Deborah Oxley, Lucia Zedner, Margaret E. De Lacy, Marjorie Barnard Eldershaw, Henry N. Shore, Antony D. Hippisley Coxe, Robert Hughes, Thomas Keneally, Jonathan King, Neil K. Macintosh, Paul-Alan Johnson, Cahal Dallat, Jonathan Bell and, not least, James Martin.

Thanks are due to Joanne Hillman of the County Local Studies Library, Redruth, Cornwall; Linda Greenwood, Irish and Local Studies Librarian, Central Library, Belfast; Sheila McGoran and her fellow members of The Glens of Antrim Historical Society; the staff of Worthing Library and the Revd A. E. Allardice.

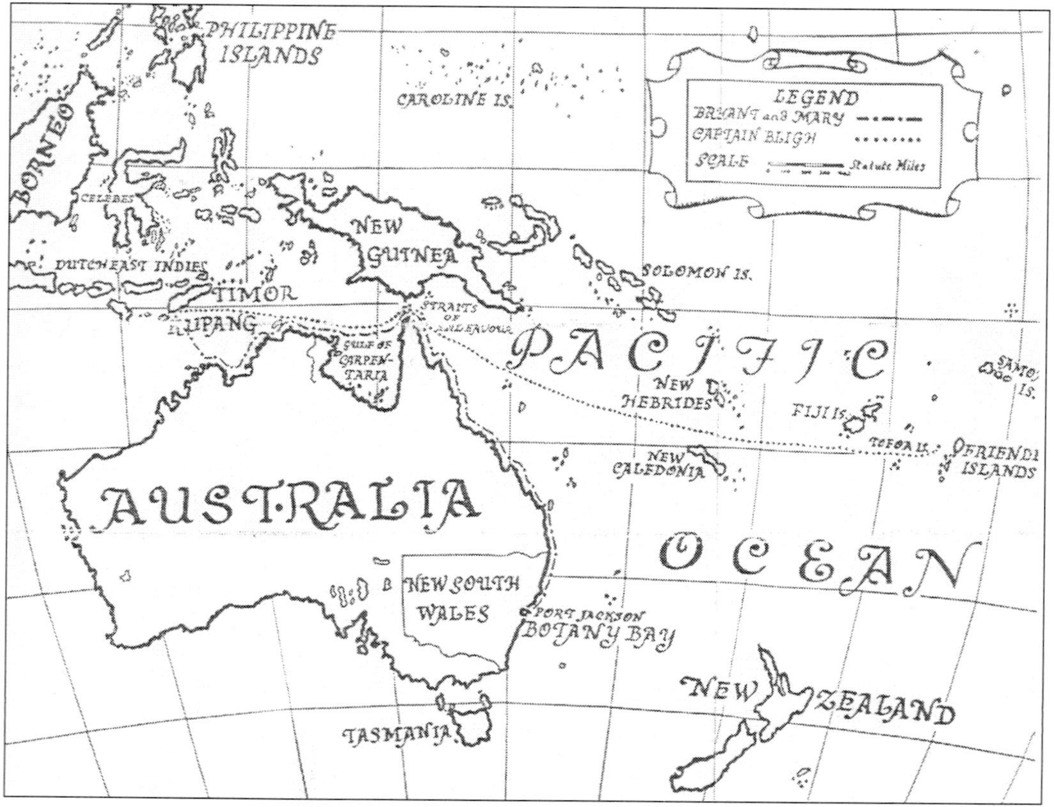
LEGEND
BRYANT and MARY
CAPTAIN BLIGH
SCALE
Statute Miles
PHILIPPINE ISLANDS
CAROLINE IS.
BORNEO
CELEBES
DUTCH EAST INDIES
TIMOR
KUPANG
NEW GUINEA
STRAITS OF ENDEAVOUR
GULF OF CARPENTARIA
SOLOMON IS.
PACIFIC
OCEAN
NEW HEBRIDES
FIJI IS.
TOFOA IS.
FRIENDLY ISLANDS
NEW CALEDONIA
AUSTRALIA
NEW SOUTH WALES
PORT JACKSON
BOTANY BAY
NEW ZEALAND
TASMANIA

CHAPTER 1

Will Bryant was his own man. Not for him the shared spoils of an organized smuggling run. Let other Cornish fishermen work for an organization, 'Cap'n Will' wanted the 'Cousin Jack', the cognac, for himself.

He had bought the two small kegs in France, 140 miles away by sea. John Copinger's warehouse in Roscoff, Brittany, had charged him just 42 shillings. To buy a pair of kegs in England would have cost 272 plaguy shillings. Customs duty alone was 60 shillings – £3! Curse the Government, those Englishmen – those bloody foreigners! – in faraway London who had the audacity to tax a Celtic Cornishman.

He had done well on this trip, selling a £3 English anvil to a Breton for £7, thus paying for the purchase of the contraband. God bless those fellow Celts.

Guided by the starlit outline of Lelant church tower, he steered the fishing boat up the Hayle estuary. In truth, he could see two church towers, as he had partaken of a bottle of the stuff to warm himself on this windy December night of 1783. The precious kegs themselves were snug at his feet. The tubs were linked by two short lengths of rope for carrying ashore on his chest and back.

His own man indeed. *He* would not be hiding *his* kegs in that lonely church, nestling in the towans, the dunes, and at risk of being engulfed by the drifting sand. That was where the organized smugglers secreted their contraband, on weekdays, with the brandy-swigging vicar's permission. Rot that! Will Bryant would never set foot in St Uny's. He was no church sheep; he was a chapel man, dammit: a Wesleyan Methodist.

His eyes scanning the water and the extensive dunes for any sign of the revenue men, he began thinking about Methodism's founder. Before Will had been born, John Wesley had preached in the nearby port of St Ives against smuggling. Brave Wesley was his own man, too, and had been struck by stones and bad eggs thrown by the local smugglers. But eleven years later the preacher had returned to north Cornwall, believing his words had been effective and 'since that accursed thing is put away the work of God is everywhere increased'. Effective? Wesley had been a danged fool to think that smuggling had ended. And if he'd thought that the likes of Will Bryant would give up drinking as well, he'd been an even bigger fool.

Will couldn't help but admire the old man, though. Wesley's life had often been in danger but, undaunted, he'd travelled a quarter of a million miles and preached something like forty thousand sermons, folk said. And, good luck to him, he was still travelling and preaching now.

Will Bryant had covered a few miles himself since those happy days as a fisherlad on this old boat of his father's, the *Jane.* Will had long since taken over the vessel from the old fellow. William Bryant senior had taught his son well, and not for nothing was the twenty-six-year-old called a master seiner. Now, nobody could teach him a thing about fishing or sailing. The St Ives revenue cutters, *Brilliant* and *Dolphin,* had deep keels, and bowsprits nearly as long as their hulls, allowing them to hoist more sail, so he could never have outsailed them in a straight race. But he'd have a trick or two up his sleeve and didn't he know these waters better than anyone?

It looked as if there were no cutters tonight, though, and he would soon be in his Lelant cottage, drinking this lovely brandy. Eight-and-a-half gallons of it would certainly help him through this cold Cornish winter.

It was a pity that he'd have to drink it untinted, till he could get some sugar to burn, for he liked his brandy honey-coloured.

'Millions of grains of sand on the beach but not one grain of sugar in the cottage,' he muttered.

Dang it, he shouldn't have thrown out Rosie Rowse last week because of her plaguy nagging. Rosie would have remembered to buy some sugar; women thought of things like that.

Having anchored the *Jane*, he slid thigh-deep into the freezing water and floated the kegs the few yards to the shore. He rolled them onto dry sand and was about to hang them fore and aft over his shoulders, when he heard shuffling in the darkness ahead.

'Stay where you are, Bryant! Raise your hands above your head.'

Revenue men! He dived to the left into the side of a dune and a pistol shot rang out. Picking himself up, he ran far along the beach, then darted between two dunes.

By the sound of the voices, there were only two officers and they were staying with the kegs. Be danged if he'd flee like a frightened sheep and let them have the brandy he'd paid for with his hard-earned money! He'd creep up on the beggars from behind and crack their heads together.

But he had lost count how many dunes back they were. Confound it, he couldn't seem to get his own head together.

Avast! They wouldn't just wait there to be sprung upon, would they? Clear your head, for God's sake! Stop for a second and listen...

Nothing. Just the pounding of the waves.

Rot it, I'll take a chance. For as sure as my name be William Bryant, they'll pinch my bloody brandy if I don't go back.

He was at the rear of the row of dunes now. Heart thudding, he crept along - and stumbled. Face down he was, spitting out bloody sand. He listened again...

Just the waves.

Something flapped past his face. A bird? No, caught in a tuft of marram grass was a piece of paper - the size of an execution notice outside Bodmin Gaol.

Bugger it if they'd get *him*! He tottered along a mite farther and had another listen...

Whispers. If the men were whispering, they'd be standing together, wouldn't they? He fondled the handle of his sheathed gutting knife.

Avast, Will Bryant! He could see the look of horror on the face of his mother: Jane Bryant, that dear Christian woman whom everybody loved. *Begone, Satan!* He snatched away his hand as if the hilt itself had cut him.

Close to each other by the kegs were two shadowy figures. Holding his breath, he stole upon them. He grabbed both heads and knocked them together and the pair fell senseless. He stooped by the kegs, lifted them and slung the ropes over his head.

Then he staggered to his feet and felt a pistol muzzle in his back.

* * *

'William Bryant, you have been found guilty of resisting the revenue officers who had seized some smuggled brandy from you. It has been proven that in the course of this resistance you were armed with a knife. Is there anything you wish to say before sentence is passed?'

The muttering mob of spectators could contain themselves no longer and roared with excitement. These whores' sons and daughters could not wait to see his legs dancing in mid-air, the macabre signal to hurl obscenities and rotten vegetables at his dying body. Will looked away from the elderly, wine-soaked judge, while the March wind rattled the grimy windows of Launceston Assize House and the crows, the Cornish choughs, cawed greedily. The shackled fisherman knew that an *unarmed* smuggler's punishment was death by hanging, outside the gaol, and then burial. But the fate of an armed man who'd injured revenue officers was gibbeting: the hanging of his body in chains after execution. He'd dangle on a gibbet atop the Lelant towans, whence his rotting corpse would be seen a great distance: a warning to all the other 'freetraders' tempted to land there. The long, sharp reddish-yellow beak of the chough would peck out his eyes before proceeding downwards. Months later, before the mocking eyes of St Uny's congregation – rot *them*! – his skeleton would be buried in the unhallowed ground of the dunes.

He was shivering, dammit! Folk would think him scared but he'd wager he was coming down with the gaol distemper raging in Launceston Gaol and throughout Cornwall and England. Hadn't the previous governor and his wife been smitten with it one night and died even before the choughs were up for breakfast?

Turning back to the judge, sitting there in robes as scarlet as his face, Will met his glazed glare.

'My Lord, I'm a fisherman – indeed, a master seiner,' he said, his voice quivering with pride as he thought of his father. 'I'm at the top of my trade, just like you be. 'Twas only my ol' gutting knife, for God's sake: I don't go nowhere without that. Surely the law allows for that? Judges need their quills, fishermen their knives. I didn't *use* it on the fellows, did I? As sure as my name be William Bryant, I ain't no murderer. I just gave them a bit of a sore head, didn't I? No lasting damage. Many's the time *I've* had a sore head, after partaking of the spirits, but I've lived to fight another day.'

The roar was deafening as the chough-like clerk placed the black cap on the judge's tie wig. Will's heart hammered.

The old man cleared his scraggy throat.

'William Bryant. It is now my duty to pronounce the sentence demanded by the law.'

The judge paused, glanced down at the wormy veins of his clasped hands, then looked Will in the eye.

'It is ordered and adjudged by this court that you be carried from the bar back to the place from whence you came, and from thence to the place of execution, and that you be hanged by the neck until you be dead by the hands of a common executioner. And may Almighty God have mercy on your soul.'

The black-garbed chaplain's sepulchral 'Amen!' echoed round the courtroom. He was a churchman, too, God rot him – and a wine-flushed one to boot.

Rich Joshua Trengrouse, himself a wine and spirit merchant, smuggling-organization venturer, and churchman, muttered behind his vinegared handkerchief, 'Mercy on his soul? The *judge* has been merciful; no mention of the gibbet, more's the pity.'

* * *

More mercy followed, both from the Almighty and His Majesty King George III. The 'distemper' had proved to be a cold, and the death sentence was commuted to seven years' transportation to America. On 6 April 1784, Will was taken to the *Dunkirk*, a rotting hulk anchored in the Hamoaze, the estuary of the River Tamar, at Plymouth, Devonshire.

Eighteen months later, he was still there.

CHAPTER 2

Jimmy Martin had been tossing and turning on his bed of straw all bloody night. 'Christ, I need a woman!' cried the little Irishman, thrusting his cold right foot through a hole in one of the thin oatmeal sacks serving as a blanket.

Nobody heard him, all alone in his tiny north-east Ulster cabin, all alone yet again in the darkness before dawn. He rubbed his eyes, which were perpetually sore from the daytime turf smoke in this chimneyless, windowless hovel. These mud-and-straw cabins were normally warm and dry but the door had several cracks in it, which he should have repaired, curse it. Soon the autumn sun would be shining on these remote Nine Glens of Antrim and his small, solitary plot of land on the west bank of the Glenariff River. The river flowed from the south-west to the north-east. The cabin was three miles up Glenariff: three miles from Red Bay and in direct line of this bitter north-east wind blowing across the cruel Sea of Moyle from Scotland. It goes without saying that he had built his little house well away from the Fairies' paths, or else he'd have been plagued by bad luck all his life.

Thanks to the recent Catholic Relief Acts, Catholics had again been allowed to buy land or to hold leases, and now, at twenty-five, Jimmy was no longer a spalpeen, an agricultural labourer, but a tenant farmer. His five acres of potatoes and oats, set in 'lazy beds', supported him and Nelly, the milch cow. Until a month ago, she and the six young cattle had grazed on the booly, the summer pasture higher up, herded by the 'bouchals', wee local lads. She would stay down here now till the spring, while her companions had been sold at Cushendall Fair. Aye, he had everything to satisfy his basic needs, save whiskey and a woman.

The youngest of Widow Martin's five surviving offspring, he was the only one unmarried. His two brothers and two sisters were living separately from each other in Belfast. That was thirty miles away to the south as the Fairies fly: up forested Glenariff, passing beautiful waterfalls with names like the Tears of the Mountain, and over the greyish-blue Antrim mountains. Máire, Déirdre, Eamonn and Séan would shortly be waking to walk a mile in their bare, swollen red and blue feet for another hard day's toil at the linen-bleaching works outside the town. 'The mammy' lived with Máire, the eldest, who had six children of her own. All his brothers and sisters had a cabinful of screeching kids, so there was no room for him – even if he could have borne it. Poor wee devils, though, they'd all be linen-bleaching long before they reached the official starting age of twelve, so they would.

He should have married Maeve McAuley all those years ago. He should have proposed to her by the Tears of the Mountain, for God's sake. Sure, 'twould have been magical, with a single shaft of sunlight peeping through the canopy of trees onto the cascading waters. Aye, while the Fairy People and the goats and wild ponies watched, he should have sealed it with a kiss and a bunch of the bluebells which grew so abundantly there, not forgetting to leave a bowlful of Nelly's milk among the mosses and ferns to please the Fairies, so that they would have protected the young couple from bad luck in their future life.

Faith, there'd been nothing wrong with the wee girl! It was just that he had thought that one day he'd find someone who would really make his heart thump. Maeve had had a nervous collapse after he'd told her that he liked her but didn't love her. She'd soon recovered, though, and within six months had married Dermot McAlister, and now she, too, had six. That's a point, though: if he, Jimmy, had married her, he'd probably be wide awake now, in any case, with six squealing brats tumbling all –

Something was moving about outside. Nelly?

A crackling. Burning! Flames bursting through the cracks in the door! Burning thatch falling to the mud floor! Bed alight!

He leapt from it and slid open the door bolts. The door wouldn't open, the bloody door wouldn't open! He tore at his straggly black beard. Choking, he sprang back to the bed. He hurled his spindly frame against the door, which shuddered but stayed shut. He grabbed the axe leaning against the wall. He struck the door and flames whooshed in. Shielding his face, he struck the door again. And again.

Then he was outside, breathing God's air. The whole cabin was alight. Straw had been strewn all around it and logs piled against the door.

'He's got out!' somebody yelled. 'The Papist's got out!'

Peep o' Day Boys!

He ran. Not fast enough, though. One of the men was way ahead of the others and catching up, for Jimmy Martin was stiff from the damp. Clumsy-footed at the best of times, he stumbled, falling over the first lazy bed. Up again. But fingers were clutching his coarse linen shirt and his belt.

'Got ye, ye scuttling little Papist!'

Jimmy still had the axe. He wrenched himself free and swung it, catching the man with the flat of the blade. Then Mrs Martin's wee lad was off again and was soon hidden in the dense woods of hazel, birch and ash, leaving the Devil's henchmen to curse among those windblown flaming straws.

CHAPTER 3

For eleven weeks now, the south-west winds had stopped the boats from going to sea. The fisherfolk in the small southern Cornish town of Fowey were starving.

It was Christmas Eve 1785. Down-along there in the moonlit town, that wealthy widow Susannah Ann Austen (born Treffry) would be fast asleep in her curtained four-poster in Place, the Treffrys' ancestral mansion. Up-along here in Farmer Tregenna's windswept field, it was plaguy freezing.

Old William Broad's gutting knife flashed across the ewe's throat and she died.

'I'm glad you stunned her before doing it, F-Father,' shuddered Mary Broad.

The fisherman groaned as he and his queasy daughter struggled against the wind to lift the carcass onto the fish barrow. They had almost succeeded when he let go, clutching his heart.

Mary's icy fingers gripped his spindly arm. 'Father! Are you ill?'

'No... no, my sweet'art,' he gasped. ''Tis only those indigestion pains o' mine, caused by the excitement. You're only twenty year old; when you're sixty-five like me, you'll find it's a struggle to keep going.'

'Aw, Father.' She forced herself to smile reassuringly as they bent down and grasped two blood-drenched legs each. 'When we get home, I'll make you a dish of hot yarrow tea to speed these Devil-sent pains away... Are you ready, then? Here we go...' She breathed deeply. 'Yo-heave *ho*!'

With a strength that amazed her, she helped haul the dead animal onto the barrow. The poor ewe's eyes stared at her accusingly and she shivered the more. But needs must when hunger drives.

'Quick now, gal,' panted the old man, 'we must pull the gurry back... across Tregenna's field... before the fat ol' varmint wakes from his pleasant dreams of making more and more money and catches us.'

Quick? It was easier said than done, battling against this shrieking sou'wester, which was determined to stop them as if it were Tregenna's ally.

She marvelled at her father's own strength, though, for in less than a minute they had reached the gate. The sou'wester fought to prevent her from opening it but this only served to make her Cornish blood boil. Damning the wind back to Hell, she tugged at the gate as she had tugged so many times at the oars since her childhood, when helping with the fishing. It was a fierce fight but she was a Broad, dammit, and managed to open the gate wide enough for her father to squeeze the barrow through to the long, steep track leading down to their riverside home.

''Tis well the ground's granite-'ard,' she puffed, 'or else Tregenna would follow our tracks home.'

They kept further thoughts to themselves until at last, thank God, the tiny limewashed cottage came into view.

'I tell you, daughter,' he wheezed, 'I tell you that, for fishermen, this is the worst winter I've ever known... Eleven week of cussed sou'westers so we can't put the *Jenny* to sea... and then rot me if those waves don't get it into their white heads to throw the poor ol' gal halfways across the mud... so she's a dead'un as near as makes no difference, because I ain't got a *farthing* to pay for repairs! And not just the *Jenny* but six other boats are like crippled old ladies, too, ain't they, including Mr and Mrs Edward Puckey's.'

'Goody-madam' Puckey, as Mary called her, was her elder sister. The Puckeys, who could read and write, thought themselves superior to the Broads.

'All of us fisherfolk are starving,' he said, 'and nobody outside Cornwall gives a tinker's cuss!

'And as for you, Mary dear... I remember well that once upon a sunny time you were my happy, romping tomboy of a daughter. And then you grew into the prettiest five-foot-four of womanhood that Fowey ever saw and, till last twelvemonth, you had all the billies whistling after you. Gor, what a merry maiden you were! With your well-rounded body, your long, windswept brown hair, the impish smile you always had on your rosy lips and in your sparky grey eyes... and with your plump cheeks like shiny red apples, you were ripe for the plucking… And now look at you, poor wretched child: as skinny, straight and dull yellow as the boathook. But at least *that's* a useful article; *you* ain't fit for hooking a plaguy thing no more!' He paused for breath.

'… And, gal, I promised your poor old mother, Lord rest her, I promised her before she died of that terrible consumption, that I'd never let you and your little sister starve.'

She was straining to catch any sounds of pursuit but could hear nothing save this fiendish wind.

'I know, Father, but if they catch you and me, we'll be hung, and then Dolly would starve for sure. It's best I leave home and get work and send you some money. You're too old for fishing anyway. I'll go to Plymouth on Matt Davy's wagon on Friday.'

'No, don't you leave me, gal,' he cried. 'Don't you leave me, for God's sake!'

'I'm twenty years of age! You'll still have Dolly in Fowey for a while yet; she's only thirteen, ain't she? I'll come and see you regular, one Sunday a month, and us three can go to St Fimbarrus's to pray for Mother's soul, just like we always do.'

He groaned. 'And it only seems like yesterday when you were baptized there, child: the first of May 1765. No, you ain't a-goin' to Plymouth. No, I forbid it; 'twill *kill* your poor old father!'

'I'm sorry, Father,' she murmured, squeezing his bloodied hand. 'It's either Plymouth for *me* or St Fimbarrus's graveyard for us all – Pincher!'

Barking madly, her skinny little terrier leapt through the gateway - the gate having been wrenched off the week before by the wind. He jumped onto the dead sheep and sniffed excitedly with this split nose of his: proud reminder of a fight with Snapper, Tregenna's sheepdog.

'Quiet, for mercy's sake,' she hissed, 'you'll wake the whole town. Dear life, you'll put a rope round our necks, you stupid animal!'

They trundled the gurry and its passengers into the garden, past the ropes, seine nets and fish tubs and the stinking cesspool. The pitifully thin Dolly was at the open door of the unlit, windowless thatched cottage, whose walls were of clay mixed with gravel and straw. Poor child, she was shivering so violently in her thin cotton-check frock and bare feet. The girls had long since sold their lovely warm woollen shawls for food money but at least Mary was wearing her fishwife mother's coarse canvas jacket and split black leather shoes. There was no fire, their turf stock being exhausted, the ground too hard to dig the tabs. Mary would have to make the yarrow tea by burning some alder twigs. Mr Pitt in London had drastically reduced the duty on proper tea to lower the rewards for smuggling but even when Father had been working, the drink was still too expensive for the likes of them. Lord, these past weeks they hadn't even been able to afford the penny for used leaves which Susannah Austin's plump rosy-cheeked housekeeper sold daily at Place's shiny black back door.

'Out of the way, Dolly, 'tis mortal 'eavy,' gasped the old man as he and Mary reached their own, humble door.

Dolly darted inside and they tipped the sheep – and Pincher – onto the rush-strewn clay floor, by the rickety little table.

Mary followed her father in and the wind slammed the flimsy door shut behind her. She turned to her sister.

'Roast sheep'll chase away that gnawing wolf inside you, Dolly. Yiss, this poor old ewe will warm you and so will her woolly coat,' she smiled, putting her arms round the girl's neck, and suddenly aware of a lump in her own throat. *Yes,* she thought, fighting back the tears, *I'm scraggy enough these days, and this old jacket and frock are hanging off me like a dang scarecrow's, but you, my poor darling, are like a skellinton.* Stroking the long, tangled sandy hair, she murmured, 'And it'll put some flesh on you, my lover. Dear life, another week of nothing but limpets trigged from the rocks and you'd be joining Mother in Heaven!'

Dolly broke away sobbing. ''Tis Christmas Day tomorrow and she won't be here. Aw, I do miss her terrible!' She flung herself onto the straw mattress, which she shared with Mary. The family's two blankets had been sold for food and the Broads hadn't even a sack to their name.

Her mother's death had hit the sensitive, tender-hearted Dolly hard. Sensitive, yes, and sensible, too: far more sensible than Mary thought she herself was. Dolly was now prone to tantrums. And sleeplessness. Even when she'd still had the warming blanket, she had slept little. When she did manage to sleep, she invariably had nightmares.

'We all do, my beauty,' said Mary, her own eyes pricking, 'we all do. It's nine months now and I miss Mother more every day.'

Their father fumbled for the flint-and-steel on the highest shelf, then, with shaking fingers, lit the rush candle in its long tin candlestick on the table. Dolly's tears glistened on her pinched, pockmarked freckled cheeks.

Mary told herself that after the sheep was roasted, they would have plenty of fat for making rush lights. All those rushes that she had gathered and treated in the autumn would be dipped in hot fat, giving the Broads lights for the rest of the winter. The light was feeble compared with the tallow that Susannah Ann Austen used at Place but, at ninepence a pound, those heavily taxed candles could never be afforded by ordinary mortals. So, it was dark in the evening, and dark during the day, for who could afford windows, with a shilling tax on each one, for goodness' sake?

Everything was taxed. Worst of all for the fisherfolk was the tax on the very salt that they used for fish curing.

Yes, thank the good Lord for rushes. What would people do without these precious plants, which lit the darkness, caned the chairs, carpeted the cold clay and gave them a roof over their heads? As always, she praised God for all nature's wonders.

And tomorrow was the birthday of His –

'Aye, 'tis Christmas,' muttered the old man. 'And a fine Christmas present your sister's giving us, Dolly.'

'What d'you mean, Father?' asked the child, sniffing loudly. Her thin blue lips opened in alarm as she saw the look on their faces. She twisted the tangles and her tearful green eyes bulged in their sunken sockets. Her right cheek twitched. '… W-what d'you mean?'

Mary Broad swallowed hard. 'I… I'm going to find work in Plymouth at the end of the week.'

'You – you're leaving us?' Dolly's eyes grew even bigger. 'You're deserting us? But you can't. You can't!' she screeched, stamping her icy feet against the wall.

The startled Pincher scuddled under the table and hid behind the sheep. It was always wise to keep out of the way when his quick-tempered mistresses fell to ramping and raving.

'First Mother leaves us and now you! You're selfish. Selfish! *Selfish!*'

'I ain't!' blazed Mary Broad, slamming her fists on her bony knees. 'How dare you say that? I'm doing it for your own good, you stupid gal. I'm doing it to earn some money so you can have some bloody bread in your belly!'

A wave of weakness swept over her and she could scarce continue.

'I… I'm going to Plymouth and that's the end of the matter.'

The old fisherman had slumped into his usual place at the table and, white-faced and trembling, stared at the flickering flame.

'Aw, my dear wife,' he cried, the tears mingling with the blood on his blue-veined hands, 'whatever's become of us Broads? Mary's leaving us, too. Mary's leaving us. too…'

CHAPTER 4

'Jeez, why did I leave Ireland?' groaned Jimmy Martin as the south-west wind blasted his hut door off its rusty hinges and his tin plate from his lap. Then nine square feet of the flimsy wooden roof sailed off into the night.

'Merry Christmas, Jimmy,' he yelled.

There'd be nobody else to wish him it. Sure, Lord bloody Courtenay and his family wouldn't. Drinking themselves silly at this time of a Christmas Eve night they'd be, having stuffed themselves with pheasant in their bloody castle.

The 'bloody' castle was Powderham, near Exeter, Devonshire, and Jimmy's hut was in the grounds, which he helped keep so tidy for His Lordship. To think that just a month ago he, James Martin, had had his own land in beautiful Antrim. Aye, king of his own castle he'd been, until members of that Protestant secret society had set light to his stout auld cabin.

In the moon's beam, the barefoot Irishman retrieved the single potato from the cold clay floor and took a bite. The thing stuck in his gullet.

'Ack, curse it, I'll not freeze to death on Christmas Eve in this biting wind while those buggers are warming their fat bellies. I'll find *something* in yer man's shed to fix this bloody door and roof. Thanks be to the man in the moon, I'll not have to wait till peep o' day…'

Three minutes later, he was back with some old sheets of lead and about a dozen rusty iron screw-bolts. It would be no easy task with this wind but bedamned if he'd spend Christmas huddled shivering in a corner, like a poor wee robin with a broken wing.

He glanced at his straw bed – well, what was left of it, now that the wind had done its worst.

'Aye, Jimmy,' he sighed, 'Maeve would have kept ye warm, even on a coul night like this.'

CHAPTER 5

Mary's last six pennies in the world were paying for this ride on grizzled old Matt Davy's tilt-covered wagon. She and her six fellow passengers were huddled in the straw, their backs against barrels of Bordeaux wine. There were four dusty young quarrymen and two young women, all looking mighty thirsty.

The wagon had headed north, then crossed the River Fowey at Lostwithiel's medieval bridge, six miles upstream. Despite the sou'wester's constant urgings, the ancient vehicle seemed to have been creaking along eastward for hours now. The desolate, grey moorland hills on the left had deepened Mary's depression, the bumpy road adding insult to injury.

'Dear life, Mr Davy,' she groaned, 'this is a rough road. Especially with a creaky cart like this'un and a bony bum like mine. You could have stowed a mite more straw in here, I'm thinking.'

The skinny old carter was shivering in this cutting wind, even though he was wearing a floppy leather hat tied well down over his face, a quilted white smock, a leather cape and thick leather leggings bound with straw above the ankles.

'You call this rough, Mary? You should have ridden along it in Granny Broad's day. But 'tis bad enough, I'll grant you. I broke an axle along here last year. 'Tis all the large stones they use for repairs. They should use smaller ones but the turnpike trustees won't spend the time or the money on breaking up the dang things.' He cracked his whip. 'Who-ho, George, who-ho, Nancy,' he cried.

The skinny young redhead beside her sniffed. Her cheeks and thin lips were heavily painted and Mary could see that beneath the brown cloak she was gaudily dressed in orange. She reeked of gin.

The green eyes flashed mischievously and the freckled snub nose crinkled. 'What about leaving us have some of this wine to make the journey more pleasant, like?'

''Tis more than I dare do, gal,' grunted the old man, his back bowed against the wind. 'Joshua Trengrouse of Lan'son expects every barrel intact. Lor, he'd have me thrown into the Tamar with my pockets full of road stones. Besides, you and your friend only got on at the Fountain at Liskeard; you ain't been travelling since cock-crow like our Mary.'

'You miserable old devil,' muttered the woman, spitting at his back. She turned to Mary, who recoiled from her foul breath. 'So you're a Mary, too, are you?'

Mary was so cold and miserable the last thing that she wanted to do was talk. Neither her father nor Dolly had bothered to accompany her to the Ship Inn where she'd joined the wagon. William Broad had even kept Pincher indoors. The poor dog's howls as she'd walked up the track from the cottage were still echoing in her head.

She would make an effort, though. 'Yiss, I'm Mary Broad.'

'I'm Catherine Prior.' She grinned, showing blackened teeth. 'My friend here's a Mary: Mary Shepherd,' she said, poking her plump neighbour's stomach through her scarlet frock.

'Pleased to meet you both,' said Mary.

The fat young woman's flaxen hair was matted, her painted face pockmarked by smallpox, like Dolly's. Her blue eyes were cold.

You don't sound it,' she said, scratching her armpit.

Mary blushed, then forced a smile. 'Forgive me. I'm just mighty tired and low-spirited. I've had to leave my young sister and widowed father, and my poor old dog, in Fowey, to find work in Plymouth. I've never been further than Lostwithiel before. And I don't go *there* much if I can help it! Us Fowey folk don't think Lostwithiel people are very Christian. They think they're betterer than us because they've got a ruined castle and a famous old bridge. And were once a more important port than us. But they weren't, once the River Fowey got filled up with sand, and ships got biggerer and couldn't reach the plaguy place.'

She was warming to her theme. 'I'll wager that if I fell into an overflowing gutter outside St Bartholomew's Church there, the congregation coming out wouldn't even trouble to pick me up if they knew I was from Fowey. They'd maybe use *me* as a bridge so as not to spoil their precious Sunday shoes!'

Matt Davy laughed. 'You want to see a mite more of the world, young Mary, and then you'll find there's good and bad in all places.'

Despite the cold, Mary Broad felt her cheeks burning. Was nobody on her side any more?

'The Reverend John Baron's a good man,' she said; 'I'll grant you that.'

Catherine squeezed Mary's wrist. '*We're* Plymouth gals; *we're* very friendly. We've been spreading comfort and joy to all those pale-faced tin-miners and quarrymen who came down from the moor into Liskeard for Christmas. We really brought the colour to their cheeks.' She winked at the men and they grinned. 'And now we're returning to Plymouth to cheer up the sailors. *We'll* raise your spirits, Mary Broad. Come and see us there this evening.'

Mary whispered, 'What sort of comfort and joy?' knowing full well what sort.

'Hey, we ain't prostitutes, if that's what you're thinking!' protested the fat woman, farting.

'Fancy thinking that,' said Catherine. 'We sing and dance in the taverns to cheer everybody. We'll cheer you, too, Melancholy Mary.'

'But I can't; I've got to find work; I ain't got no money.'

'We'll see that you're all right,' said Mary Shepherd. 'Come round to our lodging in New Street for a little something to warm your insides. It's by Sutton Harbour, just round the corner from the Mayflower Steps.'

'No, I can't; I've got to find a lodging.'

Catherine squeezed harder. 'Once we've crossed on the Torpoint ferry we're in Devonshire, ain't we, and we'll ask you again then. I don't know about *your* customs, Cornish Mary, but in Devonshire it's bad manners to say "No" when folk ask you to call.'

Was that the wind or did 'Cornish Mary' hear a sigh from fatherly old Matt?

CHAPTER 6

'Mary, you're a godsend and worth every penny of Mr Pitt's tax on maidservants! The roast chicken was delicious!'

The speaker was frail, white-haired Miss Hannah Treeby. She had spent Christmas alone in this big old Vauxhall Street house, following her maid's death on Christmas Eve from a consumption. But Miss Hannah would be alone no more. Late this afternoon, 'God' had sent her this 'angel' of a Cornish wench to knock on the front door, looking for work. It was the thirtieth house that Mary had tried in Plymouth and, with rejection after abusive rejection because of her fishwife looks and smell, the girl had almost given up hope. In fact, she had been in two minds whether to knock, the knocker being draped in mourning ribbons.

If the dining room mirror had not been crape-shrouded, Mary knew she'd have seen that her face was as red as her mistress's berouged one.

'Delicious, gal!' With white-gloved hands, the old lady brushed and collected the breadcrumbs from the white linen tablecloth and then wiped her thin, aquiline nose with an embroidered white silk handkerchief.

'I'm glad you liked it, Miss Hannah,' she said, curtseying, having come back up from the kitchen to clear the table. 'My dear mother taught me how to cook - though it's a brave long time since us Broads have had a roast.' A lie, but it had come out before she could stop it. She hated lying to such a sweet old soul, who had given her a week's wages in advance! But, for goodness' sake, she couldn't tell her the truth, could she?

Miss Hannah's faded blue eyes twinkled and she patted Mary's cold fingers, which the glorious coal fire here hadn't had time to warm.

'Well, *you* can finish the rest of it, in the kitchen. 'Twill help fatten you.' With the same hand, she stifled a yawn. 'I'm away up the wooden hill as soon as the meal has settled. I suggest you do the same for you look so *dreadfully* weary.'

'I – I promised the two gals I met on the carrier's wagon that I'd visit them at home this evening for a drin – er, a dish of tea. 'Twas difficult to refuse their invitation without seeming rude, like.'

'But I've given you some tea. And 'tis dark outside, Mary! No God-fearing young woman should be abroad in Plymouth at night, for mercy's sake!'

'Don't you be afeard for me,' she said, yawning, too. 'It's only a street away; they've shown me where it is. I won't stay long.'

An hour – and three gins each – later, Mary's new friends had persuaded her to go to a nearby alehouse; the first she'd entered in her life. After another hour, spent watching them perform sea shanties and hornpipes with all these drunken sailors, she was amazed to find that she, too, was mighty drunk. Two tankards of ale was all she'd had in here; the alcohol must have affected her more because of her tiredness. Tired or not, she hadn't felt so mischievously happy in years.

'I tell you, gals,' she said, as the three of them staggered to the street door, 'I'm so pleased I've got a job and can send some money home, that I feel like throwing my hat in the duckpond, for joy!' This was something that the 'sensible' Dolly would never have done. 'The only problem is, I don't own a hat... I s'pose I could throw somebody else's hat in,' she giggled, squiggling in the sawdust with her pointed shoe. 'Some rich Jack-a-dandy maybe. Or if there are no fops about, well, the first *lady* that sticks her nose up in the air and sniffs as she passes us will have to do!'

The first people to pass the alehouse were a sniffy marine officer of about thirty and his pink-bonneted young lady, with matching cloak over a bustled red-and-white-striped dress. The feeble light from the only window was enough to show that the redcoat was wearing his sword, so the three did nothing.

'You know, darling...' he said, removing his three-cornered hat and foppishly raking his fingers through his queued blond hair, '... you know, every time I pass this duckpond, I'm minded to return at dawn with my fowling piece to shoot a big duck for you, my dearest Betsey, and our chubby little Ralph.'

'Oh, Ralph,' chided this narrow-shouldered little woman, raising her closed red-and-white-striped umbrella to eye level and aiming at the pond. 'Oh it would be too easy to hit the poor creatures on such a small pond.' The girls could hear them greeting a 'Miss Lakeman' as their voices faded into the night. Moments later, the lady herself appeared in the glow. Thin and in her middle years and cloaked in black, she, too, was wearing a matching silk bonnet.

Not any more: Mary Broad had whipped it and how Miss Lakeman screamed. Dear life, surely they'd hear it inside, even above that din?

Catherine rasped, 'Rot the old witch, she ain't leaving go of this bloody bag!'

'No, Catherine!' Mary's shout echoed in the night. 'No, you're *hurting* her! You'll *kill* her! I've got her bonnet; that's all we wanted. I'm no cutpurse. Leave her be!'

'Help me!' shrieked their victim. 'Somebody help me!'

'My life,' gasped Mary Shepherd, 'the old bitch is screaming so much, everyone in the alehouse will be out here in a minute. Everyone in bloody Plymouth will be out here!'

'No!' cried Mary, dropping the bonnet and grabbing the girls' arms. 'I'll not allow *this*. Leave her be, you sclum cats, leave her be!'

As Catherine tugged and shook her, the lady slipped face down onto the muddy cobbles. In a trice, Mary Shepherd had wrenched away the bag.

'This'll learn you to try and stop us,' snarled Catherine, kicking the woman, first in the kidneys, then in the spine, her agonized shrieks sending shivers down Mary's own back.

Mary Broad frantically knelt down and cradled the quivering head in her lap.

'Aw, forgive me,' sobbed the trembling girl. 'Aw, I'm so sorry. I'm so very, very -'

'What in hell's happening out here?' The bald and burly landlord had flung open his door and before Mary and her companions could move, he and some of his customers had grabbed them.

'You trulls!' he roared. 'You drink yourselves bosky with my ale and then you attack and rob Miss Agnes. You cowardly trulls!'

The marine officer came rushing back, with drawn sword.

'You bitches!' he cried, helping the sobbing woman to her feet. 'You damn bitches! You'll be up before the magistrate on the morrow and then be remanded for trial at the Spring Assizes at Exeter Castle. And with all of us witnesses against you, it's a hanging job for all of you. Ha, pretty enough for any red-blooded man to kiss, you may be, but the only kissing you'll do now is kiss the world goodbye.'

CHAPTER 7

'Prisoners at the bar, my duty is to pass sentence on you,' intoned black-capped, bewigged Sir James Eyre. The black eyes of England's most feared judge glowered at Mary in the Exeter Castle dock. At earlier assizes, he had pardoned two thirds of those he'd condemned to death under the 'Bloody Code' of 160 capital offences. But by 1785, the Bloody Code had become a scarecrow that the birds no longer feared; the crime rate was rising rapidly and government and people were panicking. The crime wave was largely caused by all those starving soldiers unemployed after the American War of Independence. Determined to tackle it, this florid-faced, middle-aged judge with a Somerset accent was now sending countless poor wretches to meet their Maker long before their time. Mary had heard that when he'd presided at the Essex Summer Assizes in July last year, all ten under capital sentence for crimes like small highway robberies had been hanged. 'Mary Broad, Catherine Prior and Mary Haydon, otherwise known as Shepherd. For feloniously assaulting Agnes Lakeman, spinster, in the King's highway. Feloniously putting her in corporal fear and danger of her life in the said highway. And feloniously and violently taking from her person and against her will in the said highway one silk bonnet valued one shilling and other goods valued eleven guineas, her property...

'You shall be taken from this place and, at an appointed time, hanged by the neck until you are dead. And may God have mercy upon your souls.'

Edging beside him, the chaplain, pale and black-draped like Death himself, cried, 'Amen!'

'Aw, Dolly,' gasped Mary Broad, clutching the rail as sparks darted in the blackness enveloping her. 'My poor little sister, who will look after you and our poor old father now?'

* * *

The condemned-cell door in Exeter Gaol clanged open and the slight figure of the Reverend John Baron entered, accompanied by the armed turnkey, Simpson, and a freezing March gale.

Mary, who herself had long since lost her jacket, dragged her chain through a dozen half-naked women to reach her visitor. She clutched his thin hands – even colder than hers. The bob-wigged, bespectacled Vicar of Lostwithiel was her last link with Cornwall, for tomorrow there'd be no Cornwall and no world. *He* had reached middle age; she never would.

'H-h-how is my father and Dolly, your Reverence?' Since leaving them, she'd had a terrible gnawing in the left of her lower abdomen, which wasn't just hunger, although that was bad enough, her meals consisting of broth, mouldy bread and coarse meat.

The warm brown eyes smiled down at her over half-moon spectacles and a vinegared fine-linen handkerchief. This he had swiftly held to his bony nose because of the overpowering stench.

'My dear child,' he choked, 'they will both be happier folk tonight when I ride to Fowey to give them the news. And it will cheer the gentleman on whose behalf I have been making these visits to you: my reverend friend and colleague, and your vicar, James Benetto. Cheer him on his sickbed.'

Her heart leapt. 'You – you mean...?'

She caught her breath as, through the slit in his cassock, he drew a roll of parchment from his breeches pocket.

Gawping likewise, her two former cronies gathered round, as did the twenty other women and girls in this hellishly overcrowded cell. All, including Mary, were faeces-smeared and stiff from sleeping on the filthy cold stone floor, having no money to pay the keeper for one of his feather beds. All, too, were verminous – they spent their days lousing themselves – and many of these skinny bodies were ulcerated.

'I mean, you three, that I have brought you glad tidings.'

He held the parchment close to his spectacles and read by the faint, dusty beam of sunlight from the bars high above.

> Whereas Mary Broad, Catherine Prior and Mary Haydon, otherwise Shepherd, were at this assizes convicted of felony for which they were excluded the benefit of clergy. And His Majesty hath been graciously pleased to extend the royal mercy to them on condition of their being transported beyond the sea for and during the term of seven years, each. And such intention of mercy hath been signified by the Right Honourable Thomas, Lord Sydney, one of His Majesty's Principal Secretaries of State.
>
> It is therefore ordered and adjudged by the court that the said above-named convicts be transported beyond the seas accordingly, as soon as conveniently may be, for and during the term of seven years respectively.

Mary Broad fell to her knees, oblivious of the ordure – and the rats. Kissing the spindly fingers, she gazed up into the eyes of her saviour. The beam was stronger: dazzling.

'Aw, praise be to God! I shall feel the warmth of the sun again, and hear the beautiful birds sing, and smell the sweet scents of the Lord's lovely flowers...'

He cleared his throat and his Adam's apple bobbed over his white-linen neckbands. 'You will, my dear, you will.'

The smile in his eyes vanished. 'But mind this, and mind it well, all three of you. When you attacked Miss Lakeman, it wasn't just that good lady who was hurt. It was a wound to the body of Our Lord Jesus Christ. Those brutal kicks in the back could have been the death of that poor gentlewoman. *She* nearly didn't feel the warmth of the sun, or hear the beautiful birds, or smell the Lord's lovely flowers ever again.'

'Her?' rasped Catherine, her thin lips sneering. '*Her?* She was only a sniffy-nosed shrivelled old rich witch!'

'Yes,' said a leaner Mary Shepherd, laughing hysterically and farting. 'She was just a skinny old hag with a bag! What would *she* want with sun and birds and flowers? They're for young folk, like us: boys and gals walking out and loving one another. Not for vinegar-cheeked dried-up old dames.' She scratched her grimy chest, which the red rags scarcely covered now. 'It's *our* world, not hers! She might as well be dead anyway. We'd have done her a big favour, putting her out of her misery.'

The vicar's brown eyes studied Mary Broad, still at his feet.

'What do you, a *Cornish* maid, have to say about that, Mary? You've heard the views of these two Devonshire girls, whom you met for the first time on Matt Davy's wagon, when you were alone in strange country – straightway getting into bad company. What do you have to say, my sad-grey-eyed, brown-haired young woman of twenty years, whose cheeks, which were already sunken, are woefully even more emaciated and sallow now, after two-and-a-half months in this noisome prison? Do *you* think that a lady of Miss Lakeman's age still enjoys God's birds and flowers? And when you were snatching her silk bonnet, what were *your* thoughts?'

She felt these sallow cheeks reddening.

'Of course she still enjoys the birds and flowers! Begging your pardon, sir, but that's a stupid thing to ask! And if I'd ever got talking to her, we'd probably have shared the same thoughts about them. But that evening, I wasn't thinking about what was *in* her head. All I was thinking about was what was *on* her head! You see, I was just funning; not stealing. I was only going to throw the dang bonnet in the duckpond.'

She wept. 'I'm sorry Miss Lakeman got hurt.' She glared at the other two. 'Very, very sorry. I looked Miss Lakeman straight in the eye in court and told her that. And not a day goes by when I haven't begged the Lord's forgiveness for starting the whole business. I was so happy that I'd got a job and could send some money to my poor old father and Dolly, I just felt like doing something stupid, like. I was so bosky, you see, that if *your Reverence* had walked by, I might well have thrown your wig into the pond! Miss Lakeman wasn't *that* old, so I knew she could have waded out for the bonnet. The pond wasn't very deep or wide...'

He pulled her to her unsteady feet.

'Oh, my poor Mary. The *pond* was not deep or wide, but the oceans are, and wherever the Government decides to transport you, you won't be able to wade home to Fowey.'

CHAPTER 8

Exeter Gaol had been suffocatingly overcrowded. But this December night, on the lanternlit lower deck of the *Dunkirk* prison hulk off Plymouth, there was barely room for the rats to run between the convicts lying on the slimy, straw-strewn low shelves. It was said that one in every three prisoners died in these floating dungeons which folk called 'hell on earth'. Only the men were ironed, but in loose shackles which were useless at preventing the lecherous beggars from pushing aside the flimsy partition, creeping into the women's apartment and forcing themselves upon the occupants.

One stinking-breathed, black-bearded giant was doing so now – to Mary Broad of Fowey.

'Get your hands off me, you filthy varmint!' she shrilled. 'Go and play with the other rats!'

'Oh, come on, dearie,' he leered, fondling her breasts. 'All of us fellers will have marines stopping us from getting out of our apartments when we're stowed in the transports. Then I'll never feel a soft wench again for months – perhaps for ever!'

Soft wench? Her hard fist split his soft lips and they bled into the torn top of what remained of her cotton-check frock.

'You whore!' he roared, tearing at the rags.

Scratching at his blazing black eyes with one hand while trying to preserve her modesty with the other, she frantically, vainly, searched the apartment for help. Some folk were asleep – God alone knew how. Mary Shepherd and Catherine, though, had a man each and were rolling and giggling on the faeces-caked boards below. All around her were men's lusting eyes and slavering lips. Shouting obscenities and rattling their chains excitedly, these animals were enjoying every second of her shame, illuminated by the caged lanterns.

His tremendous weight took the breath from her and there was nothing that she could do as he had his way.

* * *

'Leave her be, Spence, ye bloody animal!'

It must have been a minute or two later. Through a mist, she saw Jimmy Martin. He had been sentenced at the same assizes and travelled, chained to her, on the outside of the stagecoach from Exeter. On hearing her cries, the Irishman had tottered through from the men's section, somehow managed to climb onto her ravisher and was pummelling away at his loathsome head.

The brute flung her aside and smashed his hairy fist into Jimmy's mouth with such force that the little fellow struck his head against the ship's side. Then before he knew what was happening, the breath was being squeezed from his throat. Mary hurled herself onto the massive back. She twisted and punched the long hairy ears. She tugged at the long greasy hair. But to this great ape she was just one more flea. Jimmy's heavy-lidded, strikingly blue eyes were bulging, about to spurt blood: a dead'un for sure.

'Damn your eyes, Spence!' yelled someone else who had staggered in. 'Leave the little fellow alone!' A big fair-haired, bushy-bearded convict of about thirty, looking like a sailor, shoved her away and jerked the brute to his knees, while Jimmy lay like a ragdoll, his frothing white tongue dangling limply from the corner of his mouth.

The quivering convict girl watched with relief, and admiration, as her second rescuer grasped her attacker by the ears and slammed his repulsive face against the side. As everyone cheered, he did it again – and again – then contemptuously flung the unconscious man off the shelf. From the corner of her eye, Mary saw that the Devonshire girls were still enjoying their own male company too much to notice what had happened.

To hell with them, she was only concerned about Jimmy.

'Aw, Jimmy, Jimmy!'

'Don't you fret about *him*, my lovely,' growled the newcomer, who was wearing a black greatcoat, several sizes too big, even for him. He wrapped his once brawny arms round her trembling body. 'Little Irishmen like him are like cats: they've got nine lives. Lor', you must get this frock mended, because it's terrible temptation to anyone,' he breathed, his rough hands pulling it back onto her shoulders. 'For, if not, Jimmy and me will be spending all our time as your bloody bodyguards!'

Jimmy... The glazed eyes were trying to focus on her.

'Aye, he's right, Miss Mary,' he gasped, forcing a painful grin. 'There should be a law against pretty Cornish wenches like ye. Sure, ye should be locked up.' He laughed, then groaned.

'Let me introduce myself,' muttered the big man. His large dark-brown, liquid eyes and full red lips caused a quivering in the pit of her belly. 'I'm Will Bryant, fisherman, from Lelant. A master seiner, in fact. And a freetrader in Cousin Jack. Two year ago I was taken after a fierce fight with the revenue men as I was smuggling brandy ashore that I'd brought from Rusco. 'Twas my own stupid fault. They'd never have caught me, save only that I'd partaken a mite too freely of the spirits myself – as I often do. And would do so now if those buggers would let us poor mortals have any spirituous liquor.

'At Lan'son Assizes I was sentenced to death. It was commuted to seven years' transportation to America, even though the colonies were independent by then. The Americans don't want us, so maybe it'll be West Africa. Aw, the Devil knows where they'll send us all...

'Tell her about yourself, Jimmy, if she don't already know. Tell her your story.'

She had been feverish on the stagecoach and although Jimmy had never stopped talking, to try to cheer her, all she could remember was his name.

'As ye may recall, darlin', I'm from... I'm from the County Antrim...' wheezed Jimmy, gingerly feeling his neck. Like the fingernails of the

English convicts, including Mary's, the Irishman's were bitten down but in his case the right thumbnail had been kept long for potato peeling. '… Ye may have heard of the Nine Glens of Antrim.'

'Yes.' She said it automatically; she couldn't concentrate on what he was saying.

'Well, I was a small tenant farmer, living on me own, like, but along came what we call "the Peep o' Day Boys", Protestants, like, and burned me wee cabin at five o'clock in the morning…'

He paused for a much-needed breath.

'… So I took ship to England and, to cut a long story short, got meself a job on Lord Courtenay's land at Powderham Castle, near Exeter. And, blow me down, didn't me wee hut nearly blow down during that mighty wind we had, last Christmas Eve? So I took some iron screw-bolts and some strips of lead from one of the castle sheds, to repair me door and roof. Well, Devil take me if His Lordship didn't have the impudence to have James Martin, Esquire, Gentleman Farmer from the County Antrim, arrested!'

The twinkle had returned. 'And on St Stephen's Day, too. St Stephen's Day, when masters are supposed to give their servants a Christmas box! Sure, yer man would have had me arrested on Our Lord's birthday itself, but nobody noticed the lead on me roof that day, being as they were all addled with the drink, the lucky devils.

'*My* death sentence, too, was commuted to seven years' transportation,' he concluded.

'Well, Mary, gal?' murmured Will Bryant. His calloused hands gripped her shoulders, which seemed to fascinate these unnerving eyes of his. 'Where do *you* come from? And what terrible deed have *you* been convicted of?'

She lowered her own eyes. 'I'm – I'm Mary Broad, daughter of William Broad, fisherman, of Fowey. Being new in Plymouth, and – and bosky with ale at the time, I – I snatched the silk bonnet from a lady's head. I was only going to throw the dang thing in the duckpond. Black Sir James Eyre sentenced me to be hung by the neck till I was dead, along with these cruel bitches Catherine Prior and Mary Shepherd down here. But King George extended his royal mercy and *we're* to be transported for seven years, too.'

'Such a terrible crime!' cried Jimmy. 'Sentenced to be hanged for wanting to throw a dame's bonnet into the pond for the wee ducks to have a peck-peck-peck at. Ack, anyone would think ye'd been found guilty of cutting off her head and throwing that into the bloody pond. Faugh, if I were a free man, I'd throw Sir James's wig and black cap into the pond, and then throw himself in after them. Treating a young woman like that!'

'It – it wasn't *just* the bonnet, though. It was her bag, you see, and – and she was kicked in the back. *I* never took it, and it was Catherine that kicked her. *I* tried to stop her hurting the poor lady.'

'You're cold, girl,' said Will Bryant, stroking her arms, exposed by the tattered frock. 'Here, come and snuggle under my greatcoat,' he grunted, pulling it round them both. 'I've got a fiery heart in here that'll warm the both of us.'

No thick greatcoat, no fiery heart could take away the inner chill of her degradation, her violation. Oh, how she loathed herself. She just wanted to wash and wash and wash, then crawl away into a dark corner and hide, and cry.

CHAPTER 9

'Prisoners of His Majesty,' the young red-coated marine officer boomed from the quarterdeck. The ship's master and a gentleman were on either side of him and about forty armed redcoats stood in lines behind. 'Welcome aboard the *Charlotte* transport on such a sunny Sunday morning.'

'God love him,' murmured Catherine Prior. 'What an 'andsome gentleman! He's got grey hair but he ain't no more than thirty years old, is he? And ain't he got beautiful big bright-blue eyes,' she breathed, 'all sparky in the sun?' She gripped Mary Broad's manacled wrist as the three girls stood, in their heavy, cutting anklets, chained to their fellow shiverers on the upper deck, this cold March day. The women had been rechained for the boat transfer.

Mary reckoned that there were eighty or ninety men and twenty women here, together with a six-year-old girl and boy belonging to the convicts. Nearly all these stinking, ragged wretches had sunken, pasty cheeks, slack jaws, vacant expressions and sloping beetle brows and were short and spindly with a rickety curvature of the legs. Some were shivering and sweating with ship fever; all were supporting each other as best they could. But at least the seriously ill of the gaols had remained there, thank the Lord.

'I am Captain Watkin Tench. This regrettably small vessel will be transporting you to Botany Bay, in New South Wales, New Holland, as part of a fleet under the command of Captain Arthur Phillip. He will assume the Governorship of that virgin territory when we disembark.

'Captain Phillip will join the fleet in about two months' time at the Mother Bank, off the Isle of Wight. However, we and the *Friendship* transport shall proceed to the Mother Bank without delay. If there is still hardly a breath of wind this evening when it is time to move, we'll have to be towed out of the Hamoaze into Plymouth Sound by the guardship's boats, and then when the wind freshens, we shall set sail up-Channel immediately.

'After leaving the Mother Bank, we shall call, in due course, at the island of Tenerife, at Rio de Janeiro in the Brazils and at the Cape of Good Hope, on our sixteen-thousand-mile passage to Botany Bay at the bottom of the world.'

'The bottom of the world!' Everyone gasped and Mary's heart thumped. Plymouth was far enough from home and that was only about thirty miles of water. Sixteen thousand miles! Did God's sun even shine there?

'You will find that summer is winter and winter is summer down there, and the summers are mighty hot,' he said, as if in answer. 'Now, the reason that we sail across the Atlantic and then back, rather than just follow the African coast southward, is to take advantage of strong winds and currents. We get the benefit of the north-east trades and then the Brazilian Current to take us down to Rio. We then continue southward on that current until we've caught the westerlies, which will sweep us across to the Cape.

'On my right is Captain Thomas Gilbert, the ship's master, and on my left is Mr John White, who will be the colony's Surgeon-General. Pray God that we do not need Mr White's services too often on the passage.'

Gilbert, a fat, bald, unsmiling man, was well into middle age. He was dwarfed by the amazingly good-looking White, a slim gentleman with black hair and barely older than Tench. Mary had already noticed the surgeon's roving eye – and *he'd* spotted *her*.

'And,' said Tench, 'I also pray God that I do not have to use the very effective firepower of my company of marines.'

He turned to the redcoats. 'You will not hesitate to fire your muskets at the first sniff of insurrection.'

Facing the convicts again, he said, 'You will shortly be taken to the 'tween deck. You women will have your own apartment, which is separated from the men's by the marines' quarters. There are strong bulkheads between these sections. At night, and during storms, of course, the hatches will be locked, bolted and cross-barred. They will be guarded at all times. A windsail will be rigged by each hatchway to direct *some* fresh air down there during the day. Save for Mr White's purposes, no candles or lanterns will be allowed, as none of us wishes to be burned alive, do we? So, it will be dark, and stifling, I am sorry to say, for, unlike the *Dunkirk*, there are no portholes.

'You men will be kept in irons while you are below. However, for those of you who behave yourselves, there is a possibility – just a possibility, mind – that Captain Phillip will have you released from your fetters. All of you, men and women, will find that your accommodation is far superior to that on the prison hulk and you will have flock mattresses. Everyone will be exercised on deck twice daily: a certain number at a time so that there will be room for you to move.'

Tench cleared his throat.

'During our two months' wait at the Mother Bank, we hope to give both marines and convicts a daily ration of fresh beef and vegetables; though, unfortunately, there is some sort of problem about obtaining these necessaries at the moment.

'After we have left England, the weekly ration for marines will be seven pounds of bread, four pounds of salt beef, two pounds of salt pork, two pints of peas, three pints of oatmeal, six ounces of butter, three quarters of a pound of cheese and half a pint of vinegar. Male prisoners will be at two-thirds allowance. Female prisoners will be at two thirds of the male prisoners' allowance and children one third.

'Besides water,' said Tench, 'the marines will have half a pint of rum and a gallon of beer per day. And when we reach Tenerife, a pint of wine instead of beer. Water alone will have to suffice for you prisoners because, except for Mr White's patients, intoxicating liquor is forbidden.'

He cleared his throat again and Mary thought that he could do with some water himself.

'The storeships will have enough provisions on board to last us for two years from our arrival at Botany Bay.

'I join Mr White in deploring the fact that the Government has not seen fit to supply some of the necessaries allowed to ships even on a common passage to the West Indies, such as sugar, currants, rice, sago, barley, portable soup, tea, spices and pickled vegetables. And all that they have provided to prevent the scurvy is an inadequate quantity of essence of malt!

'Once you are settled in your apartments, I shall come amongst you and offer any assistance that it is in my power to give. If you wish to write to your loved ones, you may do so. I am under orders to read every letter and, likewise, those that you receive.

'You are to be washed and scrubbed and your heads and beards shaved–'

'Oh no! Not our heads shaved!' Mary and the other women clasped their heads in horror. '*Oh no!*

'Silence! This is to reduce the numbers of lice and other vermin. Nightcaps will be issued to warm your bald pates. Those of you who are in need of clothes will be supplied.

'Take the prisoners below!'

CHAPTER 10

Oh, God, Mary Broad groaned to herself in the darkness of the packed apartment.

They were all swaying, squashed together under thin woollen blankets, their flock mattresses. It was a freezing night, way out in the windy Channel. How cold her body in this cotton slop frock. How cold her head, despite the nightcap.

Aw, I wish I knew how poor Father and Dolly are - whether they're still alive! Someone's sure to have taken poor Pincher by now and eaten him! Neither Father nor Dolly can write words. And Goody-madam and Edward ain't wrote, so that *sniffy pair must have washed their hands of me because I'm a felon. So I'll never get a letter unless the Reverend Mr Baron writes one for Father and Dolly. He* said *he would but he ain't, has he, all these dang long, wearisome months. Maybe he caught the gaol distemper when he came to see us in Exeter and has died. He was only a skinny gentleman; wouldn't take much to kill* him, *I shouldn't have thought.*

Well, Will Bryant can write words; he could have wrote a letter for me. But now they've put us in women's and men's apartments, I won't never see him.

'Oh yes I will!' she cried, loud enough to have woken the whole apartment, if anyone could have slept on this icy night. 'Nobody shall stop us meeting. If there's a *Will,* there's a way!'

* * *

There was a way and Will found it, as dawn broke.

'Morning, my lovely,' smiled the now beardless fisherman with the grey nightcap.

Lovely? She felt ugly.

He put down his bucket, brimful of pea soup. It certainly looked more appetizing than the nauseous boiled-barley breakfast that they had suffered daily on the *Dunkirk.*

Careful not to hit his own or Mary's head in the four-foot deck space, he lifted the Cornish girl to her unsteady feet and kissed her passionately as she swam in the warm pools of his dark-brown eyes. All these women were whistling and yelling from their mattresses but she didn't care; they were jealous. Her heart was pounding and her shaky legs would surely give way if he let go.

Suddenly he did and she sank back onto the mattress.

'Yes, gal, you knew you could trust your Will, and Jimmy here,' he grunted, winking at the grinning, clumsy-footed Irishman. Jimmy had followed him down, slopping a goodly amount from his own bucket before reaching the bottom of the steps. 'You knew you could trust us to find favour with that soft-hearted fool Cap'n Tench, to be the chosen convicts to bring down the provisions to the female apartment. I can't stay exercising my lips and my jawing tacks, though, because these nineteen screeching, starving cats that you have the misfortune to share with will claw ol' Will apart. Rot me, hark at this rare ol' dido!'

'Dear Will, could – could you write some words of writing to my poor father and Dolly? Just to tell them that I'm keeping brave, but that I miss them terrible, like...?'

He slopped the soup into her tin bowl. 'Er... er...'

He spilt some on the deck. 'Yes... yes, I... er... I suppose I could do that, my... my lovely...'

'Suppose? Stow me, surely it's not too much to ask from a – from a friend?'

Jimmy caught Mary's eye, with his 'calming-the-troubled-waters' look. He could read the Cornish couple like a book of writing and knew that two explosions were imminent.

'Ah, sure he will, Mary darlin',' he said, in this soft Antrim voice of his. 'For if *he* doesn't, I'll write it instead.'

She looked at him in disbelief. 'You can write words? An *Irishman*?'

He pretended to be hurt, putting on a pained expression. 'Sure, and why not? As a wee lad, didn't this poor misfortunate Irish-speaker have a dream? Did he not dream of escaping from his remote and near-inaccessible glen community of farmers, fishermen and fairies by learning to speak, read and write in English? To do this, did he not go to school till he was nigh twenty years of age? Did he not sit exposing his half-bare little Roman Catholic bottom to the devilish teeth of many a freezing north-easter, in one of those cliff caves at Red Bay: the driest one, eight feet up, that we call the "School Cave", like? Did he not meet there that rich and intelligent pupil James MacDonnell whose own bottom was always beautifully covered with superfine green velvet and who learned the harp music from his father's lodger, blind Art O'Neill, and taught your own James how to appreciate that lovely instrument? Aye, did James Martin not continue there until he was nigh twenty years old, learning Latin, rhetoric and philosophy from that cane-wielding Catholic, Maurice Traynor, who taught both Catholics and Protestants? Auld Maurice breaking the then Penal Law which said, "Thou shalt not teach Roman Catholics," so risking transportation.

'Aye,' said Jimmy, 'the master seiner will do it. For if your oul Jimmy were to write the letter, 'twould make our William so green with jealousy that this wee fella was worming his way into your affections that the rich green grass of Ireland would be pale in comparison!'

'Confound it, I'll do it,' muttered Will, abruptly turning his back on them and slopping his soup over the bony legs of the next ravenous group.

CHAPTER 11

'So, you come from beautiful Fowey, Mary Broad,' mused Captain Watkin Tench, his blue eyes smiling.

He had joined her, Catherine, Mary Shepherd and three other nightcapped girls leaning on the ship's starboard rail, resting after their Saturday morning deck-walking. The *Charlotte* was now anchored on the Mother Bank with the other five transports and the three storeships, under the watchful guns of the *Sirius* man-of-war and the little *Supply* brig.

'Having read your letter, and feeling as if I know you a little, I am wondering what a girl like you is doing on a convict transport.'

Her grey eyes flashed. 'And what's *that* supposed to mean, Cap'n Tench?' she snapped, even though she knew that she was risking a flogging by speaking thus. 'I'm with my own, ain't I? There are no ladies *here*. What's so special about *me* that makes you say that?'

Amazingly, Tench was blushing. 'I mean, girl, that all the other letters I have read are full of self-pity: hoping to seek sympathy from the recipients – or, more likely, from the authorities, such as myself.'

'Rot that!' she cried. 'I feel sorry for those I love but I ain't the sort to feel sorry for myself - well, not for long, anyhow. And be danged if I'd put my deepest feelings in a letter so that the likes of you, sir, could gloat over them with your gentlemen friends. Stow me, what kind of person d'you think I am?'

The smile broadened. 'There you are. You have made my point, Mary Broad. You *are* different from the others: you have a fierce Cornish independence of spirit, and a temper to match.'

'He's right there,' muttered Catherine Prior, spitting overboard, as Tench sauntered along to another group of women. 'Yes, say the wrong thing to Mary Broad and you'd soon feel the lash of her tongue, as I've found to my cost many a time these past months. And she seemed such a sweet little thing when we first saw her in the carrier's wagon.'

'If she said the wrong thing to High and Mighty Tench,' said Mary Shepherd, herself almost spitting the name, 'she'd feel the lash of the cat-o'-nine-tails! It's a wonder he let you get away with what you did say, Mary.' She fingered the pockmarks. 'Perhaps he's keeping his flower-loving Cornish whore's skin as smooth as petals so he can stroke it himself one of these nights – hi, leave my ears alone, you bitch!'

'Don't you call *me* a whore!' cried Mary, pulling down the ears so hard that both girls fell to the deck. She managed to sit astride her enemy and held her wrists to the boards. 'Say you're sorry!'

'Whore. Whore! *Whore!* WHORE!'

'Owww!' Catherine had kicked Mary in the back in a repeat of the Lakeman assault and would have done so again if somebody had not grabbed her from behind.

'Leave her,' rasped Jane Langley, the tall, strong young black woman from London's East End. She had been transferred from the *Lady Penrhyn* women's transport to be Captain Gilbert's unwilling bed-warmer. 'Don't be so bloody stupid, all of you. Get up, you two. Tench'll whip the lot of you, like what happened to me on the *Lady P* when I was caught fighting.'

Luckily the sailors had been singing their shanties and everyone, including the officers, was busy so nobody had heard or seen.

Catherine realized that there was no sense in arguing with such a powerful woman, who, by the look of her, must have won a hundred fights in that infamous quarter of London. Jane let go and Catherine jerked her friend to her feet.

Jane, likewise, helped the wincing Mary as the other pair crossed to the larboard rail, muttering.

'Thank 'ee,' grunted Mary.

They leant on the rail together.

‘Forget it, gel,’ said Jane, patting her hand with one nearly as big as Will’s. ‘What’s your name?’

‘Mary Broad. I’m from Cornwall.’

Jane’s white teeth gleamed as she grinned. ‘Really? Speaking like you do, in that fast, rising and falling, singing-like way, I thought you was from London.’

‘Ah, whist, stop funning me,’ said Mary forcing a smile. ‘Faugh, my dang back hurts, the bloody bitch.’

Jane massaged it. ‘Auntie Jane’ll make it better. I’m Jane Langley.’

‘Yiss, I know.’

‘Yeah,’ sighed Jane, ‘everyone knows me, don’t they? Captain Gilbert’s bloody bed-warmer. Like a slave on a slave ship. I should still be on the *Lady P* but he had me brought across. Instead of being in the arms of that fat son of a sow, I could be with Philip now.’

Mary stood back from the rail and looked at her in astonishment.

‘You and Cap’n Phillip?’

‘No, you noddy-head!’ she snorted. ‘Philip Scriven. He’s a seaman on the *Lady P*. I’ve always liked seamen. Well, I suppose it’s natural, being as I live – lived – in Blackhorse Yard, in Wapping parish where all the sailors are. But I’m not a prostitute, mind; though many of my mates are, being as how they’re so bloody starving, like.

‘My story, if you’re interested, is that I served my apprenticeship and am a skilled embroideress. I wanted to get on in the world. So, with the little money what I’d managed to save, I bought some luverly material for a frock and made meself tidy, like. And now look at me, dressed in sacking like most of the other *Penrhyn* women ’cos the clothes they first gave us fell to bits! The very first evening I wore my luverly frock, I met an ’andsome gentleman in the street. “Such good fortune!” thought I. “Lord Jesus is guiding me tonight!” He seemed a jolly man so I invited him back to my friend Mary Finn’s in Blackhorse Yard, where we three sat and drank together. Then we said goodnight to him because it was getting late, so he had to leave. Three days later he saw us in the street and hauled us before the justices. He said that the night us three had drunk together, Mary Finn and me had stolen five guineas, and nine shillings and sixpence in change, from his pocket.'

'But why did he want to get you into trouble?'

'*I* don't know. But he then met one of our witnesses, a man, in the Brown Bear and offered not to appear against us if he was given four guineas. Our witness passed the message to us in the King's Arms lockup, but we told him that we was not guilty and we didn't have no money to pay our accuser. If we'd really stolen the money, we'd have had some money to pay him, wouldn't we?'

'So...' murmured Mary, 'because you'd been dressed nice, he thought you *was* rich. And *you* thought *he* was rich because he was well dressed. But he'd only pretended to be a gentleman to get your money. Either that or he was rich but wanted revenge because you and Mary Finn didn't give your bodies to him... Surely not?'

'Well, whatever the reason, we found ourselves on trial at the Bailey. D'you know, in court, he had the bloody sauce to say that it was our witness who'd approached *him* and offered him four guineas.'

'So what happened, Jane?'

'Unfortunately that witness and a woman witness for us got their stories muddled and was charged with what you call "perjury", like. The judge said that the normal punishment for our "crime" was a whipping and six to twelve months in gaol. But because we'd called "perjured witnesses", he sentenced Mary Finn and me to seven years' transportation. *She's* on the *Lady P.* Lord Jesus, we ain't thieves; we've always behaved right. Are *you* innocent, too, gel? What's your story?'

'It's a long one...' said Mary, sucking in her breath as she rubbed her back.

CHAPTER 12

'What's all the excitement about up on deck this morning?' a sweating Mary asked the stubble-headed Will and Jimmy who had arrived with dinner. Hating them seeing her own stubble, she had swiftly pulled on the nightcap, despite the June heat.

Will murmured, 'A lad named Power escaped from the *Alexander* about eleven o'clock last night.'

He knelt down to hand Mary her meal, a full plate of steaming fresh beef, rice and onions: marvellous luxuries taken aboard here, in Santa Cruz roadstead, off the sunny, mountainous island of Tenerife.

'And,' he grunted, 'who can blame him with so much gaol sickness aboard her even before the wretched vessel set sail. Rowed off in her jolly boat he did. He'd been allowed to help the sailors watering the ship and hid himself on deck while the barrels were being unloaded from the boats. He stayed there when every other suffering mortal was stowed below for another boiling night. Then when everything was quiet, he must have climbed down the anchor hawser and swum to the jolly boat lying astern. Lucky beggar, I wish I could've rowed away with him.'

In the sunlight from the grating, her tired eyes searched his.

'Would you have taken *me* with you, Will?'

'Well now, my beauty, how could ol' Will do that? Once we'd got ashore, you couldn't run like the wind when your belly's full of that babby, not after being six months with child, you couldn't.'

'God damn that black-bearded son of a sow that gave it to me!' she hissed. She stroked her bloated stomach through her frock. It still fitted because, despite the regular meals, the rest of her had stayed skinny, with all her grieving.

Yes, she told herself, *if I'd given myself fully to Will, on the* Dunkirk, *like he kept trying to make me do, this babby might have been* his *for all we knew... But just because he's my protector, it don't give him the right to use my body. There's a greater protector than Will Bryant. I ain't forgot all those Sunday lessons at St Fimbarrus's!*

'If Power's foxy,' said Will, 'he'll lie low on the island for a couple of day: once he's got himself a brave long way from this northern end. Cap'n Phillip ain't going to delay the fleet to search for one plaguy convict.'

'Aw, Will, I pray he gets away, bless him. Not just for his sake but to give hope to the rest of us: that some of us might escape and be free one of these days.'

Will grunted again. 'One thing's as sure as the fact that your face is even prettier with that babby inside you. The child won't be freeborn. It'll be born in captivity on the *Charlotte*, like nigger brats on slave ships. It'll be no better than a nigger. Nor ain't you no more.'

'How dare you compare me with a nigger! *I'm* nobody's slave! We're proud, independent folk us Broads. Cap'n Tench knows it. Father's never been no mortal's slave; his only master is Lord Jesus, and He's *my* only master, too. We go – went – to Fowey parish church every Sunday morning and –'

'Parish church? Parish church! Pah. Why didn't the old fool take you to a Methody chapel? Bloody traitor to his class he is – Owww!'

She'd slapped his left cheek.

'Damn you, Will Bryant! Nobody calls my dear father an old fool and a bloody traitor, d'you hear? Nobody!'

The cheek twitched. 'You little bitch!' He raised his fist.

But before this big man could strike her own quivering face, Jimmy had put down his tray, leapt across and grabbed Will's arm.

'No, Will!' gasped the Irishman. 'For the love of God, man, have ye gone off your head?'

Will Bryant rose and shook off his friend's trembling hands.

'No, Jimmy. Not quite,' he muttered. 'But one thing's as sure as the horror in your eyes: I will do if I'm stuck on this prison ship much longer.'

* * *

'... Ninety-nine! One 'undred!' The hoarse shouts of the *Alexander's* bosun's mate carried across the twenty yards of sparkling violet-blue water, as the convict ship's red and white pennant, 'the whip', fluttered gaily in the breeze.

Mary and the other assembled convicts could clearly see the blood-washed victim slumped at the upright grating. Lord, his face was nearly as white as the houses below those high conical-peaked mountains over there!

'Poor bugger,' muttered Will, looking into Mary's anguished eyes, as everyone was herded below to the bilge-reeking, rat-infested 'tween deck to rejoin their sick companions. 'He'll be heavily ironed now. Caught sleeping among the rocks in a cove at the south of the island, eh? Damn their eyes. Damn their cowardly eyes! As sure as my name be William Bryant, the swine would never have caught *me. I'll* show them. Just you wait. I'll show them one of these days!'

CHAPTER 13

'Mary Broad, you are the mother of a fine wee girl, so you are. What are you going to call her?'

It was the middle of the September afternoon and this torturous business had been going on since the breaking of her waters at dawn. All the other women, except her midwives, Jane Langley and Catherine Prior, were exercising on deck, now that the rain had stopped. As she sat on this horseshoe-shaped birthing stool, Mary saw, through a blur of sweat, John White's smiling pale-blue Irish eyes.

Then she looked at the closed eyes of this screeching, bloodied, very slimy, very tiny, red-and-wrinkle-faced creature that he had gently placed in her arms.

Aw, poor little mite, what a world I've brought you into! So helpless you are. So small and helpless. Look at your dear soft little fingers, that'll be calloused before you're full grown. This creased little brow, that'll have real wrinkles long before its time. These pretty little feet, that are doomed to walk the cruel rocks of a foreign land. This little back, that'll be bent with weariness while you're still a child. This skin as smooth as Father's rose petals, that the scorching sun of a land at the bottom of the world will turn to leather. This tiny little heart beating like a newborn bird's, and just as fragile; God give it strength to survive!

Her own heart skipped a beat. *What would Father say, though? A babby born out of wedlock... But it wasn't* my *fault, it wasn't* my *fault! Aw, stow your self-pity, woman, stow it! Your Auntie Dolly would love you, my babby, because you're so beautiful! No other babby in the whole world's as beautiful as you, my dear little -*

'Mary Broad. Did you hear me? What are you going to call her? Now we've left Rio de Janeiro and our gallant crew are sailing us back across this wild Atlantic, they'll want to know whom to toast when they're given their additional allowance of grog in her honour. So, what are you going to call this first baby to be born on the *Charlotte*? A baby who'll grow to be a *pretty* wench if she takes after her mother.'

Her brain raced. She stared blankly at the handsome young gentleman wiping his fine hands on a cloth as he ducked under the lantern swinging from the whitewashed beam. On the orders of this lanky surgeon, all the timbers on the *Charlotte*'s 'tween deck had been coated with quicklime to prevent the slime caused by the convicts' breath. Yes, the *Charlotte* was definitely an improvement on the *Dunkirk* – The *Charlotte*...

'Er – why, Charlotte, of course, sir. What else, for mercy's sake? Charlotte, after the ship.'

He looked cross. 'Surely the name Charlotte has a greater significance for you than a mere ship?'

'Oh, and after the Queen, too, of course,' she blushed. 'God bless her.'

'Well, I suppose your first instinct was right, for 'tis fitting to commemorate the ship,' he murmured, patting Mary's sweat-drenched shoulder. 'Because on this dark, rainy day, Saturday the eighth of September 1787, aboard the ship taking us to a sunny new life, you've produced a new life. A new life for our new land, New South Wales.

'When we *get* there,' he sighed. 'This passage is so deuced tedious. My patience is wearing very thin. We only left Rio on Tuesday, and, indeed, 'twas a charming city, but it's this endless ocean that I get so impatient about. It will be at least six weeks before we even reach the Cape of Good Hope!

'I tell ye truly,' he said, his northern Irish accent coming through strongly, 'I'm looking forward to New South Wales with eager anticipation. I can't *wait* to get to know the native folk and see the different vegetation and animal life. By God, it's exciting! You lasses and I, and little Charlotte here, are making history. D'ye realize that?'

Damn his boyish enthusiasm! She wiped away the plaguy sweat from her eyes and looked straight into his.

'It might be exciting for *you*, sir, but the only folk *this* lass wants to see are her own beloved father and young sister Dolly. And the only vege – whatever-you-call-it – she wants to see are her father's sweet-smelling pink roses in his garden. And the only animal she cares about is Pincher, her grey and tan terrier with the split nose. A pox on New South Wales and everything that lives there!'

He roared with laughter, his face flushing.

'Such spirit! Sure, if Charlotte's father has as much fire in his belly as her mother, what a lass *she'll* be... Who *is* the father?'

If Mary told White that she had been raped, Spence – aboard the *Friendship* – would be hanged. She hated the swine with all her being; but she *loved* Jesus and knew what *He* had taught; she'd heard it enough times at St Fimbarrus's.

'... Er – John Spence, sir. He – he comforted me when we were on the *Dunkirk*. I was that low in spirits then.'

White grunted. 'Ah, yes, he was one of the *Mercury* transport's convict mutineers who brought the ship into Torbay and were then captured by *Helena*. Not a good choice, Mary Broad, not a good choice. The child must be given the name of both her parents, though, so welcome to the world, Charlotte Spence Broad.'

* * *

Because of the strong westerlies, it took the fleet just five weeks and four days to sail from Rio to the Cape. The *Charlotte* anchored in Table Bay at seven o'clock on the hazy evening of Saturday 13 October. The *Sirius* had been here three hours already, one of many ships of different nations.

Standing at the rail, holding her baby, with Will and Jimmy on either side, Mary sighed loudly. To the distant accompaniment of builders' hammers from the rapidly expanding town, a white mist was cascading down the huge, flat-topped mountain behind.

Tench was here now and she thrilled as these long, sensitive fingers gently pressed her shoulders.

'Yes, Mary Broad, it is a black, dreary-looking mountain, isn't it? One of the world's most beautiful natural sites for a town? Fiddlesticks! Give me Rio de Janeiro any time. The many descriptions published about this place are far too flattering.'

Jimmy patted her arm. 'Sure, she's read every one of them, haven't ye, darling?'

Hugging Charlotte, Mary muttered, 'Even if I *could* read, I wouldn't want to read about this dang place.' She could not be bothered to look any more and glanced along the rail at Jane Langley, now expecting a baby of her own. Jane was having a difficult pregnancy.

Within a week of their arrival, with John White moving to shore quarters, the screaming black girl had to be taken back to the *Lady Penrhyn* so that Surgeon Arthur Bowes Smyth could attend her. Henrietta Langley was born on Tuesday 23 October, two months prematurely.

Jane, with baby, returned to the *Charlotte* on the day of another happy event. On Sunday 28 October, before the delighted eyes of almost everyone aboard, the grey-eyed Charlotte was baptized on the transport's quarterdeck by the fleet's chubby-cheeked chaplain, the Reverend Richard Johnson. To save on water, a sprinkle had to suffice. Mary gazed up at the turquoise sky and thought of her father. What would he have thought of his granddaughter if he could have seen her? If he was alive... She knew one thing: she'd love this little girl more than anything in the world. For, as Jimmy had said, 'Ye can't blame the wee mite because her father's the son of a bachelor!'

Afterwards the two mothers sat in a shady corner, to breastfeed and share experiences.

'So, Jane, you and Henrietta will be living all the time in the captain's comfortable cabin. Comfortable in one way but–'

The big woman shrieked with laughter, making both babies cry.

'*That* whore's son? No, I'll be with the rest of you. He's had his fun and don't want to know me no more. He certainly don't want to know my poor li'l gel. Does he, my love?' she cooed, stroking Henrietta's red cheek, which would have been coffee-coloured if she hadn't been squalling. 'Everyone on the *Lady P* thinks she's Philip's because that's what they've been told, even though they know about Gilbert. I've told Surgeon Bowes the truth, though: Philip and I never lay together. Mr Bowes likes Philip; says he's a good man. But Philip didn't want to know me after Henrietta was born. It was Surgeon Bowes what sent me back here. Even though he's a friend of Gilbert's, he told me it was Gilbert's responsibility to look after me and Henrietta.'

'Surgeon Bowes sounds like a kind man,' said Mary. 'A good surgeon, too, being as how you were early with the baby, like. Kind and good like Mr White. I don't know what I would have done without–'

'Bowes kind!' exploded Jane. 'He hadn't tried to help me that time at the start of the passage when I was flogged with the cat-o'-nine-bloody-tails on my naked buttocks. Naked, and at my time o' month! I started to swear in my best Billingsgate at him and the punishment squad, so they gagged me. And then he said to me, "There has never been a more abandoned set of wretches collected in one place than you *Penrhyn* women. You whores have no sense of shame or common decency." Well, where was *his* shame or decency to witness me being treated like that? Still, what can you expect from a surgeon who won't even give us a supply of rags for our monthly flowers.'

'Bless and save us!' gasped Mary. 'On your bare buttocks at your time of month... Cap'n Tench and Mr White wouldn't allow that to happen on the *Charlotte.* Mr White gives us rags for–'

'Well, perhaps they got to hear about it and had words with Bowes and the other leering buggers, because no other poor gel was stripped *total* naked after that... You know, I've often wondered if it was Bowes what told Gilbert about me and suggested that he might like me in his bed.'

'Yiss,' breathed Mary, 'getting his revenge on you after the Surgeon-General scolded him.'

The ships had been taking on deckfuls of animals and poultry for the new colony, which meant that the *Charlotte* had to squeeze in some convict women from the *Friendship* who had been displaced by sheep. Will and Captain Tench would have preferred the sheep.

While at the Cape, the prisoners were given equal daily rations to the marines and seamen: one-and-a-half pounds of lovely soft bread and the same amount of either fresh beef or the equally delicious roast mutton.

On 12 November, they were back at sea again and, within two days, the *Charlotte*'s crew were drinking another toast: to Catherine Prior's baby boy, John Matthew. The father was Cornishman John Arscott, twenty: he who had rolled on the *Dunkirk*'s boards with the eager Catherine that horrific December night. Arscott, too, had been sent to the Charlotte but then been transferred to the *Scarborough.*

God help the poor child, with a mother like this! thought Mary.

* * *

Charlotte herself was four months old when the fleet turned away from the stomach-emptying waves of the Southern Ocean. *Good riddance to the most terrifying sea in the world,* Mary said to herself, scarcely believing they had left what Jimmy called that 'wild watery wilderness' behind at last. They had battled against shrieking, bone-chilling winds and surfed endless monstrous swells and not once had those merciless allies of Satan given up trying to send them all to the bottom.

In a violent squall, the ships sailed north round Van Diemen's Land. Then, accompanied by gulls, they slowly progressed up New Holland's east coast but well out of sight of land.

CHAPTER 14

The fiddlers were playing and everyone aboard was smiling, cheering and singing. Everyone except Mary Broad and Will Bryant.

Will gripped the starboard rail as the *Charlotte* anchored. 'So, gal,' he muttered, 'this godforsaken place is Botany Bay, is it?'

It was 8 o'clock in the morning on Sunday 20 January 1788. They'd heard that they were two days later than the swift little two-masted brig *Supply*, which had taken the Governor ahead, and a day after the *Scarborough*, *Alexander* and *Friendship*. The anchorage was two miles in from the northern and southern headlands guarding the entrance to this huge bay. The water being so shallow throughout most of the bay, the ships had had to moor far out from the shore, in direct line with the two-mile-wide entrance.

The Cornishman spat into the waves. 'Hold the babby up so she can see what a bleak world you've brought her into.'

The warm breeze was blowing the salt-matted hair into the convict girl's eyes. How painfully bright this white light! Under a clear pale-blue sky, she was peering across the rolling blue waves to where the surf pounded onto the white sands of a marshy shore and onto rock-covered spits. Beyond, shimmering in the summer sun, was a seemingly endless parched moorland of grey scrub and sparse giant white-trunked trees. Despite the heat, she shivered. *Oh, how lonely! - Ghostly!* Some of the trees were dead: charred by fire. Even the live ones looked dead, being clear of branches to an amazing height and with the merest wisps of greyish-green at the top. Long, twisting, untidy branches they were, flung out all over the place like skeletons' arms left frozen forever in the agony of death. The sun's brilliance only served to emphasize the lifelessness of the colours there: light fawns and pale yellows, and those monotonous greys stretching into the vast, dreaded unknown. Oh for the rich greens and browns of home!

'Aw, Will, what a difference from the lush greenness of my beautiful Cornish coast with its coombs and its friendly ol' trees. Dear life, the bottom of the world's a truly terrible place – a scary, *evil* place!'

No twinkling River Fowey here. Was there even a stream? If there wasn't, Charlotte would die of thirst! And what about those marshes? They looked mighty unhealthy, and imagine the Devil's fog swirling round those silver tufts of coarse grass...

Will grunted. 'As sure as my name be William Bryant, this ain't no dang good for a settlement. Cap'n Cook who discovered it must have been blind – or blind drunk – to call it *Botany* Bay. Nothing will grow here; it's too damn sandy. And it ain't no good as a harbour either; it's wide open to the sou'easters. This wind's only a moderate breeze but just look at that swell. Pah, it's plaguy useless!' The master spitter spat again.

'Bryant!' yelled Captain Tench, striding towards them from the quarterdeck steps. 'Cheer up, man, for God's sake. We've got you here safe and well and tolerably well fed, haven't we? Like most of your fellow convicts, you're looking a good deal better than when you came aboard, aren't you? Well, now's your chance to do something to repay us for all that fruit and fresh meat we gave you at the ports of call. As soon as we land, you are to be put in a position of trust. You will be assigned a crew and are to take the Governor's six-oared cutter and lead the other boats round the bay. One thing that this colony will need is a master fisherman, which you have kept boasting to me you are. If you do the job well, I am sure that the Governor will grant you special privileges, including a hut of your own, and, who knows, even someone to tend your garden.'

'Garden? *Garden?* Dang it, nothing will grow here, sir,' snorted Will. Even so, he turned to smile at him because of this unexpected favour.

Mary was astonished to see the Cornishman smiling with his eyes. In all the time that she had known him, even when he'd been about to kiss her, she'd only ever seen his lips smile.

'A hut you say, sir?… I'll surely do the job well. I surely will.'

Jimmy was here, too. 'Hey, Mary,' he breathed, 'there are some natives sitting on the rocks. See? On that jutting bit over on the far left.' There were ten of them: men and boys. 'Black as the Devil's heart, and naked as the day they were born, so they are. Jeez, I don't like the look of those spears; they must be twelve feet long! Talking about hearts, I'll wager those fellas would happily eat mine for breakfast!'

'Ah no, Jimmy...' She laughed, and felt better for it. Despite this burning need of home, this eternal gnawing in the lower left of her belly, she was so relieved that the journey was over at last after eight wearisome, worrisome months. Praise God for that and for keeping them safe. '… Ah no, *you'd* even manage to charm those savages, with that grin of yours.'

The little Irishman squeezed her arm, just above the elbow. The limb was so thin that his forefinger and thumb almost met. She for one was not 'looking a good deal better'.

'Well, me darlin', if ye don't mind, I'd rather we didn't put that to the test. This is as near as *this* gentleman wants to get to *those* gentlemen – ack, can't ye keep Charlotte quiet?'

Oh, Charlotte, whatever's going to happen to you? Mary Broad was full of foreboding again.

'I know how the poor little mite feels,' she said, sniffing back the tears as she rocked her baby. 'Aw, God, I know how she feels.'

Later in the morning, Mary and Charlotte were back here at the rail. Jane and Henrietta were with them. Even though the ship was a long way out, the clear light enabled the women to see what was happening on the southern beach. The Governor and some officers and marine guards from the *Sirius* were trying to make friends with the local tribesmen. At first, they had fled into the scrub but the Governor and the others had pretended to be indifferent and, eventually, the natives reappeared about twenty paces away. Despite Phillip's holding up some red cloth and glittering glass beads and other cheap trinkets, the black fellows were too timid to approach. He showed them his musket, then laid it on the sand. He said something to his officers and they seemed to be protesting but suddenly he advanced alone.

Seeing that the white chief had only presents in his hands, a grey-haired native gave his spears to a younger man and nervously walked halfway towards the Governor. Then the tribesman pointed to the sand and Phillip put down the presents, bravely turned his back and retraced his sandy steps for a few yards.

The black man picked up the gifts and hurried back to his companions. A younger warrior left his own spears behind and he, too, came forward, indicating that he wanted some presents. One of the officers brought forth more, put them down and then withdrew.

Eventually the natives allowed Phillip and the others to walk up to them and hand over the remaining delights.

Mary turned to Jane. 'They're like childer at Christmas. Look 'ee.'

Those with presents were holding out their hands for more, jumping about excitedly and laughing, jostling each other to get the best baubles.

Then they grew more confident and began feeling the whites' coats, waistcoats and shirts. One of the officers removed his hat to mop his brow and the natives whooped in amazement. Another officer had queued hair, which the grey-haired tribesman suddenly grabbed, telling his companions to look at this strange style. More astonished whoops.

Braver still now, they let the boat crews dress them with coloured papers and jingling fool's caps: roars of delight!

Mary looked at Charlotte, whose grey eyes were blinking in the sun.

The mother sighed. 'No baubles for you, my sweet'art.' Turning to Jane, she was astonished to see her weeping.

'What's the matter with *you*?'

The black woman sniffed. 'Seeing all them dirty, sooty fellows with red-painted faces reminds me. Seeing 'em dancing about, dressed up so prettily in their white fools' caps and red ribbons and coloured paper, reminds me of the dancing chimney-sweepers in the May Day processions, their own sooty faces smeared with rose pink. May Day in dear ol' London...'

'May Day,' mused Mary, 'birds and butterflies and flowers. Children singing and fiddlers playing while us maids with our garlands dance round the maypole on the green. Pincher barking crazily at our heels. Dolly there, laughing, sitting on Father's knee. And Mother fresh from making pasties, her dear small hands still covered with flour and smelling of onions and herbs...' A lump formed in her throat and she, too, wept.

In the late afternoon, the master seiner and his boats returned on a mercifully gentler swell. A beaming Will Bryant climbed over the *Charlotte*'s rail, to be greeted by Mary with her baby in her arms. Jimmy rushed across to join them.

'Ho, woman!' cried the Cornishman, giving her such a bear hug that Charlotte screeched in protest. 'We ain't done too bad for first go. We've caught whacks of big rays, plenty of bream and mullet and a goodly number of different sorts of small'uns. Dang me if I can't see that hut rising before my eyes. And my own little old servant sweating in the noon sun in my garden, trying to make something grow, in *Botany* Bay.'

CHAPTER 15

'Lord Jesus,' gasped Jane Langley. She and Mary were leaning against the starboard rail, on this warm Monday morning, clutching their bawling baby girls.

Captain Tench, seven-year-old Alexander Ross and a dozen armed marines were stumbling along the southern beach to meet the same number of spear-brandishing natives. Alexander was the son of Major Robert Ross, the testy and unpopular Lieutenant-Governor.

'Oh, Mary, Major Ross had no right to let Tench drag that poor little boy with him. Mercy on us, look at him, poor little devil, holding his hat on his little head while Tench's cruel hand pulls him along. Look at his poor little legs slithering in the sand.'

Mary rested her own hand on Jane's white knuckles and looked into her worried eyes.

'Don't you fret, gal, he'll be fine,' she said with a confidence that she did not feel. 'Watkin Tench ain't a stupid man – not like some of 'em – he'll keep the boy safe. They won't harm a curly red hair on Alexander's head.'

Jane tore at her own curly hair, for the captain was leaving his men behind and just taking Alexander to meet the tribesmen.

Tench stooped and began unbuttoning the boy's coarse linen shirt.

Jane shuddered. 'Look at that hideous ugly old red-painted savage with the long grey beard and great long, barbed spear. He – he's – Oh Lord love us!'

'Calm yourself, Jane. Look 'ee!'

The native had now dropped the spear and was advancing, hands open wide. He gently put his right hand on the boy's big, floppy black hat and fingered it. Then he felt the shirt and, with a great effort, somehow managed to bend slightly and stroke the side of the brown fustian trousers: like a smith with a lame horse. Alexander shrivelled back and Tench motioned him to rejoin the marines.

Freed from the officer's grip, Master Ross turned, hurtled along the sand and flung his small arms round Corporal Alexander Anderson's great big legs, clinging to them for dear life.

'Oh, merciful Lord,' gulped Jane, burying her face in Mary's shoulder. 'For a moment there, I thought he was a dead'un.'

'Stow me,' breathed Mary, 'look, Jane, look!'

The whole fleet had erupted with whistles and catcalls, as the tall, dark and handsome Private William Segar Jones strode forward, opened his white breeches and exposed himself to the natives.

'The dirty devil,' sniggered Jane. 'What's he doing that for?... Gor, the dirty devil!'

Mary Broad roared with laughter. 'Cap'n's orders. So those bearded natives know what sex our shaved boys are under their clothes! Hi, Jimmy!' she yelled at her friend. He was with his own friend, the lanky, sandy-haired James Cox, at the far end of the rail. 'Ain't you glad you ain't a private of marines under Cap'n Tench's orders?'

The Irishman's sunken cheeks blushed and James Cox grinned wickedly at Jane.

'Ye're right there, Mary darlin'. Sure, I never thought I'd see the day when I was glad to be a convict rather than a marine. Ha, poor Sugar Jones is a *private* fella no more!'

CHAPTER 16

Meanwhile the Governor, sharing Will's despair about Botany Bay, had set off on a three-boat reconnaissance party up the coast.

He eventually returned on Wednesday evening, telling his officers to inform everyone about a magnificent harbour just twelve miles away by sea. Named Port Jackson by the late Captain Cook, it was a far better place for a settlement, where ships could anchor safely, close to a fertile shore, and where there was plenty of fresh water, unlike Botany Bay's limited supply.

However, the journey northward was delayed because of the astounding discovery that they now had visitors at the bottom of the world: two French ships on a voyage of exploration. The British stayed to exchange civilities with the commander, the Comte de la Pérouse, but, in truth, there were far more important things to do than gossip with Frenchies. '*Adieu!*' and 'Anchors aweigh!' were the only words worth saying at a time like this.

* * *

Finally, at seven o'clock on the bright evening of Saturday 26 January, a light breeze carried the *Charlotte* and her companions between the towering, wave-dashed sandstone headlands guarding the entrance to Port Jackson. Inside this vast, beautiful blue harbour, where the high sandstone ledges sloped into the water, were shores covered by dense woods of a deep olive colour. From the fringes, dozens of natives could be seen watching the ships.

'Dang me, Jimmy,' gulped Will, 'the size of this here harbour. Thousands of big ships could anchor in it!'

'Aye, Will, and there'd still be room to swing thousands of proverbial cats. A wee bit bigger than Fowey's harbour, Mary?'

'Yiss, you *could* say that,' she breathed. 'In faith, it must be the biggerest in God's world!'

Passing large sharks, small islands, long sandy beaches, and thick woods occasionally broken by sandhills, the ships sailed up the southern side of the harbour for six miles, by Will's reckoning. They anchored in one of the smallest of the deep, sheltered coves, tying up to the trees on either side, just within hailing distance of the *Supply*. The Governor had arrived on Friday evening aboard that vessel, which was moored at the head of this half-mile-long cove. Everyone was ashore, clearing the woods to put up tents by the banks of the sparkling stream flowing into the cove. A flagpole had been erected but the Union flag barely stirred.

Unlike the local birdlife. At a safe distance, scores of brilliantly coloured parrots with blue bellies were screeching at those noisy axe-wielding intruders.

'And look at all those tiny green ones flying up over there!' gasped Mary. 'Swacks and swacks of 'em, smaller than my fist. Swarming like plaguy greenfly!'

'This is more like it, gal,' said Will, feelingly. 'A snug cove with deep water close to shore.'

'And with a freshwater stream,' she sobbed. 'Beautiful, delicious, fresh, cool water for my Charlotte. Lord be praised!'

'Yes, gal. Lord be praised. Amen to that.'

'Jeez!' exclaimed Jimmy, pointing. 'The size of those skeleton trees there!'

Mary could not believe her eyes. The giant gum trees seemed rooted in the very rocks. Though few in number, it was as if they had sniffily pushed past all their much smaller neighbours to reach the water's edge, saying, 'You may think you're betterer than us, being shiny green and healthy, and we're all raggy bark, like, but you can't grow on rocks like we can, can you?'

Captain Tench was behind her. 'Yes, Martin, a pleasant pinkish variety. Friendlier-looking than their miserable greyish-green cousins at Botany Bay, what? It is astonishing how they are even growing in the sparse sandy soil among the gaps in the rocks. And look at those other giants over *there.* Gad, their trunks must be nearly thirty feet round! An abundance of trees, indeed. It is a fine, sheltered cove to be sure, Bryant, but it will need much backbreaking toil to cut down all those trees to build a settlement. It will build a few muscles, too,' he said, glancing at Jimmy's spindly arms.

Mary chuckled. 'Not on a herring-gut like him, sir, I'm thinking. He'll always be a puny boy.'

'It will make a man of him,' smiled Tench.

'The impudence!' protested Jimmy, his bright-blue eyes twinkling in the evening sun. 'If James Martin, Esquire, of the County Antrim is not a man by now, at twenty-seven years of age, I don't know what he is, sir.'

'Get thee a wife, Martin,' said Tench – himself a bachelor. '*That* will make a man of you!'

The Irishman reddened and Mary thought that, for once, he was lost for words.

But he quickly stammered, 'S-s-sure, and who would be wanting a skinny wee fella like me?'

She put an arm round him. 'There's a naked native gal in among those trees. She's got her big black eyes on you.'

Tench's smile vanished. 'The temptations of Eve in "Paradise Lost": the Fall of man. Do not put ideas into his head, Mary Broad. The Governor will punish severely any man who gets entangled with the Indian women. God's my life, 'twould start a war! Clapped in irons you'd be.'

'Aye,' grinned Jimmy, ''twould be a padlock rather than wedlock for yours truly.'

'It would be worse than that, Martin. It would be execution at dawn. And speaking of dawn,' said Tench, 'all you men will be landed at first light.'

He turned to Will. 'Because, save only you, master seiner Bryant, and some mariners of your choosing, all the marines and sailors and the rest of you convicts, Martin, will be hacking away at those trees and grubbing up the roots. Great stretches must needs be cleared and, as you can see, there is thick undergrowth: ferns and the Lord-knows-what tangling weeds.'

Tench's smile returned. 'After all these months aboard a rolling and tossing ship, you will all be staggering and stumbling into each other like drunkards: straight from the longboat into the wood, with no flat, open ground on which to put your feet, because you'll be landing at a different part from where the *Supply*'s men are working. I can see it all now,' he laughed, deliberately looking at Jimmy, for Tench was well aware of the Irishman's two left feet.

Mary turned to the officer. 'And what about those *savages*, sir?' she asked, fiercely. 'Do you think they'll stay standing idly by? My life, I know what us Cornish folk would do if shiploads of armed foreigners landed on our dear shore. Hark at the beggars now, shouting their heads off, from the bottom of their throats!'

'*Warra, warra, war!*' cried the natives. '*Warra, warra, war!*'

Tench's own bright-blue eyes clouded as he looked into her anxious grey ones. 'Well, they have not attacked us so far, thank God. Admittedly those vociferous, guttural cries are the equivalent of a Cornishman's "Begone, you sons of whores!" but the Indians were sociable and peaceable enough when I presented them with that looking-glass at Botany Bay. Why, they even gave me a large club in exchange, sufficient to fell an ox.'

Will grunted. 'You were lucky they didn't fell *you* with it, sir! I don't trust those ugly black beggars. They're waiting for cock-shut, as sure as my name be William Bryant. They're waiting for black night.'

CHAPTER 17

Eleven nights had fallen but there'd been no trouble from the natives. So, on Wednesday 6 February, the women were rowed to the cleared beach. Mary and Jane were in the final group, at 6 o'clock in the evening. All women and children had been issued with clean slop clothing to replace their rags. But much of it was of terrible quality and far too small even for women of common size. Mary's new cotton frock was not only tight under the arms, it barely covered her calves, while Jane's exposed her knees.

Massing all day, the black clouds were threatening to burst, as the cutter's keel furrowed the sand. Jane, after jumping out herself, helped Mary from the boat – damned difficult with babies in their arms.

'Stow me, Jane, the bloody beach is swaying! God's my life! Hold me, for mercy's sake, or I'll drop my darling!'

'Lord Jesus, gel, I can't keep on me own bloody feet! Let's get moving before one of the marines cuffs us for being slow. That big Scotch bugger Anderson's looking over here. Oh Lor', I'm going to be sick, I'm – ' She was: into the water.

The Governor's huge canvas house with wooden frames had been erected on this eastern side of the stream. There were fifty or sixty tents nearby for the convicts. The marine camp and the other convict tents were over on the western bank. So, too, those for the sick, whose numbers were increasing alarmingly because of camp dysentery and a sudden outbreak of the scurvy.

'Lord 'elp us tonight, Mary,' shivered Jane as they tottered over to the tents which had been pitched on a patch of red clay.

'What d'you mean?' asked Mary, swerving to avoid a rat from the longboat.

'I mean that it's going to be impossible to guard us from the men now we're ashore. Even though we'll be in women's tents, we'll be lambs to the slaughter, gel.'

'Yes, but – but I've got my Will to look after me, ain't I?' He was out fishing in the *Beauty* but would soon be back.

Jane's derisive shriek caused a low-flying gull to veer upward. '*Your* Will? He ain't your 'usband, is he? This is the night what him and all the others have been waiting for, ain' it? And I heard that the sailors on the *Lady P* have been given an extra rum ration to make merry with the *Penrhyn* women – all one hundred of 'em – now that the poor souls have left the protection of the ship. *We'll* be in their lustful sights, an' all, Mary Broad. Lord 'elp us all tonight.'

'Hey, you, Langley!' bellowed the hated corporal, striding towards them. 'There's just enough room left for ye and yer black brat in that tent for six on the right there. You, Broad, take your bairn to one of those two large tents behind that great tree where Major Ross's animals are sheltering.' A stall had been built for six sheep, two lambs and a pig. There were also two pigs without any shelter, tied to a post six feet to the left of the tree. 'The one behind Lieutenant Ralph Clark's swine.'

Her heart lurched. Lieutenant Ralph Clark! One of Satan's instruments for getting her sent to this hell. Had the black-booted redcoat come to dance on her grave?

Frantically gathering her wits, Mary put on a little-girl-lost expression.

'But, Corporal, Jane and me be friends.'

The Scotsman's fearsome ginger moustache bristled.

'I canna help that. 'Tis a plaguy nightmare trying to get everyone sorted. D'ye realize there's more than a thousand of us in this cove? Now, do as ye're told or ye'll know the consequences.'

She opened her mouth to protest further but Jane's glance silenced her.

'Goodnight, Mary gel. Goodnight, little Charlotte,' said this dear woman, kissing the baby's pale, freckled cheek. 'I – I hope to see you in the morning.'

'Yes, Jane. T-take care, my sweet'art,' she sniffed, kissing Henrietta. 'Goodnight, little one. Sleep well. God bless you both.'

* * *

Just as darkness fell, a flash of lightning, followed by an almighty clap of thunder, shattered Mary's nerves and started Charlotte squalling, here in the tent. Normally, Mary Broad was not the sort of woman to be bothered by thunderstorms – heaven's sake, she'd weathered enough of them in Cornwall – but tonight there was something about this one that scared her. And hark at the wind, like a winter's night in dear old Fowey. This flapping tent was no cob-walled cottage, though.

A sudden splattering on the canvas: rain, furious rain, dashed by an angry gale. Lightning flashed again, illuminating a dozen women's fearful eyes: all looking at her. She squeezed her poor, screaming Charlotte and rocked her gently, but the mother's cooing was drowned by another tremendous thunderclap. The wind was so violent now, that it would surely blow away the tent at any moment.

'Aw, Charlotte, that was a loud'un, wasn't it?'

'Frightened, are you, ducky?' asked a deep-voiced woman from the far end of the twenty-foot tent.

'No I ain't,' said Mary, as loudly and calmly as she could. "Tis nothing this'un. You ought to be lying in my bed on the Cornish coast on a wild winter's night if you want to know what a proper storm sounds like.'

'I can't fink of nuffink better, ducky.'

The others roared with filthy laughter and – the tent had gone, its pegs ripped from the clay by the sheer Satanic force of this gale. The screaming women were scattering, struggling to hold the mattresses over their heads, as were the occupants of other tents that had been blown away, including some of the men's.

'Eek!' Some ugly bald brute had his arms round her and Charlotte.

'Let me go, you whore's son!'

Lightning flashed, revealing broken black teeth in a slobbering mouth.

'Put the baby on the ground, woman!'

'I will not!'

'If you don't, I'll hurt it!'

'You wouldn't dare; Cap'n Tench'll–'

'Cap'n Tench can go to the Devil. I've been waiting for a woman for two whole years. You'll do me just fine, lovely – put the bloody baby down!'

'Help me, Will!' she screamed. 'Help me!'

'Who's Will?' rasped this animal, stroking her streaming hair, which had grown back fast.

'He – he's my husband.'

'Well, some husband *he* is. His pretty little wife calls and he's nowhere to be found. I'll wager that at this very moment he's doing the same to some other lovely, juicy wench as what I'm going to do to you.'

'Will!' The thunder drowned her cry.

'Let's have a proper look at yer.' His trembling fingers were tugging at the top of her frock, while Charlotte kicked and screeched.

'Will, for the love of God, help me!' Where were the guards? Sheltering from the storm? 'O blessed Jesus – Charlotte!' He'd wrenched Charlotte from her arms, tumbling the mite into the mud. He ripped the cloth and, as the lightning flashed, Mary Broad was white naked to the waist. 'Oh my Christ!' The thunder crashed.

'Lovely...'

'Leave her be!' commanded a rain-drenched skeleton.

Jimmy! Her whirling brain had warned her just in time not to say it aloud. Instead she cried, 'Will, my dear husband! Thank the Lord you've come!'

Don't let the cat out of the bag, man. Don't let puss out, for pity's sake...

'Me darlin' wife, what's he done to ye?'

Thank God for your quick wits, Jimmy.

'Leave me wife alone, or by Christ I'll -'

'Faugh, you worm, you couldn't even fight a girl.'

Lightning flashed and so did the tree-felling axe that Jimmy swung from behind.

'If ye don't leave her go, I'll – I'll chop off both of yer fondling hands, ye filthy bugger,' he hissed.

The animal's hands were trembling for another reason now. Flinging her against the Irishman, he scrambled away. Off into the storm he scuddled, like a terrified ewe when the Broads were abroad.

In an instant, Jimmy had picked up the mercifully still-screeching Charlotte and put her into her mother's arms. Then from inside his sodden shirt he produced a large sack.

'Here, Mary lass, I'll put this round the both of ye. 'Tis an empty grain sack that we brought ashore with the supplies today. I took it to rest me oul head on tonight.' He choked. 'Oh, my poor darlin'.'

'Aw, Jimmy,' she shuddered, 'that's twice you've been my knight in shiny armour.'

He laughed nervously. 'Your skeleton in smelly rags, ye mean.'

'Where's Will?'

'I – I don't know,' he mumbled.

'Tell me the truth, Jimmy Martin! I've known you for far too long to be fooled by *you.*'

'He – he got put in one of the other tents... er – on the other side of the stream, I think...'

She was about to say, 'You're lying; he's with some trull,' but Jimmy gasped, 'Jeez, will ye listen to the tars?'

There was singing, laughing and swearing everywhere. The sailors were having a rain party.

'Quick now, under the trees, Mary – Jeez, the dunner's crashing like 'tis the end of the world!'

'Well, Jimmy, we are at the end of the world, ain't we?'

Helped by the fierce onshore wind, they reached the wood in seconds.

Moments later, as they huddled together, with the squalling Charlotte between, forked lightning split the tree where the tent had stood. Lieutenant Clark's swine would live to tremble another day but the squeals of Major Ross's pig and the bleats of his sheep and lambs had been silenced for ever.

'Lambs to the slaughter,' breathed Mary. 'Whist, Charlotte. Hush. We're safe here, my lover – hi, Jimmy, look over there!'

One tent after another was being wrenched from the ground by this fiendish wind, and male convicts and drunken tars were dragging the screaming women to the trees and upturned boats. Some sailors were so drunk they didn't care about the lashing wind and rain and were already making love among the rocks. The marine guards definitely must have fled to the shelter of the wood for there was no sign of them. The Governor's canvas house was still standing – doubtless, though, His Excellency himself was not, probably having drunk himself silly, too. Aboard the tossing ships, the officers were surely as drunk as the seamen on the beach. And as for the marines over the stream there, they were only concerned about saving their own tents, not the wretched women.

'Poor Jane,' sobbed Mary. 'Aw, poor gal.'

CHAPTER 18

The marines' loaded muskets and little Governor Phillip's perspiring bald head glistened as the mid-morning sun finally broke through the clouds. Standing here, flanked by the officers and gentlemen, His Excellency was finger-brushing the sleeve of his navy-blue uniform as he prepared to address the convicts, squatting round him in a circle, on the cleared ground between the men's and women's camps. The redcoats themselves formed an outer ring behind them. Mary and Charlotte were right in front of him. The Cornish girl was squeezed between Will and Jane, who was rocking Henrietta. Mary, like all these other bedraggled survivors of last night, was caked with clay almost as red as the soldiers' coats. But who cared? Who bloody cared any more?

'Prisoners of the King. The scenes of riotous debauchery that occurred last night defy description. Know you well that I shall stand no repeat performance. Any male prisoners who try to enter the women's tents will be shot on sight!'

Charlotte, none the worse for last evening's nightmare, was screeching from the heat, and Corporal Anderson's own hot breath suddenly entered Mary Broad's right ear.

'Keep yer bloody bairn *quiet*,' he hissed, his moustache tickling her.

She exchanged angry glances with the hollow-eyed Jane, who was definitely the worse for wear. So were the two trembling *Penrhyn* women between Jimmy Martin and Jane. Elizabeth Hayward, who was only fourteen, was supporting the bent-backed Dorothy Handland, who claimed to be 'a mite over sixty' but looked over eighty. Both had been transported for seven years: apprentice cloak-maker 'Saucy Lizzy' for stealing a cloak, a linen gown and a silk bonnet from her master, old-clothes-seller Dorothy for committing perjury. What had happened to these three women last night did not bear thinking about. Lizzy, hating all men, was glaring at the officers. Dorothy, grinding blackened teeth and incessantly muttering, 'Hang the buggers, hang the buggers,' had eyes only for the Hanging Tree at the edge of the clearing.

The sharp-featured, ill-looking Governor wiped a drop of sweat from the end of his large, curved nose and cleared his throat of its dryness from last night's drinking. Mary noticed that he had a top front tooth missing – from falling down drunk? White-faced, despite the heat, this middle-aged gentleman pressed his small, bony fingers onto the folding table before him as if for support.

'I have been sorry to find that there are many among you who are not to be governed by lenity. I have repeatedly forgiven crimes, which you committed on the passage out, and since your arrival here, and you have constantly abused my lenity, by similar transgressions. But for the future, the law shall take its course. I am convinced that there are a number of good men among you who, unfortunately, from falling into bad company, or from the influence of bad women, or in the rash moment of intoxication, have been led to violate the laws of your country, by committing crimes which, in the serious moments of reflection, you think of with horror and shame, and of which now you sincerely repent, and will be glad by future conduct to retrieve your characters. But I am sorry to add, that I fear there are some men and women among you, so thoroughly abandoned in your wickedness as to have lost every good principle. Therefore, from henceforth, however it might distress my feelings, every crime from the smallest to the greatest magnitude shall meet its punishment that the law inflicts. Anyone stealing the colony's animals, poultry or produce will be hanged.

'Many of you men since you have been disembarked, instead of assisting in the necessary work of forming the settlement, have been found skulking in the woods, and come to the camp only at the appointed times for the serving of provisions to you. For the future, all such idlers as are found beyond the limits, the Provost-Marshal and the patrol have orders to take up and imprison, and that in case of their running from the patrol, they will be fired at with ball.

'Those who will not work shall not eat. For the *good* men shall not be slaves for the bad.

'Because of the warm climate in this exciting new outpost of our great country's empire, your daily labour should be much easier than the common labourer's in England.'

He took out his fine-linen handkerchief and dabbed his forehead.

'There are three priorities.

'First: Clearance. More trees, rocks and stones must be cleared and the soil hoed. 'Second: Planting. We must get that seed sown. By the by, you will be exempted from labour on Saturday afternoons in order to cultivate your own gardens to increase the food stock.

'Third: Building. I am sure that none of you had ever experienced the like of last night's tempest. Well, the blowing-down of your tents has shown how important it is to build houses quickly. A hospital and storehouses must also be constructed as soon as humanly possible.'

He focused these dark, liquid eyes on Mary.

'Some of you women will help here by making pegs for roof tiles and collecting oyster and cockle shells for burning into lime for mortar.'

He licked his rather sulky lower lip.

'I shall ever be ready to show approbation and encouragement to those of you who prove themselves worthy of them by good conduct and attention to orders. On the other hand, those who are determined to act in opposition to propriety, and those who observe a contrary conduct, will inevitably meet with the punishment which they deserve. It is in your interest to forget the habits of vice and indolence in which too many of you have hitherto lived. I exhort you to be honest among yourselves, obedient to your overseers and attentive to the several works in which you are about to be employed. How lenient are the laws of England, that, though you are brought here to this distant land, you may, by your industry and good behaviour, regain the advantages of life that you have forfeited. It is in your own power by a steady perseverance in a series of good conducts to make the day of your transportation to this place the happiest day you have ever seen.'

Dabbing his brow again, he looked intently at Mary and Will.

'Be in no doubt that indiscriminate intercourse will be punished with the greatest severity and rigour... I therefore recommend marriage,' he said, in a softened tone, and the eyes, and even the lower lip, smiled.

'So, doubtless, does our chaplain, the Reverend Mr Johnson, beside me here, who himself married this beautiful young, red-haired wife of his before the fleet sailed.'

Not so young, thought Mary, pulling a face at Jane. The only person sitting, the only gentleman's wife in the colony, thin, black-bonneted Mary Johnson was surely in her middle thirties. Her black gloves and high-collared, long-sleeved black velvet gown would have looked at home in her native City of London but were definitely unsuitable down here. Blushingly smiling, she waved her large dark-green fan against the heat and flies. Saucy Lizzy, for reasons known only to herself, decided to poke out her tongue at her. Luckily for the child, none of the gentlemen noticed but Mrs Johnson looked shocked and hurt. This Christian soul said nothing, though, and Mary blessed her for that. Folk said that the pretty lady was half a Baptist and half a Methodist, whatever that might mean, but even the Methodist half of her had never attracted Will Bryant, who could not stomach her fan-dangling ways.

'This Sunday, the tenth of February, he will conduct marriage services, under that great tree near the Hanging Tree, for those of you who wish to live together. Of course, *I* shall see each couple beforehand to give, or withold, my approval... Needless to say, everyone here must attend divine service every Sunday. You shall have the rest of today to yourselves.'

Jimmy said under his breath, 'Roman Catholic priests have been legal in dear auld Christian Ireland for six years now but His Most

Protestant Majesty doesn't think that James Martin, Esquire, might have need of one in this heathen land. Not content with chaining me body, the Protestants want me soul as well. The Reverend Johnson! God save me from Evangelicals!'

'God save the King!' cried Phillip.

'God save the King!' echoed all their captors.

As the last of three musket volleys echoed round the cove, Will Bryant flicked one of these big red foreign ants from his bare foot and turned to Mary Broad.

'You heard what Tench said about me getting a hut if I did my job well, didn't you, gal?' he grunted, rising.

'Yes, Will?' She gasped from this plaguy stiffness as he helped her up.

'Well, I'm thinking that I could really turn the tide in my favour if I were to show Tench I was worthy "by good conduct": if he saw that I, being a stout-hearted master seiner, was taking the darling Guvnor's advice, by making an honest woman of you...'

Her heart thudded and the sweat poured down her face and neck into the sack still preserving her modesty.

'Yes, Mary, married in four days' time. What do you think of that? You know how much "Watkin" likes his spirited Cornish convict girl; he'd have a beautiful hut built for us.' Will's dark-brown eyes had this crafty expression now: this half-closed, gleaming look that she knew so well. 'And your darling Charlotte would have a home, and a garden with fresh vegetables. And a father!'

The baby's squalls were attracting sympathetic eyes from all around, including the sparkling blue ones of Tench himself. He was accompanying the Governor and the other officers back to the blissful shelter of the big canvas house. The convict girl cursed this infernal sun, which was getting hotter by the minute. If only the poor little mite had shelter. The shelter of a hut...

'Well, Mary Broad. Will you marry me?'

'Aw, Will... Yes, Will Bryant. I'll marry you, dammit. I'll marry you.'

CHAPTER 19

'Oh, Mary, you've got such a beautiful garden,' breathed Jane as they stood, holding their babies, in the hut doorway. It was the following February and Jane was thin now: even thinner than Mary.

The summer sun would soon be setting and the dry scent of the bush filled their nostrils, while the buzzing of insects filled their ears. They were watching a blister-footed Nathaniel Mitchell, the Bryants' rugged Dorsetshire-born gardener, slowly digging the black sandy soil to plant potatoes. A perverse individual, he was forever the crabby old man, though not yet forty. He claimed to know more about gardening than anyone in the settlement, including 'that boastful beggar', the Reverend Johnson. Mary would have supported Mitchell's claim, for he was, indeed, a mighty good gardener – and a hard-worker like herself. She wouldn't have dared remind the old moaner, though, that Johnson, not Mitchell, had been the first in the colony to use the piles of rich fertilizer from the natives' middens to improve the soil.

The ground was still shimmering with heat and swarmed with giant ants, both black and reddish-brown. Mary's own bare feet had once disturbed an underground nest of the latter and she'd been chased and bitten by those inch-long buggers. The pain had been terrible. All over her they'd gone, all over.

The ants were a pain in another way. Like the rats and fieldmice, they'd eaten what little corn crop had managed to survive in people's gardens. The same had happened on the Government farm. Of course, some of the seed-wheat had been so damaged at sea it hadn't sprouted at all, and even the corn that had shown early promise had decided to give up the ghost, in this poor soil. The seasons were so confusing down here. Folk did not know when to plant, or what crops were best suited to the climate and this wretched soil, which had first looked so fertile supporting all those trees.

All these rocks and tree roots and stumps were not making Mitchell's work any easier. For there had been no time for the colonists to dig up every rock and to grub out every deep-rooted tree in the settlement. The perspiration was trickling from his lank black hair. It ran down his ruddy cheeks into the top of his grimy white coarse-linen smock-frock, which Mary herself had frequently patched – along with the clothes of many other womenless men.

Also watching him, from a tall, bushy shrub by the low fence at the end of this short garden, was a friendly thrush. Only the top of its head was bluish-grey; the rest of the bird was chocolate brown at the back and dusky white at the front, its wings and long tail lead-coloured. One of the few of this upside-down world's inhabitants that reminded Mary of home, whenever it opened its dull-yellow beak to sing, the sound was so melodious her heart ached.

'All these pretty flowers you've gone an' collected,' said the black girl. 'Oh, it's so bloody hot!' she groaned.

'But you're a nigger; I didn't think you felt the heat like us.'

Jane laughed. 'I was born in Holborn Lying-in 'orspital, you noddy-head.'

'Where's that?'

'London, you stupe. Good ol' London. Oh, I wish I was back there now,' she sighed, leaning wearily against the cabbage tree doorpost.

This soft wood, from the beautiful, straight ninety-foot pines, was the only kind suitable for housebuilding but, being unseasoned, had begun to crack.

Suddenly Jane screamed, flinging away a huge, glossy dark-brown spider, which had fallen from the reed thatch and just missed vanishing down her emaciated bosom. This fanged monster killed frogs and lizards and, doubtless, would have had a damn good try at killing her – or the babies – but mercifully it scurried off through a colony of giant 'white ants' swarming near Mary's toes. John White had told Mary that the 'ants'' correct name was 'termites'. The darting devils, and their aforementioned mates, seemed to be the only creatures with the energy to work hard this baking summer. The termites would eat the timbers quicker than you could say '*Warra, warra, war!*' Perhaps she could ask Jimmy to find her an anteater, one of the few useful mammals down here. Though the very thought of the Irishman trying to pick up one of those prickly hedgehog-like things made her chuckle, despite her depression.

'Yes, Jane, the flowers are lovely,' she sighed. 'I must have counted thousands of different kinds growing about the colony in places where there ain't many trees: where they've got room to breathe, like. You wouldn't think they'd do well in this useless thin sandy dirt of Sydney Cove, would you?'

When the trees had been cleared, exposing the black sand to the sun's fierce rays, even the grass had died.

She went on, 'They grow much betterer than the colony's life-preserving crops, that's for sure. What a pitiful harvest! It's no wonder the Governor's farm closed and no wonder that, without vegetables, so many folk are dying from the scurvy. And anyone with any sense knows that without manure you won't get no vegetables or grain from this dang soil. And you won't get no manure without animals.'

The bulls and cows had wandered off – who could blame them – and hadn't been seen since. And nearly all the sheep had died. The only creatures left were some hogs, and a few hens, which hadn't yet been pinched by the convicts, or the plaguy dingoes.

'What we need,' she continued, 'are some good farmers from Old England to help poor old Henry Dodd teach his bunch of buffleheads how to grow things and how to save the stock.'

Dodd, a quiet, attentive man whom everyone liked, had come out as Phillip's personal servant and been put in charge of the convicts working at the farm, next to the Governor's house.

She paused to yawn.

'Anyhow, as I was saying, you wouldn't think these *flowers* would do well, would you? None of them have much of a scent, though, not like ours back home. Except for that bushy shrub there. It's my favourite.

Aw, it's a rare old showy thing when it's in bloom. It comes out in pretty white spring flowers that smell like English may, and the scent follows you into the hut. I wouldn't dare take its flowers inside, though, because it's unlucky to have English may within doors and this could be the same.'

She hugged herself. 'I just *love* flowers, Jane. When I see flowers, I see Life itself: being born, and growing, and blooming. Like a child. And I want my Charlotte to be surrounded by them, too,' she smiled.

She kissed the sweating forehead of the golden-curled seventeen-month-old little girl, snug in the canvas apron-pouch tied round Mummy's waist and shoulders.

'Yeah, Mary, you and Will have done bloody well in the twelve months since your marriage. Living better than the rest of us you are, at the top of the rising ground here. "The aristocrats of the 'ill" is what everyone calls you now, you know. You've got easily the biggest hut in either of these two streets west of the Tank Stream. And it's all good cabbage tree wood, an' all. And you've even got a glass window. Lord Jesus, the rest of us are in miserable bloody wattle-and-clay hovels no bigger than nine foot by twelve, ain't we? No windows, just lattices made of twigs, and the rain washes the clay out of the walls in winter. And many other poor mortals in the colony are still stuck in bloody tents. Even a deal of the soldiers are.'

Jane wiped the sweat from her eyes with a sodden rag.

'Yeah, Mary Bryant, living better than any other prisoners you are, and no mistake. And yet...' she looked at her searchingly, 'and yet you, gel, seem more discontented than anyone. Ah, yeah, you always keep chirpy and cheer the whole damn lot of us with your jokes and your pigheaded refusal to be as downhearted as the rest. And you even *sing* – nearly as good as this bird here – when you hear Surgeon Worgan's pianoforte in the still of the evening playing that nursery rhyme thing – well, I'll be damned, he's playing it now…'

They could plainly hear the distant notes, from across the stream. His own glass windows obviously wide open, George Worgan was playing 'Malbrouck', a plaintive little tune. Sung as a nursery rhyme in its native France, it seemed to be being sung or whistled by everyone nowadays. Even by the cultivated Watkin Tench. He had been caught whistling it last year by the commander of those French ships. Just recently, Tench had heard Mary singing it in imitation French to Charlotte. He'd told the Cornish girl that she was in good company, for La Pérouse had informed him that King Louis and Queen Marie Antoinette sang it to their own children. And even those amazing mimics, the natives, regularly sang it these days while paddling their canoes.

'... But, Mary,' Jane went on, '*I* know you better than anyone knows you: certainly more than the likes of Mary Shepherd and Catherine bloody Prior know you, because they ain't that bright, poor bitches. They can't see what's behind the twinkle in your eyes. There they go, they're twinkling now - I can see things what they can't. Yeah, I've known you long enough, gel, to know that deep down inside of you there's a bubbling volcano. You can't fool your ol' Jane.'

Mary blushed and embraced her.

'You're right, my sweet'art. You're right about both things.

'I keep cheerful because I know I'm mighty lucky to have a biggerer hut than the rest of you, and to have Joe Paget to help me with jobs inside the house when he ain't aboard the *Beauty* helping Will.

'And you're right about the volcano in me. It's bubbling fit to erupt! Because this garden ain't got no pink roses. 'Cause this cabbage tree cottage ain't my real home. My home is a beautiful cob-walled cottage. In Cornwall. They could build me a palace here at Sydney Cove with a thousand plaguy Pagets waiting on me – and with gals waving fans over me to keep off these dang pesty flesh-flies–'

She sucked through her teeth and furiously brushed this particularly persistent buzzer from her burning cheek.

'Stow me, Jane, it's one of those that don't blow eggs but huge living maggots! Aw I hate these bloody foreign insects! And foreign animals and birds. Dang great 'roos jumping all over the place, full of the joys of spring when it's nearly autumn, in this upside-down world - where the sun rises in the east but then climbs northwards! And the Devil's own king's fishers that laugh hideously at us in our misery, because *they* can fly off to wherever they dang want. Them and their "*Kook-kook-kook-ka-ka-ka!*" No one in Old England could ever imagine what it's like down here in this lonely wasteland of Creation. Where the night sky's so scarily huge and full of millions of bright stars that it makes you feel like a tiny lonely lost soul: lost in an unknown, devilish world. And where nearly everyone from our own world is so full of their own woes that they ain't got no pity left for other folk, and even steal from *each other* – there's one now.'

A shaven-headed woman wearing a canvas cap with 'THIEF' on it skulked past.

'Yes, Jane, they could make me Queen Mary of New South Wales and give me a hundred beautiful gowns so I wouldn't have to wear this stitched-up old slop frock no more, and I still wouldn't be happy. I still wouldn't be free. Free to live where I want, which is in Fowey, with its beautiful sparkling river, its cool woods, its romantic rich-green valleys and a *million* lovely flowers – whose scents you can really smell! A pox on this cussed cove and this whole cussed country!'

Jane smiled weakly after all this. 'Yeah, you've never lost your spirit, have you, gel? I seem to have lost all of mine,' she sighed. 'I've lost all confidence in meself. I hardly know who I am any more. Oh Lord, I'm so bloody lost! Faugh, you talk about flowers and life. *I've* got *no* hope. No hope at all. When the men's term finishes, they can earn their passage home by joining a ship's crew and, if they're married, their wives and children can go with them. But poor single gels like me will have to *pay* for *their* passage, won't they? When *my* term finishes, *I* won't be able to afford the fare back to England – not unless I first become the prostitute that the world thinks I am!'

She looked down at her baby and then at Charlotte.

'And my poor little Henrietta's so thin. Much thinner than Charlotte. My little mite's just wasting away. I'm afraid she won't last much longer in this hell on earth, what with food getting so short, and in four months winter being on us again, with a vengeance.

'Mary, where d'you get your fiery spirit from? And,' she murmured, 'you know I don't mean the spirit what Will likes to drink: what turns him into a fuddled fool nearly every night. I know he gets *that* from trading some of the fish what he holds back when the orficers ain't looking. And what with the colony being so short of food, an' -'

Flushing, Mary snapped, 'He don't just give the fish in trade for spirits, Jane Langley. He gives some to ol' Nathaniel here as reward for doing the garden. But none to that miserable Joe Paget who grudges everything he has to do for us. How dare you say that? How dare you!'

Jane clasped Mary's clenched fist. Both women were shaking.

'Love a duck, gel, I was only joking, for Gawd's sake. This is your ol' Jane. Gor, *I* can talk about spirits; he's kept *me* well supplied, ain't he? Calm yourself. Gawd, I've never known anyone with an angrier, quicker temper than yours, Mary Bryant. You ain't like it very often but when you are, I wonder what you're going to do next. 'Strewth, I didn't mean nothing by it.'

The volcano had spent itself – for the moment – and Mary squeezed her friend's hand.

'It's my anger that keeps me going. My anger against the court that sent me here, just for snatching a lady's bonnet from her head, when I'd told Black Sir James Eyre and his mates that I'd only been funning. I know it was wrong of me but I was bosky, and happy for the first time in ages. I would've thrown *your* bonnet in the bloody duckpond. I was so happy, I would even have snatched my own mother's bonnet off if she'd been alive, rest her. It would have been different if I'd been the one that kicked the poor lady. I would've deserved it then. Like those cruel bitches deserve to be here, at the bottom of the world. If *I'd* been one of the judges, *I'd* have sent 'em here. But, for mercy's sake, I tried to stop 'em! I told the court that, and I told them that I'd prayed to the Lord for His forgiveness. And I told Miss Lakeman that I was very, very sorry to be the cause of the whole business and hoped that she was no longer in pain. Which she wasn't, thank the Lord. And I told them that I had never ever hurt nobody in my whole life, nor would even dream of doing so. I'm a Christian, ain't I?

'I'm also angry about the look on the face of that Lieutenant Clark whenever he passes me. It's as if he thinks I'm a lower animal than his bloody pigs.' She snorted like one and Jane snorted with laughter. 'Do you know, he's never once spoken to me all the time we've been down here, though I've always spoken to him, ain't I? I've behaved like a good Christian and forgiven his trespasses against me.

'You know, sometimes when I've been on my way to the Reverend Johnson's service, by chance I've followed Clark who's been going there, too, to read the lesson. Unbeknown to him, I've seen him take one of those what-you-call "miniatures" out of his inside pocket, open the tiny little glass lid and kiss the picture, outside of its case. It must be a picture of "dearest Betsey" and he's dreaming of being back in Plymouth with her and "chubby little Ralph". I wish *I* had miniatures of my dear father and poor Dolly. I'd kiss them a thousand times a day,' she sniffed.

'Now, that's enough about me,' she said, brightening. 'Don't you fret about little Henrietta, my sweet'art. She'll be fine, just you see. Auntie Mary knows – hi, look 'ee! Will's coming up the street: back from the fishing, with James Cox, your lanky London lover, by his side. Surely *he's* brought your confidence back?'

James was a Wapping acquaintance of Jane's. Though pleading not guilty, he had been sentenced to death for stealing twelve yards of thread lace and two pairs of cotton stockings by breaking a London haberdasher's window. The items had not been found on him but his bloodied hand had condemned him. He had subsequently been reprieved. Later, though, as one of the *Mercury* mutineers, he'd received another death sentence, eventually commuted to transportation for life. Like Will, he was a Methodist, and had often seen John Wesley preaching at his great chapel in the City Road. Unlike Will, James practised what Wesley preached, never drinking alcohol.

'Yeah,' said Jane, lightening, 'James is a good'un. You know, he's always telling me to stop drinking, saying it's for me own good. But it calms me nerves, Mary. Nerves and no confidence? Why, he's as bad as me; his nerves are terrible.'

She went on, proudly, 'He can't swim and he's scared stiff of the sea. And with his fair skin, he's got such terrible sunburn, ain't he, poor boy, even though he ain't shaved his beard off like Will and Jimmy. And yet, he goes out fishing with Will every bloody day. Yeah, James is a marvel. He's always eager to learn things and do things: what with Will learning him navigation and what with him doing cabinet-making at the carpenter's shop in his spare time.'

Mary smiled. 'Like *you* were, with your embroidery: determined to improve yourself. Maybe that's why you get on so well together.'

'Yeah, Mary, perhaps you're right. He's certainly good with his hands. And,' Jane grinned, 'when I say "good with his hands", I don't mean what *you're* thinking, you dirty bitch. He even carved that little boat for Henrietta, didn't he? The only toy the poor little beggar's ever had.'

Jane lowered her voice as the two fishermen drew near. 'You'd think James would just give up, wouldn't you, being as he's down here on a life sentence. *Our* term is bad enough but, if we *don't* die of starvation, we *might* be able to get a ship back home *one* day – even though I've been moaning and groaning about it and feeling sorry for meself just now. But, poor dear, he's got no future at all. Yeah, Mary, what I admire most about him is that he's scared stiff of the sea, yet he keeps going way out there in the harbour day after bloody day, even though he's been awake half the night fretting himself sick about going. He told me that even when he does manage to fall asleep, he wakes up with the sweat pouring off of 'im because he's dreamed that the sharks are tearing 'im to bloody bits!'

Mary chuckled. 'I well remember the colour of his face when he saw those twelve-footers when we sailed up the harbour. Us Cornish folk sometimes see basking sharks off Cornwall but our London lad wasn't used to seeing them off Wapping, was he? I mind well, too, that thirteen-footer that was caught last year...'

The shark had been nearly seven feet round. Back at the cove, after its jaws had been cut out, its seamen captors had played games with Will and some of his crew by passing those enormously wide fearsome things over the lads' heads and bodies without even scratching them.

'Poor James was so terrified,' said Mary, 'he wouldn't go within thirteen *yards* of the carcass, would he? And what about that other time? The shark that followed our old *Beauty* when she was coming up the harbour. The bugger jumped out of the water four times, shaking its head from side to side, then got hold of the blade of James's oar. And when poor old James somehow managed to shake him off, that ol' bone-crauncher went to the rudder and didn't leave go till Will threw all the catch overboard.'

Having wiped Henrietta's brow with the rag, Jane continued with her theme.

'All *seamen* are brave, of course, like your Will. That's why I've always liked seamen; I admire them. But Will was brought up on the sea, like you. The bravest bravery of all is when you're someone like James, who's scared stiff and yet he still goes out there and faces waves twice as high as this hut.'

'Hi, Mary!' panted the beaming Will, just yards away now and struggling with a large fish-box. James was carrying the small one, containing Will's own allowance. 'Us got a tidy catch today, didn't us, James?'

'Yeah,' grinned the Londoner, opening the gate.

'Make way, both of you,' Will grunted, 'before cat's eyes Anderson sees me with this extra bit of fish and his whiskers quiver!' Squeezing past, he thankfully put the box on the table.

Once everyone, except Mitchell, was inside the hut, an anxious Mary slammed the door.

'Here, Jane,' said Will, 'stow these two fat'uns down the front of your frock to take home with you. It'll do your child good, poor little runt.'

He handed her two slippery, brown-striped, pale-yellow mullet, about five inches long. 'Eek!' she cried, sliding them down. She turned to her wide-blue-eyed man. 'Lor' love us, James, I'm so bloody thin that I have to shove a couple of fish down me frock to show the world that I'm a woman!'

He kissed her sunken cheek.

'You're still a comely wench to me, J-J-Jane Langley,' stammered her twenty-nine-year-old lover, whose own cheeks, above his beard, were like raw meat. 'How's little Henrietta today?'

Her shiny black eyes clouded. 'She's not very well at all. She's tireder than ever.'

James smiled encouragingly. 'Will's right, duck: the f-f-fish'll do her good.'

'Here, Jane,' grunted Will, lifting a floorboard, 'this'll cheer you.' He handed her a bottle.

Her right cheek twitched as she glanced at the disapproving James.

'Now, J-J-Jane, you know I–'

'Let the gal take it, James,' snarled Will. 'Dang me, the poor bitch needs *some* bloody comfort in this godforsaken hole!'

'I'm only thinking of her own g-g-good. It'll rot her guts.'

'It'll help keep her going, Lor'sake! Stop acting like her bloody mother.'

James's right cheek was now twitching like Jane's and his hands were shaking. He turned to leave.

Before he could, Mitchell rushed in.

'Will,' he cried, 'Anderson's come up from the barracks! He looks mighty mad. I've only just seen him, he's nearly here!'

Mary shuddered and her eyes met Jane's, while Will frantically slid back the floorboard.

'Aw quick, Will,' she gasped, 'put the big box by the table and sit on the thing. We'll all sit round, pretending we're having a jaw. We'll say–'

Mitchell fell into her arms as Anderson burst in. The half-squashed Charlotte screeched.

'Bryant. William Bryant,' rasped the now kilted redcoat who was even bigger than Will. The Scotsman had permission to wear the kilt these days because his breeches had been badly torn and the colony had run out of thread, having had to make so many repairs this year. His right hand held his drawn sword; his left proceeded to stroke the ginger moustache. 'Ye're under arrest, mon. Stand up!'

Will Bryant stayed still; so did his mouth.

'Damn your eyes, Bryant, stand *up*, I say!'

The Cornishman looked at him defiantly, then eased himself to his feet.

'Mitchell,' said Anderson, 'open the box and produce the evidence.'

Mary bit her lip and hugged the squalling Charlotte as the gardener reluctantly pulled out a mullet.

Anderson shoved Mitchell aside and looked into the box. 'Full of fish!' he cried. 'Outside, Bryant. Ye know what the Governor thinks of scum like ye who steal food when the colony's on the brink of starvation. Mary Bryant, kiss your husband goodbye. 'Twill be the last chance ye'll get, afore he's launched into eternity!'

Clutching the table, Mary staggered round to her Will and kissed his stubbled cheek. Her thoughts returned to that terrible day two weeks after her marriage, when the first man, Tom Barrett, had been hanged from the Hanging Tree and buried only a few yards from it. Tom, a leader of the *Mercury* mutineers, had had his original death sentence in England commuted because he'd saved the steward's life and prevented the captain's ear from being cut off with scissors. There had been four executions since Barrett's but his still stuck in her throat as if the knotted rope were squeezing her own Adam's apple. Friendly old Tom had been about Will's age and a rebel just like him.

The Reverend Mr Johnson had said prayers with the condemned man at the foot of the ladder, during which he'd admitted his guilt. Dear life, the Reverend John Baron would surely have calmed Tom more than that well-meaning but hopelessly inadequate chubby-cheeked chaplain! Tom, in a broken voice but loud enough for the assembled convicts to hear, had said that he hoped his fate would be a warning to them. For he acknowledged that he had led a very wicked life and long merited the death he was about to suffer. His offences, of making counterfeit coins from buttons, buckles and spoons between Tenerife and Rio and stealing beef and peas from the Sydney Cove store, had been only the latest in a long line.

After Tom had mounted the ladder, the hangman pretended to be having trouble fixing the halter, for his heart had gone out to the poor wretch. Eventually, Henry Brewer, the Provost-Marshal – he of the troubled brow and gloomy countenance – had had to climb the ladder to secure the rope.

There'd been a beautiful sunset that summer's evening, too, but the white-faced Tom never witnessed the sun's final moment, because his own had come seconds before as the ladder was pulled from under him.

As Will, head held high, was hustled down to the lockup, she saw him gazing at the red ball in the sky.

CHAPTER 20

'Joseph Paget, what is your relationship with the accused?' The speaker was the incredibly handsome, dimple-chinned David Collins, marine captain, Judge-Advocate, Justice of the Peace and Secretary to the Governor. Sitting behind the long table on the platform, with his fellow JP, Augustus Alt, the Surveyor-General, 'Curly' Collins was frowning with those thick black eyebrows of his. Frowning down at the first witness.

As the wind flapped the marquee, the slant-shouldered, weaselly little former seaman from Yorkshire darted his one-eyed look at the shackled Will standing at the bar of the court. Head erect, the proud Cornishman stared contemptuously down his nose at him.

'I've been working in the fishing boat with him and in t'house, and been shouted and sworn at by him many a time, your Worshipfulness. I've shouted back at him, though, don't thee fret.' He rubbed his sweaty palms on his dark-brown fustian trousers – patched by Mary.

'And what happened, in the course of these employments, that relates to the charge against him?' demanded Collins.

He seemed so young to be Judge-Advocate, thought Mary, seated at the back with Jane and their sleeping babies on Cape orange boxes. Certainly the big, broad-shouldered gentleman was little more than thirty, despite his greying golden curls. Paget, who was about the same age, sniffed his snotty hook-nose noisily. Then he wiped it with the ragged cuff of his faded green jacket.

'He ordered me to find out who wanted to trade with him: to give him spirits in exchange for fish. Then when I'd found this out for him, he gave me some fish to take to them, and afterwards I brought him back the spirits.

'Like what happened on Christmas Eve when he sent me to

Zachary Clark, the victualler, with a big bottle, that I brought back full of rum, that Zachary gave for a huge flathead, every inch of four feet. Eeh, that old fish must have been real delicious!

'It weren't not always in exchange for spirits, mind. Because, on Bryant's orders, I gave a two-foot blackfish to Mitchell, him that works in Bryant's garden. It were a payment, you might say, for the work he's doing there. Never gave *me* a lovely blackfish, though.'

The bespectacled Augustus Alt must have been in his middle fifties. Fat when he'd arrived in the colony, he'd shed several stone since. The sweat was running down his pasty cheeks and he didn't look well. He cleared his throat.

'How... how long has this practice of exchanging fish for spirits been going on?'

'Eeh, ages and ages.'

Alt's spectacles glinted in the sunlight through the open flap. 'What do you mean "ages and ages"?'

'Eeh, months and months, your Worshipfulness.'

Alt really didn't look well at all. Did he have the strength to ask any more questions?

'Right,' he sighed. 'That is all... Call Mr John White, the Surgeon-General.'

Mary's heart jumped. She glanced at Jane and gently squeezed Charlotte, who, thankfully, was asleep despite the suffocating heat. So was Henrietta.

'Mr John White,' bellowed the skinny little bewigged clerk.

After taking the oath, the young surgeon faced the court.

Jane gripped her friend's trembling hand. 'Lor' love us, Mary,' she whispered, 'when he was holding the Bible and them sunbeams shined on his lovely brown face, he looked more handsomer than ever! I'd share a bottle of rum with *him* any day of the week. Or night! Don't you tell James, gel; it'll make him lose even more of his confidence.'

Collins looked up from his notes, to address the gentleman who was nearly as handsome as himself.

'Mr White, what is your connection with, and knowledge of, the accused?'

Mary's heart fluttered.

'Sir.' The northern Irish voice was loud and confident. 'I have known master seiner Bryant and his wife since that first day aboard ship at Plymouth. I believe him to be strictly honest.'

Gasps in the packed marquee. Mary smiled delightedly at Jane, who blew a kiss at her handsome surgeon.

'I repeat: strictly honest. I shall explain. The court has already heard that, back in Cornwall, Bryant did his share of smuggling. But what Cornishman, of whatever station, has not? The accused has leadership qualities and trustworthiness. That is why he was put in charge of the fishing boats and why, too, he had previously been given the job of issuing provisions to the other prisoners aboard our transport. William Bryant is a brave mariner.'

White paused to wipe the perspiration from his eyes.

'His wife, too, sir, is a brave, Christian soul: a poor fisherman's hard-working daughter. From the day *her* daughter was born, this proud Cornishwoman has been determined to rear her as best she can, in near-impossible conditions. Sure, it has been difficult for all of us in this place, but how much more so to raise a *child* here! *I* shouldn't like to try.'

He swung round and smiled at Mary and Charlotte.

'If proof were needed, just *look* at the child. How healthy she is: clean-faced, clean-clothed – in a coarse-linen smock frock that that skilled needlewoman has made with her own work-calloused hands.'

He turned back to Collins.

'Compare this with the way that many of the other convict women have treated their babies. They are a disgrace to their sex. Never washed the poor wee mites' faces in their lives so that the excrementitious matters of the nose are congealed on the upper lip in rich clusters of dry bubbles and continually augmented by fresh drippings. Just like on the natives' filthy flyblown faces. The way that Mary Bryant does her best for the child, under trying circumstances – and with her own appearance, too – shows strength of character. It shows how *she* was raised: in a good Christian home. Indeed, she is one of the few – convict or marine – who have continued to obey His Excellency's orders about attending divine service. She has risked life and limb to attend Reverend Johnson's services in that dilapidated boatshed which isn't even fit or safe as a stable or cowhouse. To survive and prosper, this "exciting new outpost of our great country's empire" needs more women like her: industrious women, supportive of industrious husbands. Indeed, she has mended the clothes of many male convicts who *have* no wives. And marines' clothes, too, may I add.

'As you know, sir, *I* delivered the baby, bless her. And, as you will also know, she's called Charlotte: a royal name indeed. I can recall Mary Bryant's words when I asked her what she was going to call her. "Why, Charlotte, of course, sir. What else, for mercy's sake? After the Queen, God bless her."'

'Ooh, Jane,' whispered Mary. '"Charlotte: a royal name indeed... After the Queen..." I told him first that it was after the ship. The Queen was afterwards, after he looked cross at me. And he's sworn on the Bible!'

'Sir, the point of my laying stress on *her* character is this. Such a strong-minded, hard-working, *patriotic* woman would hardly marry the sort of man that'd steal from his fellow countrymen for personal gain at a time of near famine. As you know, the accused has always been given some of the catch, for his own family: to keep his bonny child and pretty wife healthy. I submit that the alleged trade was in that alone.

'And as for the additional box that he took home yesterday, well, you have heard his version of why he did that. He said that, as his boats had had a much bigger catch than usual, he wanted to give a reward to his team: all those stout-hearted fellows who daily brave the waves. It is his way of encouraging them to work even harder at the fishing, for everyone's benefit.

'Oh, I agree, sir,' said White, 'I agree that he has flouted His Excellency's strict orders that everything should go to the public store.

But, like all Cornishmen, Bryant is an independent-minded fellow, who, as he himself has said, might bend the rules a little but with the best of motives. The Cornish are independent-minded, yes, but they are also very *community*-minded. In this case, the motive was for the ultimate good of the community: the colony. Thus, in his way of thinking, the end would justify the means. Misguided, but... Well, I have made my point, I think. Like the captain of a ship – or, dare I say, the governor of a colony – a Cornish master seiner knows the importance of encouraging a team spirit.'

Mary was horrified to see that Collins and Alt were losing their patience with this 'independent-minded' Irishman, who had obviously realized this, too, but continued, looking the Judge-Advocate in the eye.

'You have heard from Paget that there have been many rows between the accused and himself. Can we, therefore, rely on Paget's testimony? There could be a case of spite here. Indeed, I –'

Collins's black brows shot up. 'Mis-ter White!' he roared. 'It is not your place to speculate, sir!'

John White's brown face reddened but the cause was surely his well-known quick temper, not embarrassment. 'I'm sorry, sir. May I just say one more thing?' he put in before Collins could speak further. 'Captain Tench has known the Bryants since Plymouth, too, and agrees with me that both Bryant and Mary Bryant have always been distinguished for good behaviour. Oh, and where would we be without master seiner Bryant's dauntless courage in fishing, in all weathers? Close to a cut in rations by now, I would submit. If all the convicts were as industrious as this couple, the colony's future would be a brighter one.'

* * *

'Here it comes, Jane,' gulped Mary, rocking the screeching Charlotte. 'Aw, dear life, this is the end of everything!'

Henrietta joined in, as if agreeing.

'*William Bryant!* Collins's voice resounded in Mary Bryant's brain. 'From having been bred in your youth to the business of a fisherman in the western part of England, you were given the direction and management of such boats as are employed in fishing here at Sydney Cove. Every encouragement was held out to you to keep you above temptation. A big hut was built for you and your family. You have always been presented with a certain part of the fish that you have caught. And you have wanted for nothing that was necessary, or that was suitable, to a person of your description and situation.

'But you were detected in secreting, for the purpose of selling, a large quantity of fish. And when the necessary enquiry was made, this practice appeared to have been of some standing with you. For this offence you are to be severely punished...'

'Aw, Will!' shrieked Mary, as Jane prevented her and Charlotte from falling. 'Will!'

'... You are sentenced to receive one hundred lashes on your bare back with a cat-o'-nine-tails.

'Notwithstanding your villainy, however, you are too useful a person to part with and send to a brick cart. Therefore, you will still be retained to fish for the settlement, though you will no longer be in charge. Yes, because of your selfish acts, you are being deprived of your special status.

'This also means that you and your family are to be removed from your hut, with its large, pretty garden that everyone, including His Excellency, has remarked is a credit to Mary Bryant and her helper, Mitchell. You will now have a small hut as your fellow convicts have, and you'll be at the *bottom* of the hill!'

Will was buggered if he'd look downhearted.

'Dammit, Bryant, stop smirking, you insolent beggar! Think yourself damn fortunate that you are not also being deprived of your "bonny child and pretty wife", by your removal from this world!

'Your punishment will take place at sunrise tomorrow, when the whole settlement will see the humiliation of a man who sought to deprive them of food at a time of want. Take him away!'

CHAPTER 21

Everyone was assembled here in the clearing at the foot of the rising ground. Corporal Anderson had pulled the shirt over Will's head and flung the patched garment into the dust. Now, young Private John Easty was tying the Cornishman's wrists to two of the three posts of the dreaded Triangle, having already splayed his legs and secured his ankles. The Triangle had been erected in front of Zachary Clark's provision store as a deterrent, following Governor Phillip's theft warning last February. Also tied to a post outside this large reed-thatched storehouse was Hector, Zachary's black, bear-like, Newfoundland water dog, his tongue already dripping in the heat.

'Oh, Mary,' sobbed Jane as they clung together at the front of the murmuring throng by the 'Marriage Tree', thirty feet away across the clearing. 'Oh, his beautiful brown back. Poor man. You're a hard'un, Mary Bryant; your husband's back's about to be torn to bleeding red ribbons and you ain't even shedding a tear.' Unable to look any more, she lowered her trembling head and gently hugged the sleeping Henrietta.

Rocking her slumbering Charlotte, the convict girl held her own head high, as the golden sun spread its rays through the trees. She stared defiantly at the glistening head of the little Governor who was sitting with the officers and gentlemen on the platform opposite.

'I won't let that swine Phillip see me cry,' she muttered. 'He won't succeed in making my man cry and I'm damned if I will either!'

The 'swine' was speaking. '... and so let punishment commence.' He thrust on his three-cornered hat. 'Major Ross!'

'Corporal!' bellowed the red-haired and red-faced Robert Ross. 'Do your duty!'

'Aye, sir,' grunted Anderson, twisting both ends of his moustache before taking the cat-o'-nine-tails from John Easty.

The straw-haired little cockney turned and gave Mary a

sympathetic look, bless him; Catherine Prior and Mary Shepherd were smiling, damn them.

The Scotsman stood back on those big ginger-haired legs and stroked the cat: stroked the six hard knots on each of the nine lashes.

Suddenly he swung the abominable thing wide and brought it down sideways with such whistling force that a crimson gash separated the top from the bottom half of the tense dark-brown back. The sickening sound of hemp on flesh was accompanied by a mass sucking-in of breath from the crowd and a loud, sympathetic bark from Hector, but nothing from Will despite his contemptuously refusing a leather mouthpiece.

'Two!' cried Anderson.

Again he swung wide. Again the coarse rope cut into the soft flesh. And again the spectators sucked through their clenched teeth. Hector barked even louder, while Mary stifled a groan, clutched her own back in sympathy and squeezed Charlotte.

'Three!'

Each time the cat tore the flesh, Anderson licked his whiskers, like a bloodlusting cat himself.

'Aw, Jane, the whore's son's enjoying every splash of blood. Just you wait, Corporal,' she murmured in her friend's ear. 'One dark night this Cornish cat will sclum out your merciless green Scotch eyes and feed 'em to the hogs!'

'Four!'

The blood, flesh and skin flew, her nails dug into her friend's skinny arm and Jane stifled a scream.

* * *

'Ninety-nine!'

His back was blue and black, and as bloody as meat in the shambles, the backbone itself exposed between the shoulder blades, and his legs would have buckled long since if he had not been tied. But Will Bryant, proud Cornishman, had stayed as quiet as the sleeping babes in their mothers' arms.

'One hundred!'

And he remained so, God love him.

The grinning Anderson twisted his moustache again and stood back to admire his handiwork. The moustache, like the rest of him, was splattered with shreds of Will's flesh. John Easty's trembling fingers untied the fisherman's ankles and wrists and he slithered to the bloodstained ground. Immediately, a swarm of those plaguy maggot-blowing flies swooped upon his wounds.

A white-faced Private Tom Jones – himself once reprieved from three hundred lashes – emptied a bucket of seawater over Will's back. The crumpled body did not flinch.

'Corporal, have a look at him!' barked Ross, and Hector seconded this.

Anderson's kilt stirred up the dust as he stooped and felt the side of Will's neck. Then, lifting the body slightly, he put a bloodied hand to the heart.

Mary's own heart sank. Thrusting Charlotte into Jane's arms, she hurtled towards her husband. She pushed the kilted corporal into the dirt, enabling the whole colony to see what was under his kilt, knelt down and raised her poor Will's head.

'Aw, Will...'

She lifted his right eyelid. The dark-brown eye stared at her: stared like one of Will's own dead fish. She shut it in horror. It opened of its own accord, as did the left.

Then the right shut, in a reassuring wink.

'Aw, Will, my sweet'art,' she choked, ''tain't the time for funnin', you ol' buffle'ead.'

Now she did cry.

* * *

Four days later she was trying not to cry again.

Young Lizzy Hayward had been saucy once too often. Despite, or perhaps because of, the tongue-poking incident, 'Christian Mary'

Johnson had taken her in as a servant. But Lizzy hadn't wasted much time before showing her contempt for the chaplain, who was 'no better than the rest of his bloody sex'. The more he had turned his chubby cheek, the more insolent the mousy-haired minx became and eventually he'd had to do something. Renowned for his kindness to the convicts, he regularly fed the hungry, from his own stores and garden, and cared for the sick. But this physician of both soul and body had finally realized that there was only one cure for her. A dose of the cat. Brought before 'Curly' Collins, the child had been sentenced to be tied to a cart's tail and flogged up and down the clearing.

Stripped to her skinny waist, flat-chested Lizzy looked far younger than her fifteen years. And now, as the thirtieth and last lash echoed round the clearing and the cart stopped, she fainted beside the barking Hector, her tied wrists keeping her on her feet. She, too, had scorned a mouthpiece but not once had the tough little Londoner cried out to Anderson for mercy, not once. Hector licked those pale, sunken cheeks and the tears trickled down Mary's own, while the contemptuous blue eyes of 'Christian Ralph' Clark flitted between both 'damned bitches'.

CHAPTER 22

Jimmy Martin had been ordered to watch Will's punishment, like everyone else. That was a month ago, though. The Irishman was glad that his friend's wounds were healing well but there had been little time to 'brighten the Bryants' in their new home. Since he'd arrived in this cursed land, wasn't his own back doing its share of suffering, while he was working from dawn to dusk, while he was digging and carrying clay or cutting and fetching wood, under a punishing sun at Brickfield Hill camp? The nearest trees, those that would have provided shelter while he worked, had long since been felled to fire the kilns. The worst job was pushing the wheelbarrow after digging up the tile clay. The brick clay was close to the kilns but the tile clay was two hundred bloody yards away.

Making the lazy beds up Glenariff had been easy compared with this. They weren't called lazy beds for nothing. The ground there hadn't had to be dug over; all that he'd had to do was mark out a four-foot-wide strip and spread Nelly's manure over it. Then cut a two-foot sod on each side, fold it over onto the strip and dibble his potatoes into it. The soil on his farm was shallow, unlike here and Sydney Cove and, indeed, most of Glenariff. So by folding it over, he'd given it double depth. The two-foot trenches left by the sods had allowed him to walk without treading on the crop and also served as drainage channels. But lazy beds weren't everyone's idea of good gardening; sure, hadn't he shown Dorset Mitchell how to make a lazy bed and been called 'a lazy Irish beggar' for his pains?

The camp, a mile south of the settlement, was run by convict Sam Wheeler, a master brickmaker. Sam had nineteen men and two boys working for him. With one 'moulders' shed' for bricks and two for tiles, he had been tasked to make 30,000 bricks and tiles per month.

Jimmy paused from digging the tile clay. Panting, he pushed the black felt hat back from his sweating brow. His ragged shirt and breeches clung to his ever-thinner, sun-browned body as he rested his chin on the spade handle. Och, if only there were some sweet tea vines left around here. There were none left anywhere near the cove now because the convicts, seamen and common soldiers had drunk gallons of the stuff. Surgeon-General White had recommended it, as a powerful tonic. Aye, a hot dish of that would have quenched his thirst and given him renewed energy. As for real tea, neither he nor any of the other Glens folk had had it in their lives. Mary had told him about the used tea leaves from Place's back door. With boiled spring water and sweetened with brown sugar, proper tea was 'beautiful an' thirst-quenching' and she missed it terribly, as she did the yarrow tea, but the colony's sweet tea was 'betterer than nothing'. Watkin Tench had compared sweet tea to the liquorice root of the shops but James Martin, Esquire, had never tasted liquorice root either. Jeez, he'd better get some water from the barrel by the kiln over there.

He needed food, too, though, for how could anyone do this sort of work without breakfast? Judging by the sun's height, it was only nine o'clock: another three hours before dinner. Dinner? How could you call a bowl of rice a dinner?

'Jimmy.' Sam Day, the sawyer, was passing with a barrow of logs from the sawpit. A short fellow, Sam was seven years his junior and married to convict Mary Bishop. His once-sturdy body was thinning by the day; so, too, the brown hair on this overlarge head. Aye, even a fellow with a great big head could get a woman but Jimmy Martin couldn't. The head was not so large, though, to have prevented Sam once from climbing through a Gloucester clothier's small kitchen window and stealing two pounds of warp yarn.

'Yes, Sam?'

Sam put down the barrow. 'Me and the fellows are starving. We're going to catch some fish. There's whacks of 'em in Botany Bay.'

Jimmy laughed. 'What, with your bare hands?'

'No,' said Sam, his tired light-brown eyes narrowing. 'We'll attack some natives there and pinch their fishing tackle and spears. There's fifteen of us going. We'll creep away in a minute while Wheeler and his mates are still in the moulders' shed. That bugger's so afraid of losing his privileged position, he'd never join us. You're one of *our* mates so you can come along and help us. I know you're not much of a fighter, Jimmy, but the two boys are coming, so if they can do it, so can you. I've got a barrowload of logs here that John Turner and me have sawn to use as weapons. What with them and the axes, pickaxes and knives, we'll send them black devils scuddling off like rabbits.'

Jimmy looked at the logs: as big as large clubs. God help any tribesman whose skull was hit by one. He had a vision of the brains of the recently captured Arabanoo, the Governor's pet, splattered on the ground.

Heart thudding, Jimmy Martin looked Sam in the eye. How best to tackle this?...

'Ack, Samuel, ye know the Governor's orders about not straying from the settlement and the camp.' He saw contempt here. 'Don't be misunderstanding me now, *I'm* as fond of freedom as the next fella. But just think what will happen if we're found out. We might all be hanged, including the two boys.'

'Faugh, nobody's going to find out. Even if Wheeler got to know, he wouldn't tell, would he? Because it'd look bad for him: showing that there was no discipline in his camp.'

Jimmy decided to come straight to the point. ''Tis cowardly to attack a bunch of natives going about their lawful business, fishing. 'Twould be a case of murder if any of them got killed.'

'Lawful business?' jeered Sam. 'Lawful business! We're talking about bloody savages!'

'I'll have nothing to do with it.'

'There's such a thing as standing by your mates, Jimmy Martin.'

'Not if they might commit foul murder,' said Jimmy quietly.

'Well, stow *you*, then,' muttered Sam, as his heavily armed mates approached.

Dammit, as soon as they'd gone, Jimmy would run to the settlement. If he could warn Watkin Tench, the marines might be able to avert a tragedy: the deaths of convicts as well as the natives. If the marines reached Botany Bay before the convicts had found any natives, there was a chance that when they subsequently came before the criminal court, Sam and company might be let off with a flogging. Especially if Jimmy had told Tench that the fellows had gone looking for the sweet tea creeper and had armed themselves against any attack. For hadn't one of their mates gone searching for sweet tea in the woods the other day and, having never returned, was presumed to have been killed?

'Grab him,' muttered Sam.

'What the–' the spade fell as Jimmy found his hands being tied behind his back, with a rag.

'We're taking you with us,' said Sam. 'If we knocked you senseless and left you here tied up, you'd wake up and tell Wheeler. And then you'd run off to tell your mate Tench.'

'You–' Jimmy gagged on a stinking rag being stuffed into his mouth.

'Right, come on, boys,' said Day. Jimmy found himself surrounded and hustled along. Then he was slithering with them down the hill, towards the path across the sandfields, leading to Botany Bay, five miles to the south.

Only when they had left the hill far behind did Day remove the gag but he left Jimmy's hands tied.

'Ack, Sam,' he spluttered, 'will ye free me hands, for God's sake? I can't run off, with all you beggars round me, can I? Jeez, ye're as thick as a bloody ditch; didn't yer Gloucestershire mammy put any sense into that great big head of yours? If ye keep me tied, 'twill slow ye *all* down; I'll be stumbling all the bloody way.'

'He's right, Sam,' said jug-eared Henry Humphreys, a young-looking twenty-three. The Devonian had known, and liked, Jimmy from their days in Exeter Gaol and on the *Dunkirk* and *Charlotte.*

'No,' said his fellow sawyer, taking the top from the wooden canteen.

Just two canteens between sixteen. Jimmy bowed his head. Madness, utter madness; it was becoming viciously hot now and they'd got to get back after all this. What if there was no freshwater stream at this side of Botany Bay?

And then, thank Heaven for small mercies, Sam gave him a drink. Bliss!

It seemed hours before they were finally squelching through the stinking marshes near Botany Bay. Jimmy Martin was being bitten to death by mosquitoes and could do nothing to stop them.

'Lads, for pity's sake untie me,' he groaned, vainly twisting his head to avoid yet another whining devil.

WHO-OOSH!

No mosquito that. He spun round. Terrifying yells from a score of natives with spears, less than twenty yards away through the reeds. The convicts scattered, every man for himself, leaving no one to untie him.

WHO-OOSH! WHO-OOSH! WHO-OOSH!

'Mother of God!'

One of the axes lay at his feet. Kneeling down, he rolled onto his back and rubbed the rag against the blade. Nothing happened. Rubbed harder. Cut his wrist. Still bloody tied. *WHO-OOSH!* 'Jeez!' Rubbed again. *WHO-OOSH!* Past his cheek! If he failed this time, he'd be – done it! Up on his feet. Running. Running as fast as his aching legs allowed. Where to? Anywhere away from the hollering horde. Dead convict here, face down in the mud. Jimmy Martin's turn next. Stumbling! Hands and knees in mud. Up. Running. Must go faster. Faster! *WHO-OOSH!* So close! *Jesus!* Mustn't slow down, mustn't slow down!

Hollering getting fainter?... Yes... Yes! Seemed to be concentrated back there, around the dead man. The vultures, the bloody black vultures! Thanks to that poor wretch, he was getting away. No sign of the others; pray God they'd escaped.

Yes, the hollering had almost ceased. Thank God, oh, thank God!

* * *

God alone knew how long it had taken but Jimmy Martin was at the barracks at last. John Easty was on sentry duty outside these unfenced huts.

'Fetch Tench,' wheezed Jimmy, collapsing into his arms. 'The brick kiln lads need help... The natives have killed one, maybe more!'

Within minutes, Watkin Tench had sent First Lieutenant John Poulden with a detachment of marines to march to the convicts' aid. Even before the marines had left, several other, unwounded, convicts had staggered into the barracks, including Sam Day, John Turner and Henry Humphreys.

* * *

Mary Bryant ran to the barracks when she heard that Jimmy was there, having survived a native attack.

'Is – is Jimmy Martin hurt?' she panted, rushing up to Easty.

'No, Mary, thank Gawd,' he said, giving her a reassuring smile

'Oh, thank the Lord!' she cried. 'Where is he?'

'You can't see him; he's confined in the lockup with those of his mates that ain't been hurt. Some others are in the 'orspital. The rest ain't come back yet. Please Gawd they'll be all right.'

Her legs were shaking. 'Please God,' she murmured, but she was only half listening now.

CHAPTER 23

It was the following morning. For the second time in little over a month, Mary and Jane were sitting at the back of the marquee, with their sleeping babies in their arms. Once again David Collins and Augustus Alt formed the Bench of Magistrates.

Jimmy Martin was lined up at the bar with Sam Day, John Turner, Henry Humphreys, James Neal, James Stow and John Cross. The others were in the hospital.

By the time Poulden's patrol had arrived, the natives had gone. The marines had found the dead convict's body stripped and mutilated. They had been too late to prevent more casualties. Nobody else had died but one of the two boys had been badly wounded and had his left ear nearly severed. He, too, had been stripped, and left for dead, though John White said that he would recover.

Jimmy knew that if he told the truth, he'd be freed but the others would probably be hanged. The men had had murder in their hearts yesterday but did *he* have the right to condemn them to death? No, only God could judge these sinners. But in this earthly court, Collins and Alt were deciding their fate based on the evidence. Should he, Jimmy Martin, bear witness against his mates, even though they had treated him contemptibly?

After Lieutenant Poulden had given his evidence, the Judge-Advocate frowned down at the Irishman. 'Martin, what do you have to say in your defence?'

Jimmy took a deep breath.

'Well, sir, 'twas like this, see. 'Twas such thirsty work, that the lads and I decided to take a wee walk to Botany Bay to look for some sweet tea. For, as I'm sure you know, the sweet tea vines were all picked around Sydney Cove and Brickfield Hill ages ago. The Surgeon-General himself has recommended sweet tea as a powerful tonic, has he not? Sure, it gives us the strength to make even more bricks and tiles for the good of the colony.'

Collins glared at him. 'Is it not so, that several days ago a member of your brickmaking gang strayed into the woods for the purpose of collecting sweet tea and never returned? And is it not also the case that, as he has never returned, it is supposed that he must have fallen in with a party of natives, who killed him? I put it to you that sixteen of you quitted your place of employment and, providing yourselves with stakes, set off toward Botany Bay with a determination to revenge, upon whatever natives you should meet, the treatment which that poor wretch received?'

Jimmy looked him in the eye. 'Sir, I swear on the mammy's life that we did not go to Botany Bay for the purpose of seeking revenge.' *Which is true, Mammy, isn't it? Sam and the lads wanted to steal some fishing tackle so they could do some fishing themselves.* 'Sure, I know very well that the dear Governor has expressly forbidden me to interfere with the natives. 'Tis for me own good, so it is.'

'Spare me your Irish cajolery, Martin.'

Jimmy felt these tanned cheeks burning.

'Samuel Day,' said Augustus Alt, 'what do you say on the matter?'

Wiping his nose with the back of his hand, Day shuffled his feet.

'It's like what Martin said, sir. We were thirsty, working so hard. The sweet tea would have done us a power of good.'

Jimmy could see that Collins was already losing patience with them. Mary, too, realized this and clutched Jane's arm.

The Judge-Advocate, a tall man even when sitting, straightened then stared at each man in turn, before resuming.

'Lies will not help your case. The reverse!... Now, everybody in the colony should note what I am about to say. His Excellency was justly incensed about yesterday's events and immediately instituted the most rigorous scrutiny into their cause. He judges it highly necessary to make an example of anyone who disobeys his orders about interfering with the natives, and says that this calls for the severest punishment.'

'Sir,' cried Henry Humphreys, 'if us promise to tell you the truth, will you spare us from the severe- the severest punishment?'

'You have *sworn* to tell the truth!' thundered Collins.

'Y-yes, s-s-sir,' said the trembling fellow, the sunlight shining red through his jug ears. 'The truth is, that we went to Botany Bay to pinch the natives' fishing tackle and spears so we could catch our own food. In the marsh, we *fell in*, as you might say – ha-ha – we fell in with the natives but there was far more of 'em than we thought. Fifty of the b-b-buggers! Us will get an easier sentence now that I've told you the truth, won't us, sir?'

Collins conferred with Alt and a minute later the Judge-Advocate pronounced sentence.

'This court finds you and your brethren in the hospital guilty of a most serious crime. His Excellency has already made his wishes known if a guilty verdict were given. He judges it highly necessary, as I said, to make examples of you misguided people. You have so daringly and flagrantly broken through every order that has been given to prevent your interfering with the natives, as to form a party expressly to meet with and attack them. He directs that those of you who are not wounded shall each receive one hundred and fifty lashes. You shall each wear a fetter for a twelvemonth, while continuing to work at Brickfield Hill. The same punishment will be inflicted upon those who are in the hospital as soon as they recover from their wounds. In pursuance of this order, you seven are to be tied up in front of the provision store this afternoon and punished in the presence of all the convicts. It will be a timely example to everyone. Likewise, the native Arabanoo will be present so that he, too, will understand the cause and necessity of the punishment. Back to the lockup with them!'

As Jimmy was led away, he caught the look in Mary's eye. Such anguish there! Well, at least somebody cared about Mrs Martin's youngest.

Watkin Tench was at the back here, too, standing.

'I must say, that you have disappointed me, Martin. I would never have believed it of you.'

'Ack well, the sun must have addled me brain, sir.'

Three hours later, the sun was beating down on his bare head. Ever since Will's punishment, Jimmy had wondered how he himself would stand up to the lash. Here, outside Zachary Clark's store, he discovered what real pain meant. While Hector barked in sympathy, Jimmy Martin, without a leather mouthpiece, suffered in silence.

He never heard the final barks, fainting long before Anderson had finished his work.

The next thing he knew he was flat on his bare belly, on the straw-stuffed mattress which served as his bed, and home to countless bugs and fleas. The tiny hut that he and the wee creatures shared with James Cox had been taken over by women and screeching babies. A kneeling Mary and Jane were washing his torn back as gently as they could but it was bloody torture. Writhing involuntarily, he found that his right ankle was weighed down by a leg-iron.

'Oh, Jimmy,' murmured Mary, 'your poor back is even worse than Will's, being as you're such a skinny fellow.'

'Aye,' he grimaced, 'thanks to the Kilted Corporal, I'll not be doing much brickmaking for a wee while, darlin'. And with this bloody iron, I'll not be able to run after and catch a lass now, will I? Though 'twill give me the time to read the Bible which oul Johnson lent me. And the *Instructions for the Indians.* Perhaps I can convert that good fella, that "good pella", as he calls himself, auld Arabanoo. 'Twill please His Reverence if I do some reading; he says he hasn't had many requests for his books since he's been here. Over three thousand he brought with him, to enlighten us "poor benighted souls". But what did he expect, when not many of our poor brethren can read. Three thousand! Think what they could do with *them* at the Cave School. I can just–'... he had exhausted himself.

'So, Jimmy,' mused Jane, 'you're "a timely example to everyone". You're such a gentle fellow, why did you go with Sam Day to attack the natives? After all the recent attacks by the savages, and especially the disappearance of your mate, I could understand *him* doing it for revenge. But not you. Gawd, I've even seen you laughing with that ugly Arabanoo. So what's made you want to kill his relatives?'

Mary jerked her head at Jane to go outside and leave them. Looking baffled, the black girl picked up Henrietta from James Cox's mattress and complied.

With the door safely shut, Mary whispered, 'What's your game, Jimmy? I've known you too long; you're no murderer.'

'Ack, leave me alone, Mary; I'm near *screaming* with pain, for God's sake.'

'If you want me to tend your wounds till you're betterer, you'll answer me.'

'Then I'll tend them meself. And the word is "better".'

'You?' she said, ignoring that last remark. 'You wouldn't even be able to sclum your nose at the moment.'

'Jesus, Mary, will ye please leave me be?' he groaned.

'Only if you tell me what really happened.'

He sighed. 'Promise me you won't tell anyone.'

She crossed her fingers behind her back. 'I promise.'

'Sam and the lads forced me to go with them. They knew that, otherwise, I'd run off and tell Watkin Tench.'

On hearing this, she decided to tell Watkin herself. She ruffled Jimmy's sodden hair: sodden from Private Tom Jones's failed revival attempt.

'Oh, Jimmy, you're too nice. None of those men would've lied in court to save *you.*'

'But I feared they'd hang, lass; I feared they'd hang if I told the truth.'

She picked up Charlotte. The child had finally stopped screeching, as if realizing that they were discussing mighty serious matters.

'Say goodbye to your brave Uncle Jimmy,' said Mary, waving Charlotte's hand.

Jane was waiting outside and whispered as Mary shut the door behind her, 'What was that all about?'

'I can't tell you. Look after Charlotte, will you?' she grunted, laying the child on some parched, ant-free grass. With Charlotte's cries ringing in her ears, she ran round the corner to the barracks.

Watkin was sitting in the shade of a cabbage tree, writing his journal.

'Begging your pardon, Cap'n Tench,' she puffed. 'I can guess what you're writing but it won't be the truth.'

His blue eyes twinkled. 'I always tell the truth, Mary. Unlike somebody else we both know.'

'Yiss, Jimmy always was a useless liard.'

'Liar.'

'Liar,' she said, feeling even hotter. 'But it's not what you and everyone else think, sir. He told the story about the sweet tea because–'

He rested the quill on the pot and, without thinking, put his inky finger to his lips. 'It's our secret, Mary. And will remain so for ever.'

'You – you mean to say you know?... But – but how? He's never told a living soul until just now and that was only because I promised not to tell anyone.'

'I visited them in the lockup last evening and heard their stories. He didn't reveal the truth to me but I *know* the man. And so that others wouldn't discover the truth, I pretended to be disappointed in him as he was led from the court. I can read him like a book. But, sadly, I won't be able to put it in *my* book, based on my journal, when it's published by Debrett of Piccadilly.'

'And why not, sir?'

'Because James Martin, Esquire, Gentleman Farmer of the County Antrim, would not want me to, and I respect his wishes.'

She looked at him incredulously. 'But he's only a convict, sir. How can a *proper* gentleman like you respect a convict's wishes?'

'Because, unlike most of my class, *I* don't class all convicts together as one class. From your good self onwards, I've got to know many convicts in all those months we spent together on the good old *Charlotte* and every day since. Each of you is different. One only has to see how some convicts have become respectable in the colony by working hard and with skill, whereas others have stayed at the bottom of the dunghill. Men of privilege and property back in Britain may talk of a "criminal class" but that is stuff and nonsense. Faugh, if that were true, you'd *all* still be stealing.

'And,' he went on, 'just because many of your women friends have the unladylike habit of looking male strangers in the eye rather than averting their gaze, that doesn't make them whores. Nor does it when they look back after a handsome fellow has walked by. Nor if they sing, dance, whistle and swear all the time.'

'Tell all that to Lieutenant Clark and Surgeon Bowes,' she sneered; 'they think we're all bloody whores.'

'Now now, Mary, you can go too far.'

'Well, 'tis true! How is it that *you* know so much about us, sir, and the other gentlemen don't?'

'Ever since I was a boy, I've studied human nature. My father was a dancing master in Chester and we had all sorts of people at his academy. And as a marine officer, I have to deal with all sorts.'

'Yiss, from friendly Private Easty to that bug- to that beast Corporal Anderson,' she muttered.

'Quite,' said Tench, grinning.

'So a word from you to the Governor…'

'Would do no good if Martin denied your story. And he will, Mary, he will. All that you can do is tend his wounds and, when he has recovered, give him one of your blushing smiles as he goes about his daily toil with a leg-iron for company, poor wretch.'

CHAPTER 24

Although the *Sirius* had brought flour and salt from the Cape in May 1789, rations were reduced to two thirds in November. By January 1790, famine's fingers were pinching every stomach.

Will Bryant was definitely indispensable and was reinstated as master seiner, for if anyone could produce fish from the sea, 'The Cornish Conjurer' could. But Bryant would always have to be accompanied by an officer these days – and nights – to ensure that all the fish were taken to the public store.

Thanks to The Conjurer and his assistants, enough were caught on one night this month for each man, woman and child belonging to the marine detachment to be given two pounds of them. The delighted Governor had so much confidence in The Conjurer's repeating the performance that His Excellency directed that everyone should henceforth receive a weekly ration of two pounds of fish, in addition to their pitiful fare.

Mary had done her bit to encourage the fish by nailing a lucky horseshoe to the *Beauty*'s keel.

Torrential rain fell throughout most of February. For the Bryants, having their small garden turned into a quagmire was bad enough but one tempestuous night insult was added to injury, when half of their melons and pumpkins were stolen.

The rains continued into March. By this time, food stocks were so low that the Governor despatched Lieutenant-Governor Ross with two companies of marines and over two hundred convicts on the *Sirius* and *Supply* to the fertile Norfolk Island. It was more than a thousand miles out into the deep-blue Pacific. Mary was sad to see Lizzy go and, like James Cox, mourned the departure of Jane and Henrietta. But she was glad to see the red-coated back of Ralph Clark. He'd always curried favour with the hated Ross and now every evening the womanless pair could gaze at the Pacific sunset together for all she cared. All would be joining the little colony that Lieutenant Philip Gidley King, a thirty-year-old Cornishman, had set up on the Governor's orders in February 1788.

John Spence had himself been sent there two months ago.

'And a good riddance, you whore's son!' Mary had yelled when the bearded rapist scrambled down into the longboat.

There was also a small settlement called Rose Hill, which had been established in November 1788 on rich clay soil nearly fourteen miles inland from Sydney Cove.

Despite this reduction in population, rations at the cove had to be cut again on 1 April. To stop people eating their whole week's ration within three or four days, the provisions were now served daily. The new weekly ration was four pounds of flour, two-and-a-half pounds of dry, foul-tasting pork, and one-and-a-half pounds of rice crawling with weevils.

A revolutionary change: every man, woman and child in the settlement would receive equal amounts, whereas before, only the male convicts had had the same as the officers and marines. Little Charlotte Bryant would have as much as Governor Phillip.

Though it hardly made any difference to the stock, there was now another mouth to feed: baby Emanuel Bryant's. An Easter joy for the Bryants – including Charlotte – but 'Dear life, Will, what a time to arrive!' And he was 'so tiny – oh so tiny' because of his mother's meagre diet.

On Monday 5 April, the day after Emanuel's Easter baptism, the *Supply* returned with the disastrous news that the *Sirius* had been wrecked on a Norfolk Island reef. God had mercifully preserved everyone; but the old flagship, which was then to have proceeded to China to try to save the Sydney Cove colony, would never sail anywhere again.

So the weekly ration had to be cut once more: to two-and-a-half pounds of flour, two pounds of salt pork, a pound of rice and a pint of peas. Children under eighteen months had the same, except that they only had a pound of pork.

All private boats had to be surrendered to the public use, for fishing, and Will told Mary that, with such a fleet, he felt like 'the most important cove in the cove!' Working like a madman he was, as were his loyal crews, day and night, whereas all the other convicts, being so weak with hunger, only had to work in the mornings now, and then to do no more than their strength allowed.

All the other officers and gentlemen, including the Reverend Richard Johnson and Mr John White, volunteered to take turns sailing with the night fishing fleet.

'This,' said Tench to the indignant Cornishman, 'is to see that every exertion is made and that all the fish is deposited with the commissary.'

As all the other ships had long since returned to England, Lieutenant Henry Ball's little *Supply* was now the only link with the outside world. She sailed for Batavia, Java, on Saturday 17 April, carrying with her the prayers of the whole colony. She was their sole hope now, for The Conjurer's powers were failing. He was barely producing sufficient even for himself and his assistants to eat. This was no surprise, because catches were low every year at winter's approach.

The soil was so poor that in the colony's two years, only enough grain had been grown to feed the people for three weeks. As for the scraggy animals, most had died long ago. The only food in the public store was eight months' supply of flour and biscuits, less than five months' rice and peas and four months' salt meat, all with the severest rationing.

Who would survive the winter? Indeed, would anyone at Sydney Cove be alive when the *Supply* returned, in six, seven, God knew how many months' time?

CHAPTER 25

'The flag's up, Mary!' panted the skeletal Will, bursting into the hut while his wife was breastfeeding Emanuel, in the middle of this Thursday afternoon in June. 'The flag on the South Head's been hoisted. A ship's sailing into the harbour! With winter upon us, we've got food at last. Food for my babby boy!'

'Aw, Will,' she choked, buttoning her frock-of-many-patches, 'it's well timed, because there's little enough milk here for my poor mite. God *damn* this New South Wales! In Fowey I would have gathered fennel seeds and made fennel tea to give me more milk. Stow me, why I bother to cover myself, I don't know, because half the dang settlement's tottering about near naked.' The convicts had traded their rags for a few more morsels of food.

'Quick now, woman, outside with you!' he cried, taking Emanuel. 'Let's show my babby boy the ship that's brought his deliverance!'

Picking up Charlotte, she followed him out. Heedless of the windswept rain, half a dozen other women with infants in their arms were rushing about like lunatics: passionately kissing their children, hugging their neighbours and praising the Lord.

Within minutes, Captain Tench, Mr White and Captain Collins were being rowed in the longboat out into the harbour. The waves were angry whitecaps but Watkin Tench was a fighter after Mary's own heart. *Just listen to the man!*

'Pull away, my lads, we'll reach her, never fear! It's far too soon for the *Supply*, so this one'll be from Old England. Hurrah for a bellyful and news from our friends! Pull away!'

* * *

It was an hour later, with winter's darkness falling fast, before the gentlemen returned to the wave-lashed jetty. As they clambered wearily from the boat, they were greeted by a jostling throng of convicts, which the equally barefoot, and nearly as ragged, marines were having difficulty in holding back. Watkin Tench was battling with the wind for possession of a sackful of letters.

'I know you are all anxious for news from home,' grunted Tench, shoving his way through, 'but we must needs give the *Lady Juliana*'s master's news to His Excellency post?haste. We shall sort this lot in the morning.'

'W-w-what's the news from Old England, Mr White - *s-s-sir*?' gasped James Cox, as the Surgeon-General elbowed him in his skinny ribs.

'The master of the transport says that His Majesty was afflicted with a dangerous and alarming illness, but happily has recovered.'

'God save the King!' cried Private Easty, raising his hat high. 'And a happy birthday to His Majesty tomorrow!'

'And a revolution has occurred in France,' muttered White. 'The Bastille has been stormed and the prisoners freed.'

'*Liberté!*' roared Will, the former French-brandy smuggler, lifting Emanuel as high as Easty's hat. 'God bless those French people! God bless 'em, I say!'

The starving Charlotte was howling and Mary clutched Tench's frayed red sleeve.

'What about the stores, Cap'n Tench? My poor babbies are *dying*, for mercy's sake! Why ain't us had no food from England all the time we've been here?'

'For a very good reason, Mary Bryant,' he said, resting his bony hands on her shoulders, Easty having taken the sack. There was just enough light to see the despair in the exhausted officer's kind blue eyes.

'When the ships that brought us here returned to England, they delivered His Excellency's urgent request for more provisions. In response, the Government sent HMS *Guardian* with salted meat, fruit trees, plants and seeds and two years' supply of stores. She took on many breeding animals at the Cape and more trees, etcetera. However, thirteen days after leaving the Cape, it was the frigate's fate to strike an iceberg, and to save her from sinking, much of that precious cargo, including all the livestock, was thrown overboard. The salt provisions and some flour *were* saved and eventually ended up in Cape Town warehouses after the crippled *Guardian* sailed back there. But for that accident, the near starvation and utter misery we have suffered this year would have been brought to an end much earlier. And we would not have sent the *Sirius* to Norfolk Island and lost *her*! The *Guardian* was such a fast-sailing ship that she would probably have arrived here in the latter part of January or at the beginning of February. So you see, His Majesty's Government had not forgotten us.

'All is not lost, though,' he said, sarcastically. 'The *Lady Juliana* has brought a small flock of sheep and as much as she could hold of the *Guardian*'s flour: seventy-five barrels. Enough to add a pound and a half to each person's weekly ration. Pah, what a pitiful amount! And even saying there will be a pound and a half is probably estimating it too highly, for by the look of the stowage conditions in that leaky old tub, I would wager that the contents of a good score of casks have been ruined.

'Oh, by the way, she has also brought many more useless mouths to feed. Another two hundred and twenty-five *women* to *burden* the colony, rather than men to *farm* and *build* it. Faugh, women. Plaguy *women*!'

CHAPTER 26

Seventeen days later, the *Justinian* storeship arrived and, thankfully, she was fully laden with provisions. At long last the full ration was restored.

Within another nine days, three more transports, the *Surprize, Neptune* and *Scarborough*, had anchored in Sydney Cove, bringing, as well as convicts, two companies of the New South Wales Corps. The soldiers were to take over guarding the convicts, a job which the marines had always hated.

The creaking old *Surprize* had been the first to arrive and, horror of horrors, word quickly spread that of the 252, male, convicts, 42 had died and another 21 were very sick. All 252 had lain shackled in pairs in her stinking hold, without once going on deck.

As for the occupants of the *Neptune* and *Scarborough*, on this freezing Tuesday morning at the end of June, they were in no better state. Some of the poor wretches had died while the two ships were sailing up the harbour last night, and their bodies had been thrown overboard, washed ashore and were now lying naked on the rocks out there. Others were dying at this minute in the boats bringing them to the jetty, where Mary was standing with Emanuel in her arms and Charlotte and Will on either side. Some, with thousands of lice crawling over them, were expiring on the very quay.

'Lord rest 'em,' choked the trembling convict girl, reeling back from the stench. 'Aw, Lord rest 'em. For sure, these poor souls couldn't have had a good, kind Mr White to look after 'em like what we did, like him giving me laudanum for my morning sickness. Nearly eight hundred of us lot embarked on *our* ships and only twenty-three died at sea, didn't they? Whoever's in charge of those ships should be hung from the Tree!'

'Dang me!' The Cornishman spat into the water. 'As if this cussed colony ain't got enough trouble! Four useless shiploads of ill or old or female prisoners in three weeks. How long's the food going to last now? It's madness! We'll soon be dead like these poor mortals!'

The *Scarborough* had been with the First Fleet but had returned to England soon after. Her captain, John Marshall, was Hector's original master, and now, that once-powerful animal was excitedly swimming towards the ship. The starvation years had taken their toll and Marshall would be shocked to see how thin his old friend was.

'Aw, Will, after more than two year, that dear ol' dog still remembers his *old* master! I wonder if little ol' Pincher remembers me after four-and-a-half.'

Jimmy had joined them. 'Ah, sure he does, Mary darlin'. *Who* could ever forget *ye*?'

She squeezed his bony arm. 'Aw, Jimmy, you're as loyal as an old dog yourself, ain't you?'

'Your loyal servant, ma'am,' he said, shyly lowering his heavy-lidded eyes as he bowed gracefully – well, as gracefully as a clumsy cove like him could.

She groaned. 'Even as we're talking, Pincher's probably waiting at the gate like he always did: old faithful friend. If, that is, they survived their own starving time.

'Aw, Will,' she sniffed, 'we must get back to England! We've just got to get away from here somehow, even though if we're caught escaping, it'll mean death. The old *Beauty* can do it; I know she can!'

'You've taken the words right out of my mouth, Mary,' he whispered. 'Though *my* term will be ended next March the twentieth, the danged Guvnor's said that no one can leave who's got wives or children not capable of maintaining themselves and likely to become burdensome to the settlement. And *you'll* still have two year to do, woman. Satan's horns, I can't survive another two year from next March!

'And,' he went on, 'one thing's as sure as my name be William Bryant. I can't be contented like Jim Ruse, the husbandman from Lan'son way, whose term ended last year and who got the Guvnor to give him some land at Rose Hill in hopes of living independently of the public store, happily growing wheat, and maybe getting married and raising children. Yes, folk do say he has his eyes on that pretty Lizzy Perry, her that came on the *Lady Juliana*. Faugh, growing wheat at Rose Hill! It would be like chawing cud: ruminating on things past, back in Cornwall. Ruminating ain't no life for William Bryant; *he* wants to *be* back in Cornwall. Yes, we must escape!'

'Ye're both joking, aren't ye?' breathed Jimmy. He glanced round anxiously to see whether anybody had overheard, but no one was near enough. 'Ye're not seriously thinking of escaping, are ye? 'Tis impossible!'

Will's look hardened. 'What about those victims of the *Bounty* mutineers that the *Lady Juliana*'s crew told us the story of? Dang me, if Cap'n William Bligh of the *Bounty* and those brave billies of his can sail in their ship's launch across well over three thousand mile of ocean and live to tell the tale, why can't his fellow Cornishman, Cap'n William Bryant of the *Beauty*? Yes, if that gentleman can reach the island of Timor in a twenty-three-foot open boat, so can we in an eighteen-foot'un! Then we can get a Dutch ship from there.'

The Irishman stared open-mouthed. 'But at least yer man had about a dozen tough tars with him: trained crew. Who have ye got, ye half-starved skeleton? Just ye, Will Bryant. Just ye!'

'And me, Jimmy,' said Mary, quietly. 'Don't you forget that I've helped Father on our old *Jenny* since I was a child. Feel the palms of my hands.'

Blushing, he did so and his own hands shook.

'Aye... Aye but – but ye've got two childer to take!'

He looked down at the smiling, bare-topped Charlotte in her bright-green skirt. 'Mmm, I must admit, though, that this wee brat is quite expert at throwing buckets of seawater at poor unsuspecting Irishmen, so I suppose she could do the bailing out. Ye could throw out the water, chick.'

Her sunken grey eyes lit up and the smile broadened across the pinched freckled cheeks.

'Iss, Charlotte do it,' said this bright little girl who was not even three yet.

Jimmy stooped and kissed her forehead. 'Of course, even though I've only got a year to serve, *I'd* go with ye. But ye'd need a good few more.'

Will gripped his comrade's arm excitedly. 'How many folk can we trust, Jimmy?'

'Well, let me think... There's James Cox, of course. He's a fine carpenter, if we have to make repairs, and he's getting good at navigation, thanks to ye.'

'But, Jimmy!' gasped Mary. 'What about Sarah?' Beautiful, raven-haired Sarah Young, twenty, was James's new love, having arrived on the *Lady Juliana*. Her death sentence for stealing nine yards of muslin had been commuted to seven years' transportation as part of the thanksgiving for George III's recovery. '*She* can't go; she gets even worse seasick than James.'

'No,' grunted Will, 'Sarah can't go. Anyway, we don't want no more dang women. Especially drunken whores like her. Cox'll have to go without her.'

Mary sighed. 'Poor James keeps losing his sweet'arts, don't he?'

Jimmy was scratching his mop of black hair. 'Sam Bird can handle a boat well; he's helped ye enough times on the *Beauty* – aye, I know, Will: Sam's a rascally oul bird, but he's so desperate to get away, he'd never betray us.

'Sure,' said the Irishman, 'there's a good few others who're able mariners, thanks to your teaching, and they've stayed loyal to ye through all these bad times, but I can't think of any of them I'd completely trust not to blab. Ye've made many enemies here, as ye well know. Jealous of yer favoured situation they are. And mighty resentful, too, of some of the things ye've yelled at them when they've done something stupid during the fishing – ack, Will, calm yerself, man. Look at yer face: 'tis as red as a maid's when she's receiving her first kiss, so it is! Don't get me wrong; I'm speaking as yer friend. But not everyone has the gift of being a fisherman. The fisherfellas of Red Bay were born with it, like yerself. But even they need help: from the Fairy People – the "Good People", we must call them so as not to offend them. Aye, the fisherfellas can *charm* the salmon and the trout from the water, along with the turbot and the mackerel and the cod and the herring, to name but a few. Where's *your* charm, Will Bryant? The way ye shout at some of the lads, especially when ye've been swigging spirits, ye put the fear of God into them, so ye do. Sure, it makes them lose their confidence.'

Before Will could say anything, Jimmy went on, 'Why, ye've had poor James Cox trembling like an auld maid that's found a lusty tar under her bed, and there never was a man trying harder to please! James, I mean, not the lusty tar. He's been a loyal friend to ye ever since those terrible *Dunkirk* days.

'Aye, Will, I know what ye're going to say. "*You* can talk, Jimmy Martin; you've got a quick temper, too." I'm the first to admit it. But the difference between you and me is that ye don't suffer fools gladly, and ye really hurt them with that fierce tongue of yours.' He concluded, chuckling, "Tis a wonder ye've suffered this oul fool of an Irishman gladly these past three-and-a-half years.'

Will paused, considering the home truths. Abruptly he growled, 'Well, that's as maybe, but, anyway, it'll take time to plan proper, like. Maybe James and Sam can think of someone. Tonight I'll invite 'em into the hut for a little hugger-mugger talk, like plotters in the French Revolution. *Liberté!*

CHAPTER 27

'Yes, it's Providence that all of us lads'll be out in the *Beauty* on fishing duty tomorrow,' whispered Will in the flickering candlelight, this Monday evening, 21 February 1791.

'It'll give me a chance to see how fit the three newcomers are for our brave long journey. If those five *new boys* from Rose Hill could manage to get away to sea last September and still ain't been caught, we can do it. It's eight dang month since I vowed to escape. Eight month too many, but the opportunity wasn't there, was it?

'It will be shortly, though,' he muttered. 'Circumstances will never be as good as they'll be at the end of next month. Because then the *Supply* and the *Waaksamheyd*, that Dutch snow she chartered at Batavia, are sailing again, leaving no ship here to chase us.

'Now, you're *sure* we can trust Allen, Butcher and Lilley, Bill?'

Apart from the Bryants and Jimmy, there were three others huddled over the table in the stifling little hut: James Cox and Sam Bird, and the quietly spoken Bill Morton who had come with the Second Fleet.

'I'd trust them with me *wife*,' declared this cadaverous, bare-chested Northumbrian navigator, wiping the sweat from his bald head in a vain effort to stop any more trickling into his hollow brown eyes.

'Your *wife*?' snorted Mary, looking up from patching his shirt-of-many-patches, using some thread brought by the *Lady Juliana*. 'Ha, it's easy for *you* to say you'd trust 'em with *your* wife; you ain't got no wife!'

'It's only a manner of speaking, bonny lass,' grinned the candlelit death's-head – with which, surely, no woman would ever dream of sharing a pillow?

'What about my wife?' demanded Will. 'Can I trust 'em with her, or her with them, when my back's turned?'

'Will Bryant!' She flung the shirt at his head, which, if truth be told, was itself becoming scaringly skull-like.

Morton's grin spread, stretching the parchment-dry skin so tight that it seemed about to split. This deep and rather mysterious man had never revealed his age but despite his appearance, he was probably no older than Will.

'Aye, Will,' he said, 'ye can trust them with your beautiful boat and your beautiful wife. Although *I* came in the *Neptune* and they came in the *Scarborough*, I've since got to know them well. "Old Bill" Allen's a widower, fifty-four years of age. He told me that his wife died of a broken heart, a week after he was given a seven-year transportation sentence at Norwich for stealing some pretty embroidered cotton handkerchiefs for her fiftieth birthday. Poor old fella, he never stops talking about her. He's determined to end his days in Norfolk so he can be buried next to her. And he's a right good seaman is Old Bill. Aye, ye can trust him, no bother.'

'Wot's this John Butcher cove like?' The questioner was the aptly named Sam Bird. His black beady eyes glinted and his curled black fingernails scratched this long, greasy black hair half covering his gaunt face.

A twitching little bachelor was beaky-nosed Sam, as if he was forever expecting to be pounced on. Only Jimmy liked this perpetual whiner. But the twenty-nine-year-old Thames waterman certainly knew how to handle a boat and had proved his worth on countless fishing expeditions these past three years. Sam had been sentenced to seven years' transportation for stealing 1,000 pounds of saltpetre from a Wandsworth warehouse. It was hard to imagine now but, according to him, he had once been stout. 'Two bloody years' in 'bloody' Southwark Gaol and on the *Justinia* hulk had reduced him to a scrawny bird indeed and he'd remained so.

'Comes from Wales way, didn't yer say? Well, us Londoners don't trust bloody foreigners. Whitechapel's swarmin' wiv 'em: shopkeepers, innkeepers, brothelkeepers. Robbin' vultures, the lot of 'em!'

'He's not a foreigner, Sam,' said Jimmy, soothingly. 'Sure, he comes from Shropshire, near Wales.'

'That's wot I mean: bloody foreigner. Shropshire? Never 'eard of the place.'

Bill Morton sighed. 'Eeh, my. Well, would it reassure ye to know that sometimes he, too, uses the name Sam: Sam Broom?'

The beady eyes stared in disbelief and the thin lips opened wide, revealing four rotten teeth, all that remained of his front ones.

'Gor... Well ain't that funny? *My* real name's John Simms but I always call meself Sam Bird. *His* name's John and he sometimes calls hisself Sam. Sounds like he's a cove arter me own 'art!' he said, rubbing his bald spot.

Mary chuckled. 'So you think you can trust him, then, Sam?'

'Yeah…' He sniffed noisily, then spat on the floorboards. 'Yeah, I s'pose so...'

Morton resumed. 'Like me, John was sentenced to seven years' transportation. He had stolen three pigs from his master, Farmer Harsbury...'

Jimmy laughed. 'Sure, 'tis an appropriate theft for a man named Butcher.'

Morton wiped the sweat from his eyes.

'… And our other crewman, Nat Lilley, from Suffolk, stole a fishing-net, a gold watch and two silver spoons. He told me he'd lost his wee fishing boat and his net in some terrible winter gales in '86, when the sea came right up the beach. He took the watch and spoons from the house of a Mr Benjamin Summerset, fer to buy another boat, or else Mistress Lilley and the children would have starved. He was reprieved from hanging because of what were called "favourable circumstances" and he, too, was given seven years' transportation. The poor fella's hair went as white as snow, with him pining for his wife and bairns. And that was in the two years in gaol and on the hulk before he even set one fettered foot on the *Scarborough*, mind.

'Aye,' he concluded brightly, 'ye'll have a right canny crew, Will.'

The Cornishman was restless. 'Satan's horns, it's so suffocating hot! Those few showers of rain we've had since last July would scarce add up to twenty-four hoursworth. The soil's rock hard and the tetties I planted last March were a sorry sight when I dug 'em up in September. There are only a few vegetables in the whole settlement, and the wheat was so poor last harvest that very little, except Indian corn, has been sowed this year, ain't it?

'And to cap it all,' he said, 'those bloody blacks come here every day, kicking up more dido an' caprouse than Bedlamites, and *demand* bread and meat. Bread and meat! Dang me, we've got little enough for ourselves!

'As for that greedy, pampered, bosky, gap-toothed rascal Bennelong. His gap-toothed "father", as he calls him, the darling Guvnor, has already had a brick house built for him and his mates on the eastern point of the cove, ain't he?'

Liquor-loving Bennelong had been captured in November 1789 and escaped in May 1790. Having learnt a little English, he was now a useful mediator for Phillip, a role formerly performed by Arabanoo. Gentle Arabanoo, along with countless numbers of his fellows, had died from *galgalla*, smallpox, in the epidemic which raged among the natives in April and May 1789. He was mourned by many in the settlement: particularly by Phillip, Jimmy and the colony's children.

'And that ain't all,' Will went on. 'Tomorrow, to keep the natives friendly, Cap'n bloody Tench has ordered me to take Bennelong's stinking sister out in the *Beauty* with us "to *help* with the fishing"! And where she do bloody go, so, too, do her stinking brats, all three of 'em.

'Sink me, what's become of me? What would my old billies back in Lelant say? Gor, what would ol' Caleb Pascoe and Reuben Tamblyn say if they could see me now? I can just hear 'em. "Will Bryant, once-proud Cornishman, now nursemaid to a bunch of stinking blacks down at the stinking backside of the bloody world!

'Aw,' he cried, 'hark at my cheelie! Hark at him, poor li'l babby, bawling on his sack mattress there because his mother's milk's dried up. Rot an' perish this bloody New South Wales! As sure as my name be William Bryant, I won't let my boy die!'

CHAPTER 28

'Lord save 'em!' shrieked Mary, squeezing Emanuel to her useless breast. 'Aw, Sarah, look! Aw, dear life, dear life!'

The two women and Charlotte were standing on Point Maskelyne jetty, at the cove entrance, watching the gale-battered *Beauty*'s return at sunset. The cutter was still about two hundred yards away but Mary could clearly see what had happened.

'The hook of the foretack's given way in the wind and the foresail's got sternway. The *Beauty*'s filling up!'

'James'll drown!' screamed the red-faced Sarah, swaying with rum. 'He can't swim, he can't swim!'

Everyone was about to jump overboard. Bennelong's sister had put her infant daughter on her shoulders and was now the first to slide into the white-crested, greyish-green waves. Swimming in that dolphin way of all the natives, she struck out for a point about thirty yards from her. The boys, aged about seven, were swept in behind their mother. Sam Bird clung to the side for another second, then followed. The new crewmen, Nat Lilley, grizzle-bearded John Butcher and grey-haired Old Bill Allen jumped next, with Bill Morton following. This left Will and Jimmy, and James who was clinging to the mast. They seemed to be arguing.

'For God's sake, you buffle'eads, jump!' shrilled Mary, knowing full well that they could not hear. 'Don't just stand there arguing! Jump and swim to the point over there!'

'But, Mary, they can't leave my James... They – they are leaving 'im... They're leaving 'im to drown, poor boy! They're going to jump. You cowards!' she screeched. 'You bloody cowards!'

Suddenly Will and Jimmy turned and grabbed James before he knew what was happening and snatched him from the mast. Then with James in the middle, all three fell into the turbulent waves. The mast toppled over the other side and was swept away.

Meanwhile, Bennelong's sister, a strong swimmer, had already reached the point. With her daughter still on her shoulders, she was clinging to an overhanging ledge. The rest, though, were making for the beach over there, having been carried well past the point.

'Hi, look, Sarah, look!'

Along Maskelyne Beach here, a dozen blacks had slid three bark canoes into the water and were furiously paddling to the rescue. One canoe was heading for Bennelong's sister, the others for the stricken *Beauty*.

'Jesus Christ, Mary,' wept Sarah, 'they ain't bothering about the *swimmers*; they're only thinking about the bloody boat!'

'Dear life!'

The two black boys had almost reached that beach there and were obviously safe. Sam Bird, John Butcher and even Old Bill were not far behind, and Bill Morton was gaining on them. Will and Jimmy with the thrashing James were still a hundred yards back.

'Oh, Mary, they won't do it; James is dragging 'em down! O God, please help them! Help them, please! I always knew my poor James would drown. It's his fate, poor boy. His nightmares have come true. I knew they would, I always knew they would!'

Mary's heart had gone cold.

'Mummy, you're hurting Charlotte! Your nails are hurting Charlotte's hand!'

'I – I'm sorry, my lover,' she sobbed, her eyes fixed on the desperate struggle. Will and Jimmy were good swimmers but the pair of them were so weak with hunger. They were sinking. It was all over. Their escape plans had remained just dreams. The two friends were cursed: cursed from the day they'd been born. Old Scratch, the Devil, had been laughing at them all this time: all their lives: when they'd been children in Cornwall and Ireland, playing and praying; and as prisoners, planning and praying...

No, dammit, I will not let them die!

But how to save them? No other boats anywhere near on the beach...

Wait! The scull had been brought ashore yesterday for caulking. Perhaps she was finished.

Mary put Emanuel into Sarah's arms and, leaving the wailing Charlotte to bury her crimson face in her hands, hurtled along the sand.

Yes, there she was, at the back of the beach: upturned, her bottom freshly coated with pitch.

The convict girl staggered across. She reached her at last. Heaved her upright. Picked up the oars. Feverishly put them in the rowlocks. She was panting madly, half blinded with sweat, as she pushed the scull down to the water.

She was aboard now.

'Now, damn you, move!' she cried, grasping the oars.

'Move!

'*Move!*

Over her shoulder, she saw that Will and James Cox still had their heads above water... but – but 'Jimmy! Where's Jimmy?... Drownded?... Aw... aw, don't let him be drownded. I can't bear it... Please God, don't let dear Jimmy be drownded!

'These bloody waves! Damn you, damn you to hell! I'll never get there in time... Never. Impossible... Aw, Christ, I'm so dang weak!'

It must have been four or five minutes later when she drew near.

'Hi, Mary,' wheezed Will, from just ten yards off now, swimming on his back, with one arm round the still-struggling James.

At the sight of her, Will Bryant had somehow found the strength to continue fighting the angry, hungry waves. 'Curse you... you greedy beggars,' he gasped, 'you won't swallow *me*... or my... or my crewmate.'

'Aw, Will,' she puffed as the Cornishman's arm clutched the oar at last. 'Aw, m'dear.'

With Mary pulling and Will shoving, they managed to get the spluttering James aboard. He lay on his side and puked over her feet. He'd live. Unlike darling Jimmy...

'I'll stay in the water, gal,' panted Will. 'I'll hang on to this rope here. I'll only... I'll only capsize you if I try to get aboard in this... in this sea.'

'J-J-Jimmy's gone, Will,' she choked. 'Jimmy's gone!'

Through a curtain of tears and spray, she vainly looked for a bobbing head. The curtain was red now as she turned to a setting sun which Jimmy would never see again.

'Dear little man,' she sobbed. 'Aw, dear little man! Aw, God, why are You so cruel?'

She felt a tug at the other oar.

'Jeez, Mary darlin', are ye... are ye going to keep us out here all night while ye get all romantic over the sunset?'

Her heart leapt.

'Jimmy!' she breathed, looking into his blinking blue eyes. 'Aw, thank God! Thank God!'

'Yes,' gulped Will, catching another mouthful. 'Yes, thank God... But why... why didn't those bloody blacks help us?'

'Ah, Will,' spluttered the Irishman, 'they knew... they knew we were good swimmers, like... And even ye should be pleased... by what they're doing.'

'What – what d'you mean?'

'Look: back there.'

The first canoe had picked up Bennelong's sister and her daughter. The other two had rescued the oars and mast and were now towing the crippled *Beauty* herself.

'Dang me! Whoever would've believed it?'

'She'll make it,' puffed Jimmy. 'She's... she's low in the water... but the auld *Beauty* will make it.'

'And so will we!' roared Mary Bryant. 'We'll set sail for Timor in March!'

'But Lor' God Almighty, Mary,' groaned Will, 'the ol' gal's in a bad way. She's such an old boat,' he panted. 'She was old before they brought her down here... She should never have left England!... How can we ever get to Timor now?'

Her teeth clenched, her jaw jutted.

'We'll do what we planned to do, Will Bryant... With a strengthened mast and a proper going over of the whole boat, we'll make her proper shipshaped and fitty for her brave long journey across three thousand and more mile of ocean.'

'But she's–'

'She'll be fine, Will. 'Twas maybe the Lord's way of reminding us that we're in His hands. Never mind three *thousand* mile, we'd never have got more than three mile the way she was. And–' She faltered. 'And *my* poor children would have been the ones in the water... and drownded.'

'You're right, of course, my sweet'art. You -' he swallowed yet another mouthful. 'You always are... I'll ask your darling Watkin to get the carpenters to do a real proper job... Yes, she won't let us down, the ol' gal... Like Bligh and his billies, we'll get to Timor, Mary. We'll get there.'

CHAPTER 29

Four Mondays later, there was another candlelit meeting in the Bryants' hut and this evening all the plotters were here.

'Well, my billies,' whispered Will, 'I've spent every farthing of the money you brought from England and every farthing I've managed to save from my dealings since I arrived in this confounded colony. That foxy old Dutchman, Cap'n Detmer Smit of the *Waaksamheyd*, has sold me a compass, a quadrant, a rought chart, two muskets with full bullet pouches and powder horns, and some pork and rice. James has pinched some tools and nails. And Mary here's been a-picking more sweet tea leaves from the creepers growing on the rocks, though she's had to go miles to find any.

'The fishing's been a dang sight better again these days, ain't it?... Well, when the Reverend Richard Johnson's been supervisor and had his mind on God – or, more like, on that fan-waving wife of his – and not on me, I've managed to smuggle away several boxes of fish, sell 'em, then buy flour from the baker.

'So, we've got one hundred pound of rice, one hundred pound of flour and fourteen pound of pork. And we'll take eight gallon of water: four in each breaker. We've also got that seine net Mary's been making, some fishing lines and hooks, some blankets, a big tent and a small'un and some cooking things... Oh, and – and some rum. For medicinal use, like,' he grunted.

Mary and Jimmy exchanged grins but Will pretended not to notice.

'All this stuff, save the net, is under the floorboards, in canvas-covered boxes wrapped in bark. It's a bloody tight fit.

'Charlotte don't know about it,' he murmured, indicating the sleeping girl, who had one arm round her sleeping brother. 'She'd give the game away with her chitterings an' chatterings.

'The night before we go, we'll bury most of this stuff in the sand in that little ol' cave next to Maskelyne jetty, so we'll have a quick flight from our huts.

'Oh, one more thing. I'm also taking a writing book, because Captain William Bryant's going to write a journal of the journey.'

Bill Morton bowed his death's-head and, in the candle-flicker, his sunken eyes peered at the chart.

'Show us where we're bound, bonny lad.'

'Here, Mr Navigator,' said the Cornish mariner, unable to keep the excitement from his voice. 'Here's Timor,' he breathed, prodding the chart with his shaking forefinger.

Sam Bird spat on the floor, missing the baby by an inch.

'Tell 'em all how far it is, *Captain* Bryant.'

'Something like three thousand two hundred and fifty mile.'

'Law!' gasped John Butcher, brushing his thick, greying black hair from these sad dark-brown eyes. 'We'll never do it! We'll never get there, look you,' he said, fingering this mass of grizzled beard. He looked all of his forty-nine years.

'We must, boy,' muttered Old Bill, scratching his own wholly grey hair with his right hand. 'Woe's my old bones, oi can't die down here at the bottom of the world. When my toime comes, oi want to be buried next to my dear old Betsy in Norfolk, not thousands of miles from her. If Bligh could reach Timor, so can we!'

He'd been scratching with increasing ferocity and suddenly slammed his right fist on the table.

'Bless her heart,' he sniffed as Mary clasped his trembling hands. 'Oh, bless her dear heart.'

'Old Bill's right,' said the red-faced and mighty skinny Nat Lilley. His shock of white woolly hair made him look like the wild man of the woods – save only that Nat was clean-shaven. 'He's fifty-four years of age and oi'm forty-eight, and oi won't live to be even as old as him if oi hev to slave and starve for much longer in this hellhole. We must get there, we must! My wife and children need me. If they're still alive,' he added, his voice breaking.

'And I'm d-d-down 'ere for life,' stammered the sorely sunburnt James Cox, who, though only thirty-one, looked forty-five these days. The sandy hair was so much lighter now, bleached by the cruel sun and grey from worry. 'Thanks to Will Bryant 'ere, I've learned some navigation especially for this occasion. He's – he's been very p-p-patient with me.'

Mary and Jimmy exchanged sly glances.

Cox clenched his fists. 'For mercy's sake, how else will I ever get away from this plaguy place? Not by lawful means, that's for certain. A life sentence *means* life and I'd never be a free man again. Never!

'So desperate am I, that I'm willing to leave my darling S-S-Sarah behind at a time when she's fretting herself silly about her health – and *drinking* herself silly, an' all! Poor gel, she's welcome to what little property I have. And when she's served her term, pray G-G-God we'll meet again in Old England.

'I can't f-f-face telling her that I'm going, though. So I'll write her a letter just before we go, and hide it in my other toolbox, in the carpenter's shop, so she can read it the next morning, after we've gone. In the letter, I'll beg her to give over the pursuit of the vices what prevail in this cussed place – in her case: drink.'

His raw right cheek twitched in the glow.

'As you well know, I'm a landsman what was forced by circumstances to go to sea. I can't s-s-swim and if it weren't for Will and Jimmy and Mary, I'd have drownded. If it's the Lord's will, I'll survive the sea again, and the sharks won't gobble me up. But nothing's more certain that if I do stay here, the *sun* will *shrivel* me up!'

A sudden draught caught the candle flame and a thin swirl of smoke formed, escaped and sailed off into the darkness. An omen? wondered Mary.

She sighed and gazed into her husband's tired brown eyes.

'So how much longer, then, Will?'

He hawked the phlegm from his dry throat and, aiming at Sam's spittle, the Master Spitter of Sydney Cove hit his target. Another omen? Would he also succeed in his aim for Timor?

'Well, gal, yesterday, Sunday the twentieth of March, 1791, I finished my term. Tomorrow Lieutenant Ball's sailing the *Supply* to Norfolk Island again, taking a detachment of those brutal buggers of the New South Wales Corps to act as bloody gaolers there. And next Monday morning the *Waaksamheyd* sets sail for England.'

He paused and the only sound inside the hut was the children's steady breathing.

'All of us boys will be on fishing duty together in the *Beauty* that day. And that *night* will be lovely and dark, because as how there won't be no moon. 'Twould be an ideal night for some freetrading. So we'll set sail from Point Maskelyne that very night, when there'll be no ship to chase after us.

'As soon as it's eleven o'clock bell at the barracks, we'll be out of our huts as quick as spit, because that's the only time when the guard are thinking of other things. The lads going off duty will be a-dreaming of their beds and their women, and those coming on duty will be a-cussing an' a-swearing and a-moaning an' a-groaning about having to be awake all dang night. The guard will be off guard! But only for ten minute. That's all the time we've got: to run, on our poor old weak, skellinton legs, from our huts, past the back of the barracks, past the parade ground, storehouses, bakehouse, 'orspital, and Lieutenant Ball's house. And Lieutenant William Dawes's dang observatory at the point itself. Pray it's a cloudy night and Dawes is in bed early there, because we don't want that devil-mad astronomer pointing at us instead of at shooting stars and the like!'

'Aye,' muttered Jimmy, 'yer man and his *shooting*-star eyes could get us all shot.'

'Now, my billies –'

'But, Will,' protested Mary, 'what about the night-watch convicts? They're on all night, from the beat of the nine o'clock tattoo to the morning work-drum.'

'No, gal, I ain't forgotten those bloody beggars that that one-eyed traitor Herbert Keeling trained before he was sent to Norfolk Island.

There are six of 'em on our side of the Tank Stream, right? Well, they, too, will be in the barracks at eleven o'clock for ten minute of orders.

'Now, my billies, mind this and mind it well. We're a team and must keep together whatever happens. If we don't stick together, we're sunk. So anyone who disobeys my orders gets left behind.'

CHAPTER 30

'There goes the bell, Mary,' breathed Will. He picked up Emanuel in the tiny canvas-covered crib which James Cox had made for the journey, then grabbed the musket from the table.

'Bring that box with the scales in, gal,' he whispered, easing open the creaking door. 'We'll need 'em for rationing the food.'

'But I'm carrying Charlotte,' protested Mary, feeling danged uncomfortable with this canvas scarf tied round her head. 'She ain't a little babby now; she's three-an'-a-half year old, even if she *is* only a skinny old thing.'

'Do as I say, for God's sake, woman, or we'll run out of food before we're halfway to Timor.'

'But –'

He was outside now, keeping the door open with his bare foot.

'Stow it, you stupid bitch,' he rasped; 'we're wasting precious time.'

So with her daughter under her right arm and the scales under her left, the convict girl tiptoed out. It was cloudy, thank the Lord, with no sound except the frogs from the stream and the wind in the gum trees.

'Now, woman, don't you let this daughter of yours make a sound or we're done. I still think I should've stuck some oiled paper over her mouth, like Emanuel.'

'Hush now, Charlotte,' murmured her mother. 'Mind well what I told you. We're playing hidey-peep with the soldiers. They mustn't hear us nor see us.'

'Iss, Mummy,' whispered the little girl, peeping from under her canvas bonnet.

'Here we go,' muttered Will. 'Run!'

She ran. Oh, how she ran. But, dear life, the cursed scales were rattling louder than chains!

Then the barracks loomed. Surely someone in there would hear the clatter? *Aw, please God, no! please God, no!*

'Those bloody scales, woman!' He was some yards ahead. Surely someone would hear him, too?

'I can't help it,' she hissed. 'You told me to bring 'em.'

Any moment now a shot would ring out. But folk did say that you never heard the bullet with your name on it. *Holy heavens, this is madness,* she told herself. *We'll never get past this open parade ground. Someone's behind!... Pray God it's the others.* If so, it would be John, Old Bill, Nat and Bill Morton, because their hut was at the *bottom* of First Street, level with the Bryants' Second Street home. Whereas Jimmy, James and Sam had to run down the whole length of First Street.

'Mary!' Thank God, it was Bill Morton. 'For the love of Christ, pet,' he panted, 'you're making such a din!... Leave 'em! *We* can't carry 'em for you... 'cos we're loaded with those bits an' pieces we didn't get time to bury... in the cave last night.'

Sensible advice. Will could stow his objections! Barely pausing, she stooped and left the scales in the dirt, then accelerated. Will was way ahead now, a shadow hurtling like a hellhound. Faith, he'd have put everything in the *Beauty* before anyone else reached the jetty – if they ever did.

The shadowy storehouses were over on the right here; and coming up now, over by the water, was the lighted bakehouse.

'Mummy!'

'Shhh, Charlotte!' gulped Mary. 'Dear life, cheel', you'll be... you'll be the death of us!'

'But, Mummy,' she wailed, 'your bones be sticking in me! Them's *hurtin'* Charlotte!'

'Be brave, my lover,' she puffed, 'be brave. We're nearly there now.'

Think: think of something to take Charlotte's mind off herself.

'We'll be passing Lieutenant Ball's house... in a minute. He must be halfway to Norfolk Island now... I wonder... I wonder if he's got... if he's got another big 'ouse there.'

'Shall us have a big 'ouse, Mummy?'

'Yiss... yiss... with pink roses... in a great big... garden.'

'Be pink roses pretty, Mummy?... Be pink roses got lovely smells?'

'Yiss, my sweet'art... The loveliest... the loveliest smells in the... in the 'ole world.'

The ground was sloping. The water was slap-slapping just ahead there. She was running on timber now: the boards leading to the – 'Praise be!' The jetty at last. She turned sharp left and – 'oops!' slid headfirst into the sand. Frantically she searched for Charlotte's mouth and clapped a hand over it.

'Hurry, Mary,' whispered Will from the cave. 'Give me a hand here.' He had lit a candle but, as the entrance faced away from the darkened observatory and the settlement itself, no one would see.

Within seconds, Bill Morton and his hutmates had joined them and after Mary had sat Charlotte on the cave floor, they formed a human chain stretching to the jetty.

Within a minute, the remaining shadowy figures had arrived and began stowing everything into the boat.

Within another minute, Will was handing Mary the last canvas-covered box.

'We'll leave the big seine, gal. It's too large for our needs and we're loaded like a miller's plaguy 'orse. I've already stowed the small'un you made.' He grunted as he bent down and picked up the crib and musket, then blew out the candle.

Just seconds later, Mary Bryant was snuggling her children in the straw at the stern of the boat, in front of Will's tiller seat.

A few more seconds and everyone was aboard, save Old Bill waiting to cast off... Everyone? She caught her breath. The starboard after-rower's seat was empty; Sam Bird did not have a rowing mate.

'W-where's Jimmy, Sam? I thought he came to the cave when you did.'

'Bloody foreign fool! He stopped to search for the handsaw and bag o' rice wot cack-'anded Cox had dropped just before you get to the bake'ouse. We got separated, like, 'cos Martin had to lie low 'cos one of the night-baking gang arrived for work just then.'

'Satan's horns,' groaned Will. 'Satan's bloody horns! And he's got the other musket, too!'

'Oi can hear voices along there, Will,' gulped Nat.

'Oi can see a loight, boy,' muttered Old Bill.

'Cast off, Bill,' said Will grimly.

'Will!' Mary's fingers gripped his bony knee behind her. 'You can't! He's your friend, your best friend!'

'Cast off, Bill! You ain't that deaf, you old beggar.'

The Norfolk seaman still pretended not to hear his captain's order.

Captain William Bryant blazed, 'Talk of mutiny on the *Bounty*, it's mutiny in the *Beauty* now, is it? Cast off, you damn ol' swab!'

'Please, Will,' sobbed Mary.

'Jimmy knew the rules, woman. I told you all, that we must stick together or we're sunk. We can't have one man spoiling everyone else's chances.'

'But – but he's doing it to save *us*! We'll need that saw.'

'Maybe, but it's too late. The guard's changed and they'll have found Jimmy by now and be here any second. They'll – hi, Mary, where're you going – aahh!'

With her other foot, she'd kicked his hand from her ankle and was on the jetty before he could stop her. Brushing past Old Bill, she ran along the boards, then stumbled up the slope and tore along the path.

'Jimmy, where are you?' she gasped. 'Where are you, my sweet'art?'

Soon she could see the lights; yes, from near the bakehouse.

'Jimmy, where – oops!'

'Ack, Mary... Ack, are ye trying to knock me back the way I've come? That hurt!'

'Jimmy... you stupid... buffle'ead!' She was gulping for air. 'Quick, man!... quick, for mercy's sake!'

'Ah, don't panic, me darlin',' he murmured, turning her round. 'Sure, there's nobody after us.'

'But the lights over there!...'

'Sure, 'tisn't Keeling's Killjoys or Tench's Troops; 'tis only the Bakehouse Brigade going to work. They haven't seen us... Mind ye, I gave up the idea of looking for the saw and rice. 'Tis a pity about the saw...'

She choked. 'I – I thought the soldiers had caught you. What would I – what would Charlotte have done without her "Unca Jimmy"?...'

'Hurry, you two!' Will had nearly caught up. 'Rot an' perish you both! Hurry!'

After the three had reached the jetty and scrambled down into the *Beauty*, Old Bill cleared his throat.

'Now, weren't there something that yew was wanting me to do, Cap'n?'

'Don't try my patience.'

Without another word, the old man untied the rope and clambered aboard.

'Timor, here we come,' breathed Will. 'The rowlocks have been greased and the oars muffled, so, if we can just get past the lookout on the South Head, this fair southerly will give us a night's start and the longboat will never catch us.'

CHAPTER 31

'South Head to starboard,' murmured Old Bill at the prow. Mary shivered and peered over the gunnel. There, darker than the darkness, was the towering, menacing, headland, atop which was the unseen lookout post, commanded tonight by sharp-eyed Sergeant James Scott. His own children, Elizabeth and William, were the same ages as Charlotte and Emanuel.

'Aw, Will, pray God that Sergeant Scott's eyes are sleepy this night.'

'Mummy?' whispered Charlotte. 'Mummy, be us still playin' hidey-peep?'

'Yes, my lover, with Elizabeth and William's daddy. Hush now, till Mummy tells you.'

'Wossat?' gulped Sam Bird.

'What?' asked Jimmy nervously.

'I fawt I saw a moving light on the 'ead. I'll wager it's that eagle-eyed Scotchman wiv 'is bloody lantern,' said the beady-eyed cockney. 'He'll see us! I just know he will.'

'Aw stow it, Sam,' muttered Mary.

'Easy now, my billies,' said Will softly. 'Take her gentle, round the head... Gentle... That's it... Gentle... We'll soon be past and breasting the Pacific and staring Mam'selle Liberté in her beautiful face!'

The nervous Irishman snorted. 'Staring her in the beautiful breast, ye mean, don't ye, William?'

Nobody felt like laughing, even if they'd dared.

'Nothing will go wrong,' breathed the leader, 'nothing will go wrong so long as you all keep calm, and quiet.'

'Mummy, Charlotte be a-goin' to atishoo.'

'Dear life,' gasped Mary, pulling the child's head down. 'Keep your face in Mummy's lap and don't make a sound or the Bogyman will get you. And get the rest of us, too.'

'Easy, boys... That's it... Easy...'

The convict girl held her breath and surely the others were holding theirs. A muffled sneeze shook the little body, and Mummy's nerves, and Mary stroked the spray-soaked hair where the bonnet had slipped back.

Mary Bryant lost track of time. The Lord alone knew how much later it was when she saw the 'bloody lantern'. Only a glimmer, being so far away. For it was already behind them; they had passed the head. They were in the ocean now, buffeted by much fiercer waves.

She felt strange. Excited, yes, of course, but also mighty scared; not just for herself but for these poor little babies. To risk her own life was one thing, but theirs...

She had never thought she would regard that shore as friendly, but now that it was receding... As for Sergeant Scott's light, would it be the last any of them ever saw? Three thousand two hundred and fifty mile! She strained to keep it in sight... Yes, it was still there, but only just: the merest spark.

The stinging spray forced her to shut her eyes. When she opened them, the spark had gone.

CHAPTER 32

'Hey, Will!' cried Old Bill on this sunny, and mighty windy, Wednesday afternoon. 'Look, there's a little creek over there, and at the back is a cabbage tree swamp. Tree-choppin' toime, boy.'

'Praise be,' sighed Will, gazing at the tall, straight, furiously waving palm trees, which extended back into a rainforest. The older ones were sixty to ninety feet high, the younger no more than ten or fifteen. 'We've done well so far: about a hundred mile. We've got up to six knots when the wind's been favourable. So after two days' sail, at last we can rest and shelter for a time, because this 'ere wind sure is a cussed contrary one at the moment. While some of you are chopping down some of the smaller trees, then cutting out and boiling their hearts, the rest of us'll maybe have caught some fish to go with 'em.' A favourite food of the natives, the heart, or growing bud, found inside the crown, had the white and rather spongy texture of a cabbage-head and the sweet taste of a chestnut. 'It'll be dang difficult to get into that creek, though, because of those sandy shallows across its mouth. But to hell with 'em, we'll do it.'

Mary squeezed her children delightedly.

'Mummy?' whispered Charlotte from behind her face-protecting kerchief. 'Mummy, will there be *bad* blacks there? Not nice ones like what help us with the fishing? Will they boil Charlotte an' *eat* her?'

Mary removed her own kerchief and kissed this salt-crusted little forehead.

'Naw, my beauty, of course not. Don't you fret your tiny head about that. We've got two guns, ain't we? Will can fire one and Jimmy can fire t'other.'

Hunched over his oar, the Irishman glanced up over the floppy brim of his black felt hat which was tied on with string. The child studied the forced grin on his unshaven face.

'Mummy, could – could Unca Bill Morton fire Jimmy's gun? Jimmy be such a buffl'ead, he might shoot one of us! Might shoot li'l Emanuel... Might shoot Charlotte!'

Her mother smiled. 'Or even Mummy!'

Jimmy looked at the pair of them gravely.

'Och, 'tis lucky Jimmy is, that the women in his life have so much confidence in his manly abilities. But just ye wait till the savages attack. Sure, ye'll be glad ye've got James Martin, Esquire, with ye then. He'll show ye both, so he will.'

* * *

'Mummy, Mummy!' cried the bare-topped Charlotte, running from the shade of the trees at the back of the beach, to where the late-afternoon sun shone upon the encampment, at the creek's mouth.

'Mummy, look at Charlotte's hands. Them got black chalk on 'em!'

Having stuffed the 'cabbage' into the pot, Mary turned from the fire and reached for her panting daughter, whose sunken little chest glistened with sweat. The child was holding out her left palm.

'Stow me! Will, look'ee here. Charlotte's palm's as black as a native's bottom!'

Will and Jimmy were sitting a few feet from the fire, muskets across their knees. Jimmy, agonizingly stiff from the rowing, stayed where he was, as Will rose.

'Give me the other hand, child,' grunted the Cornishman.

'N-n-naw, Charlotte show Mummy,' she mumbled, swiftly hiding it in the deep front pocket of the ragged coarse-linen skirt which Mary had made from an apron.

'Give me it, you bitch,' he rasped, jerking out her spindly little arm, so that she squealed. His calloused fingers forced open her smooth ones, revealing a small piece of a hard, shiny black substance.

It was the first that Mary, or anyone else in the colony, had seen since landing in New South Wales.

'Coal,' gasped the convict girl. 'Coal!'

'Dang me,' breathed Will. 'Hi, you boys at the back of the beach there,' he hollered. 'Come out from under those trees; you've slept enough. Come and see what the brat's found!'

All the 'boys' staggered to their feet except James Cox. The sunburnt carpenter's shore duty these days was to keep an eye on Emanuel, asleep there in his crib.

Jimmy squinted in the sun's glare. 'Jeez, Will, d'ye realize what this means, man? Little Charlotte Bryant has discovered coal in New South Wales! If they knew about this at Sydney Cove, they could have coal fires for the whole colony this coming winter, because there's sure to be masses of the stuff about here somewhere. Auld Governor Phillip would be delighted. I can just see his dark eyes lighting up like coals themselves.'

Will Bryant was ablaze himself. 'Damn his dark eyes!' he roared, hurling Charlotte's 'black chalk' into the water and spitting after it. 'Who bloody cares about that bald-'eaded ol' son of a whore? I never want to hear his cussed name again, d'you hear?'

Jimmy flinched. As for the trembling child, she went crimson, burst into tears and ran back up the beach.

Mary glared at him. 'That's a selfish way of thinking. What about those folk we've left behind? What about poor Sarah, and Mitchell, and Cap'n Tench, and Mr White, and–'

'To hell with 'em!' Will Bryant was definitely in one of his coal-black moods. 'This whole dangblasted continent can bloody sink for all I care, once we're safe away from it. Now, how much longer will dinner be? I'm perishin' starving. I can't wait to eat those beautiful mullet we caught this morning.'

While waiting for the 'cabbage' to boil, Mary screwed up her eyes against the sun to watch Charlotte. The child soon found some more coal and after rubbing it into her hands, she proceeded to smear her tear-washed face. Then she picked up a long stick and started jumping about.

'Wooya! Wooya! *Wooya!*' she bellowed, kicking up the sand. 'I'm a *bad* black an' I've comed to eat you! Wooya! Wooya! *Wooya!*' Everyone was looking at her, obviously liking her performance. This was fun: betterer than being on that horrid boat.

But... nobody was laughing. Nobody was even smiling. They were open-mouthed, as if they were about to shove in some food. But... Mummy hadn't served it yet. What was the matter, for goodness' sake? Mummy was staring – staring with a scared look on her face. But – but Mummy wasn't looking at Charlotte now. No one was looking at Charlotte. They were looking behind Charlotte...

Slowly... ever so slowly... she turned her blackened face... She was looking up at the bearded black face of a filth-and-fly-covered savage. Though he had put down his spear, his eyes were wide open as if he was about to grab her. She reeled back from the stink as much as from fear. He extended a thin, branch-like arm and grasped her shaking shoulder. Then, humming loudly, he began stroking it.

His eyes wandered down her helpless, glistening little body until they rested on her bright-green skirt. '*Budgerigar! Budgerigar!*' he cried, ripping it off.

'The dirty -' hissed Jimmy, gripping his musket and struggling to his feet.

'No, Jimmy,' breathed Mary. 'No! Don't do nothing stupid, you'll get my poor little Charlotte killed!'

Bill Morton rested his skeletal hand on Mary's shoulder.

'The savage don't mean nothing, pet,' he murmured. 'Look.'

The black was holding the skirt round his naked loins. He was grinning, the gap-toothed beggar, grinning he was.

Suddenly the bushes behind him parted and five of his countrymen joined him, and he flaunted his prize, curveting and caterwauling triumphantly. Spying Mary, he stopped and pointed at her frock.

'You're joking,' muttered the Cornish girl. 'You ain't a-gettin' *me* naked.'

Jimmy laughed nervously. 'He just wants some clothes, Mary: to show off in front of his fellas. Let's fetch some of those shirts from the clothes box.'

On jellied legs she accompanied the armed Irishman as he hobbled to the water. To hell with hoisting the frock to her knees, she walked straight in and waded the few yards to the anchored *Beauty* and, helped by Jimmy, pulled herself aboard. With trembling fingers she untied the canvas, opened the box and removed six shirts, and two of the dozen tiny boats that James Cox had patiently carved for just such an occasion.

Jimmy took the lot from her, one at a time, with his free left hand, putting the boats in his trouser pocket and hanging the shirts over his shoulders.

'*I'll* deliver them to the black, Mary. Jeez, if I leave Will do it, in his present mood he'll likely shoot one of the beggars and then we'll have the whole tribe hoopin' an' hollerin' out of the trees.'

'Yes,' she grunted, sliding into the water, 'you could be right, Jimmy. But you must leave your musket behind,' she said, pressing his wrist; 'we don't want no accidents.'

'I wonder what the darlin' Governor would do if he were here,' he said. 'He certainly has some kind of power over them, doesn't he? Sure, it must be that missing tooth. They think of him almost as one of their own, like.' Nearly all the native men that they'd ever met had had the same fore-tooth, the right incisor, knocked out. 'Perhaps I should ask ye to knock mine out.'

Back on the sand, Jimmy gave her the heavy gun, and what he thought was a comforting grin. Then despite his torturing stiffness, he ambled up the beach as if he were taking a midday stroll on Red Bay's sand. Dear life! Mary could not believe her ears. He was even whistling 'Malbrouck' now; doubtless thinking, *A wee whistle might help to convince them that I'm a friendly wee fella. And, also, it might calm me a wee bit.*

Whistling he might be but Mary could see that he was shaking as much as her. Amazingly, Charlotte began to whistle, too. In truth, the little girl never ceased to amaze her. Far older than her tender years she was and as brave as anyone here.

Jimmy held up both hands, imitating the usual native greeting.

'Your servant, sir,' he said in a loud, firm voice, bowing as gracefully as a clumsy booby like him could, then placing the shirts on the sand at the black's feet. Standing up straight, the Irishman clutched this wretched back of his, then grasped Charlotte's blackened hand.

'Me Jimmy,' he said, prodding his chest. 'Jim-my.'

'*Damèeli!*' cried the native, stooping and picking up one of the shirts. He stepped into the bottom of it and, feet together, pulled it upside down as far as his waist.

'Ack no, ye eejit!' exclaimed Jimmy, chuckling in spite of his terror. 'Let me show ye.' The pair of them tumbled to the ground as the Irishman tried to pull down the shirt.

Both now laughing helplessly, they tried again.

'Jeez! I thought *I* was the most ham-footed pudding head hereabouts but ye sure take the ship's biscuit!'

The black man pointed at Jimmy's left foot and giggled. '*Jina.*'

'Aye, I know I have two left feet but sure ye're just as clumsy.'

'*Damèeli*, Jim-my *Jina-jina*,' he giggled again, wrapping his arms round Jimmy's tortured back and squeezing tight. '*Damèeli!*' he laughed, squeezing even tighter.

Jimmy Martin grimaced. ''Jeez, 'tis grand for oul Jimmy *Jina-jina* to be welcomed with open arms but he can't take too many *Damèelies*,' he gasped, breaking free and patting the scarred, filth-caked shoulder. 'Over *head*,' he smiled, tapping his own forehead. '*You*, bend down.' He forced himself to do so, to show him. 'Right, *I* put over *your head*.' He did.

'*Nùl-lo*,' beamed the native, tapping his greasy forehead.

'Aye, *Nùl-lo*,' said Jimmy.

'*Mala*,' said the black fellow.

'Aye, *mala*,' grunted Jimmy, grasping the native's left hand and pushing the arm into the left sleeve.

The tribesmen were laughing. Charlotte was laughing. Everyone was, even Will.

'Aw, Jimmy,' roared Mary, holding her aching right side, 'you make me die!'

'I hope not, darlin',' he yelled.

When Jimmy had at last forced the right arm into its proper place, he stood back to admire the result.

'Beau-ti-ful! *Beau-ti-ful!*

'Beau-ti-ful! *Beau-ti-ful!* mimicked the native, twirling like a white-gowned rich bride before her admiring guests.

Then, having accepted the carvings and picked up his spear, with a parting grin at Charlotte and a final 'Beau-ti-ful!' at Jimmy, he returned to the trees. His fellow tribesmen snatched up the other shirts and hastily followed.

Charlotte retrieved the torn skirt and raced back to Mummy, who swept her up and gave her the biggest kiss of her life. When she was finally put down, the child made no attempt to obtain similar treatment from Will, and, indeed, turned her glistening back on him.

He ignored her. 'Right, woman, hurry with that cooking – Jimmy,' he said to his friend, who'd just staggered back, 'let you and me see if we can find some *big* lumps of coal for the fire. Bill,' he yawned loudly, turning to Morton, 'I think we'd best rest here for a couple of nights. I'm fair davered, I can tell you.'

'We all are, bonny lad,' sighed the skeletal navigator, looking more 'davered' than any mortal that Mary had seen for many a day.

The Cornishman yawned even louder. 'We're too far away now for any pursuers from Sydney Cove to catch us. So, savages, animals, reptiles and monster insects allowing, we should be quite safe here.'

CHAPTER 33

On this warm and sunny Sunday morning, as they slowly rowed ever northward, Mary had suddenly felt damp. 'Will, I've got a wet bottom!' She shifted her position slightly. 'The sea's as calm as that plaguy Plymouth pond and we've shipped no water but the straw's wet. She's leaking!'

'Satan's horns, so she is! Rot an' perish it, we should've payed her seams on Friday before we left the creek!'

Charlotte's sun-browned little fingers were white-knuckled as she gripped the tattered hem of her mother's frock.

'Mummy, Mummy, be the ol' *Beauty* a-sinkin'? Be Charlotte drowndeding?'

'Naw, my lovely,' murmured Mary, stroking the salt-matted curls. 'There's no need to be scared and give yourself the shrims. It's only a little leak, that Will can fix with the beeswax and rosin we brought along with us.'

Old Bill's thoughts, and eyes, were on other things.

'This bay we're in is endless, ain't it? It runs up the coast as fur as yer eyes can see. 'Twould make a damn good harbour for ships. Even better than Port Jackson, oi'm thinking.

Will smiled. 'It'll make a fitty harbour for the *Beauty*, too. We'll pull into a nice little cove somewhere. Providence brought us here, just when we needed it.'

* * *

After helping to haul the *Beauty* ashore in the sandy, tree-fringed cove, Mary and Jimmy decided to stretch their painfully stiff legs for a few minutes along the beach, and to take Charlotte and Emanuel. The Irishman held his musket at the ready as they set off.

The little girl beside her was soon crying, 'Mummy, Mummy! Water! *Water!*'

'You've just had some before we left the camp.'

'*Naw,* Mummy!' The child's grey eyes mocked her mother's stupidity. 'There's water. Look'ee! *Look'ee!*' She pointed at a dip in the sand twenty paces on.

'She's right, Mary!' exclaimed Jimmy, tottering ahead. 'There's a wee stream, about six inches deep, flowing from the higher ground. Jeez, there's something else here, too! Footprints, and quite fresh, by the look of them! And made by just one person: a male, by the size of them. Now, I ask meself, is yer man friendly, like auld Damèeli?' Whipping off his hat, he bent down and scooped up a little of the precious sparkling liquid.

'Here, Mary, give some to Emanuel first,' he grunted as she reached him.

He folded the wide brim and she directed it into the eager little mouth. Emanuel Bryant's big dark-brown eyes smiled and he gurgled joyfully.

'Faith, Jimmy, he looks like his father, when Will's just swallowed his first rum of the day!'

'Ye're right there, darlin',' he chuckled. 'But methinks our William's getting more and more irritable now that all his precious rum's gone.'

'Get *me* some, Jimmy,' ordered Miss Charlotte Bryant.

'Och, 'tis James yer servant I am now, mistress, is it? Take me hat from yer mammy and get some for yerself!'

She grabbed it and, kneeling in the sand, reached out and managed to half fill the hat. And spilt it all.

She had another try, this time successfully putting it to her salt-sore lips. Salt-sore because, early on, kerchiefs had proved useless against windblown spray. The child shut her eyes and gulped and gulped till her alarmed mother snatched the hat.

'Mercy on us, child, you'll drown yourself!'

When they'd all had their fill of God's wonderfully cool and fresh water, Jimmy said, 'Well, 'tis thinking I am that we should go back and tell the others, rather than do any more dandering about. There's breakers and pots to fill, not to mention men's thirsty mouths. What a difference from what we brought with us. So fresh, so cool. So blessedly cool...'

* * *

Weary Will decided to treat himself and his crew to a lazy day on the beach, saying that the *Beauty*'s seams could wait till the morrow. And everyone deserved an early night, he declared.

So, soon after dark, and a supper of pork and boiled rice, washed down with sweet tea, the Bryants settled in the small tent and Jimmy and the others prepared to stagger across to their large one. The Irishman was on first watch: a lonely vigil, if one discounted the pesty mosquitoes.

'Nigh'-nigh', Jimmy,' yawned Charlotte, peeping from the flap.

'God bless ye, darlin',' he said, stooping to kiss her blistered forehead.

'Shut the bloody flap, Charlotte,' rasped Will, already under the blanket with Mary. 'We don't want to be awake all dang night with whining mosquitoes shattering our nerves which are shattered enough already!'

'Nigh'-nigh', Mummy,' said the sleepy girl, crawling in under the blanket, on the outside, next to Mary.

'Nigh'-nigh', my lover,' murmured Mary Bryant, kissing the hot little cheek, still so hollow. 'God bless.'

As always, Charlotte had not said a word to Will. He'd never scolded the child for this, though. It was as if she had ceased to exist as far as he was concerned, except when he chided her about mosquitoes and things. In fact, since Emanuel's arrival, the Cornishman hadn't had much time for anyone else either, and certainly not his wife; as if all hope for the future lay in this tiny mite in the crib. Yes, for the millionth time, the Cornish girl's tormented brain told her that the father of Emanuel Bryant had no interest in Mary Broad of Fowey, apart from satisfying his needs at mealtimes and bedtimes.

He never discussed their future lives together. Indeed, hadn't he told her after the wedding rite that he did not regard their marriage in New South Wales as legally binding, because the banns hadn't been read? Dammit, she'd tried her best to make him happy and, despite all their sufferings, had fought to keep cheerful. She'd often laughed with Jimmy, but Will had never laughed; rarely even smiled, except at Emanuel. Will Bryant now had a son: that was all that mattered.

Well, in truth, Will did sometimes laugh with Jimmy, and at him. Everyone did. Dear, sweet Jimmy. The picture of the Irishman, the Savage and the Shirt would stay with her for the rest of her days. Yes, Jimmy seemed to have a way with all mankind. Why, even Corporal Anderson liked him – well, as much as that brute could like anyone, she thought, remembering his gleeful use of the cat-o'-nine tails. Sure, James Martin, Esquire, from the County Antrim could charm the birds from the trees, and the natives who'd come from the trees.

* * *

She could not sleep and such thoughts were still occupying her into the early hours of Sunday. She just could not turn her mind to any – 'What's *that*?' She gripped Will's arm.

He woke instantly. 'W-what's amiss?'

'I - I heard something: in the trees.'

He roughly shook her off and clutched the loaded musket, then, kneeling, hung the bullet pouch and powder horn round his neck.

'Mummy. Mum- '

Mary had clapped her hand over Charlotte's mouth. 'Shhh. Will's going outside. He – he's going to chase away an ol' kangaroo. Don't you make a sound now, Charlotte. Mummy's taking her hand away...'

'He bain't,' whispered the child, sitting up. 'There ain't no 'roo. He be a-goin' to see if there be big *bad* blacks out there.'

'Stow your clack, brat,' hissed Will, opening the flap and creeping out into the dark, cloudy night.

Mary followed him but the sand deadened her steps and he didn't hear. More than one shadow was moving among the trees over here, near the other tent. Will crept closer, still unaware that his wife was at his heels.

'Aahh!' he cried. The thing that he was tangling with was lashing out like a black demon. Will dropped his musket and grasped the 'demon's' neck. 'Yeeoww!' screamed the Cornishman. The 'demon's' knee-jerk had caught Will Bryant where he was most vulnerable and he let go.

''Tis sorry I am, William,' wheezed Jimmy, 'but ye never gave... ye never gave me a chance to identify meself... before squeezing me Adam's apple.'

'You dangblasted bufflehead – Mary! What're *you* doing out here?'

'I came to help you.'

'They're scuttling through the trees, Will,' said Jimmy. 'We've scared them off with our hoopin' an' hollerin'. I was having a wee sprinkle and no sooner had I finished than I turned and saw several skulking shadows, with spears and shields. Those blacks meant business. We'd best leave – this very minute.'

'W-what's happening out here?' stammered James Cox as he and the others scrambled from the tent.

'We're leaving,' said Will. 'The Devil knows how many more of his black children are out here. Take down the tent –hurry, for God's sake! It's lucky we left nearly everything in the *Beauty*.'

Mary raced back to their tent and grabbed the crib. Will was close behind and snatched it from her.

'Into the boat, woman! We'll have to leave *this* tent because there ain't time to -'

WHO-OOSH! WHO-OOSH! Spears!

The night erupted with bloodcurdling shrieks and Mary shivered, her scalp crawling. She whisked Charlotte into her arms. Stumbled outside. Slithered down to the *Beauty*, lying tilted to larboard twelve feet back from the water, and lowered Charlotte into the straw. Will shoved the crib beside the little girl.

WHO-OOSH! A barbed spear thudding between Mary's feet. *WHO-OOSH!* Another slamming into the starboard side. Husband and wife pushed. *WHO-OOSH!* That struck the mast. Some of the crew were here now, pushing with them, pushing like crazy men. *WHO-OOSH!* Mary clambered aboard, Sam following. The *Beauty* was floating. James tumbled into the stern, just missing the crib. *WHO-OOSH!* A veritable horde of savages was hurtling down the beach. Nat was aboard now, and John. *WHO-OOSH!* Bill Morton, too. Jimmy still had a few yards to run, but – but had stopped! Helping Old Bill who was clutching his left leg. Will and Sam stretched out their hands and - *WHO-OOSH!* - Old Bill was here now, gasping for his life's breath as they hauled him over the stern.

'Come *on*, Jimmy!' screeched Mary.

The ducking rowers heaved and the beach was gone.

WHO-OOSH!

'*Ack!* My *leg!*' screamed Jimmy.

Somehow Will and Sam hoisted him aboard and all three rolled over the after-rowers' seat into the straw. But straightway they scrambled back into their places. Keeping their heads down, the two rowing-mates grabbed the oars and pulled for their lives.

Curled up with both children, having taken Emanuel from the crib, Mary told herself that the men's leg wounds must have been only grazes. For the Irishman was rowing manfully, bless him, and the dear old mariner was hauling at the foresail halyard. As for Will Bryant, he was now crouching over all three members of his family, doubtless thinking, *Damn your pagan black eyes! If your murderous spears are going to kill a Bryant, it'll be me, not my family!* This man usually had a mighty strange way of showing his love for the female Bryants but his true colours were revealed now.

'*Aaahh!* My *arm!*' he cried.

'Will! Will, are you–?'

'Naw, it's nothing, gal,' he winced. 'It's nothing, just a scratch. Dang me, if Old Bill can stay at his post at the prow, then the least Young Will can do is keep from blubbering when he's–'

'Huddled like a hedgehog in the hay,' said Jimmy.

WHO-OOSH!... WHO-OOSH!... Three... four... five spears striking the stern.

WHO-OOSH!

'Holy Mother of God,' gulped the Irishman. 'Number six missed me nose by a nostril hair. I know they need trimming but this is ridiculous, so it is!'

From the shore, those angry shrieks must surely have terrified the creatures of the night, as the savages realized that their prey had escaped.

'Aw, thanks be to God!' sobbed Mary, covering Charlotte's tear-wet cheeks with kisses. 'We're safe, my sweet'art. We're safe, Emanuel,' she sniffed, kissing him, too.

'Aye, thanks be to God,' echoed Captain William Bryant of the *Beauty.*

'Amen,' chorused his relieved crew.

CHAPTER 34

'We must land or we'll sink,' said Mary, screwing up her sore eyes against Monday's early-morning sun.

The Fowey fishergirl was fretting mightily and it was no good telling herself that she was always more anxious when she felt as tired as a tortoise. This time, she knew that she would have been just as troubled if she'd felt as fit as a ferret.

Sam, who, as usual, was sharing the after-rowers' seat with Jimmy, sniffed this beaky nose of his.

'But if we land, we'll be dead'uns,' he puffed. 'We can't bloody win neither way, can we? We should've repaired the boat yesterday.'

On the seat behind, James Cox stared at Sam's painfully sunburnt bald spot.

'I'll t-t-take my chance with the land any time. At least the creatures ashore are half *human*. Rather *them* grinning at me with evil intent than a sh-sh-shark doing it!'

'You're right there, James,' yawned Will. 'Those savages came from the trees at the *north* end of our small cove and we've been rowing back down the coast since the early hours, ain't we? We've come far enough south now. If we keep going like this, we'll land back at Sydney Cove! I feel it in me bones that *that's* a safe haven over there. It's a tidy little cove.'

Jimmy rested his weary head on Sam's left shoulder and squinted at their captain.

'Sure and I hope yer bones are sending the right messages to yer brain, William. Because if they're not, that "tidy little cove" will be a haven for your sun-bleached bones for all eternity!'

Charlotte rubbed her puffed, red-rimmed eyes and looked up at her 'Unca' Jimmy.

'What be "bleached", Jimmy – an' what be t'other big word: "eter-eter- "?'

'Ack, ye and yer enquiring mind, Charlotte Bryant. Does it *never* rest from wanting to know things, even when we're in mortal danger?... "Bleached" means whitened by the sun, and "eternity" means for *ever*.'

'What be "for *ever*"? Is'at a long time? Is'at past Chrismiss?'

'Aye, darlin', and past the next Christmas and the next and the next.'

Mary just had to release the tension or she'd scream. She decided to sing the old carol that Mother used to perform in that happy, toe-tapping way of hers. The Cornish girl could see that dear woman now – in the good times, before work and fretting had greyed her golden-brown hair and dulled her sparkling greyish-blue eyes – see her dancing her small fingers on her fish-stained coarse-linen apron.

'As I sat on a sunny bank,
A sunny bank, a sunny bank,
As I sat on a sunny bank,
On Christmas Day in the morning.

I spied three ships come sailing by,
Come sailing by, come sailing by,
I spied three ships come sailing by,
On Christmas Day in the morning.

And who should be with those three–'

She choked. She just couldn't go on. *Aw, Mother. Mother!* Tears pricked her eyes.

Jimmy's own eyes moistened. 'Ah, Mary darlin', ye can fairly sing. Why have ye never sung to us before?'

'Because I've not felt like singing since the day my poor mother died, apart from nursery rhymes to Charlotte and Emanuel.'

Seeing the pain in these grey eyes, the Irishman said gently, 'And I'd be the same if the mammy died, so I would. D'ye know any other wee songs to cheer us?'

She sniffed. 'Er... Yiss, what about this one? I've changed the words a mite to fit my own situation, like...

'Oh, Fowey is a fine town, with ships upon the bay;
And I wish with my heart I was only there today,
And I wish with my heart I was far away from here,
A-sitting in my parlour, a-talking to my dears.

And 'tis home, dearies, home! – Oh, 'tis home I want to be!
My topsails are hoisted, and I must out to sea.
For the oak and the ash and the pretty cherry tree,
They're all a-growing green in the West Countree.
Oh! 'tis home, dearies, home!'

Through a mist she gazed into Jimmy's eyes. 'Do you think we'll see *this* Christmas, Jimmy?'

'Ah, sure we will, Mary. And the next and the next.'

* * *

Ashore again, while Charlotte watched her at the cooking pot, Mary mused on Jimmy's prophecy. Like him, she felt that she would see Christmas and the next and the next. She felt it in *her* bones. God *had* given this brave little band the courage to escape from the colony, hadn't He? And He *had* protected them from the savages. No, He would not desert them now. He –

'Mummy, Mummy, Mummy! Look'ee!'

The child's screams caused everyone to look where she was pointing. Fifty paces away, just beyond those bleached dingo bones, thirty or more red-daubed blacks, armed with spears, shields and shell-sticks, were advancing from the trees. The shell-stick, or spear-thrower, acted as an extension to a warrior's arm, enabling him to throw with greater force and accuracy.

Shaking violently, Sam clutched his friend John's arm.

'Gawd 'elp us, mate.'

Mary snatched up Emanuel and crib from the makeshift shelter of branches and blanket.

'Will, me and the childer will never make it down to the boat. Those devils can throw those spears from one end of the beach to t'other with no trouble.'

'Yes, gal, and even if we were lucky to shoot two of the savages, that ain't going to stop the rest, is it? Jimmy, you'll have to parley with 'em.'

'Me?'

'You did mighty well with Damèeli.'

'Aye, Will, but he was a friendly auld soul, so he was. Those fellas with their barbed twelve-foot spears mean business.'

'It's our only chance of saving Mary and the children. James, fish out a couple o' those little boats from your trowsy pocket and come along with me and Jimmy.'

James shuddered and fumbled in his pocket.

'I'll come, too, bonny lad,' said brave Bill Morton.

'No, Bill. If anything happens to me, the *Beauty* will need all the mariners she can get, to reach Timor safe – especially her navigator.'

Mary murmured a prayer as the Cornishman and the Irishman led the way, loaded muskets at their sides.

With thirty paces still to go, Jimmy stopped, put the musket between his shaking knees and removed his shirt. Even at this distance, Mary seemed to feel the tremor in his fingers and the hammering in his chest.

Aw, Jimmy, you might just as well try to stop a rainstorm with a handkerchief as stop those spears raining down on your skinny chest by holding up your shirt!

The natives' leader howled defiantly. Will aimed and fired, spattering the sand just a yard in front of the man's feet. But if William Bryant had thought that this would quieten him, he was mistaken. Roaring like an enraged beast, the black raised his spear.

'Run, Mary!' yelled the Cornishman. 'Run like the Devil!'

Mary and Charlotte turned and fled. Bill Morton and the others overtook them. The chief's barbed spear missed Charlotte's head by the tiniest golden curl. Mary gasped as she herself felt the hissing wind of another. Sam had already reached the beached *Beauty* and was putting his rounded shoulder to her stern. Bill Morton joined him. Then the bearded John. Then the white-haired Nat. And, lastly, Old Bill.

With the boat starting to float, Nat and Old Bill frantically climbed aboard. Mary was wading now and Old Bill leant over and plucked the crib from her. She lifted the panting Charlotte into Nat's arms. Then John pushed Mary herself up and over.

As Sam, John and, finally, Bill Morton scrambled onto their seats, Mary peeped over the gunwale.

'Aw God, Sam, they're going to die!'

A spear ripped the shirt from Jimmy's hands. She watched in scalp-shrinking horror as another spear grazed Will's right arm, making him drop the musket.

'Leave it, Will!' she screamed, for, instead of running, her crazy husband had bent down. A spear spiked the sand between his feet. Whisking up the gun, he turned and ran after his friends.

The chief was running as fast as any beast and within seconds had retrieved his own spear. Just twenty paces from Will he was, just twenty paces now. James was in the water and Sam and Mary hauled him up, the tiny boats falling from his hand into the surf. A spear slammed into the side, inches from his head, the splinters piercing her quivering cheek. Shirtless Jimmy was next – with his musket – and as Sam grasped him under the arms, a spear thudded between the Irishman's legs, just below his rump.

'Jeez!'

The chief aimed.

'Look out, Will!' she shrieked.

The rowers were tugging at the oars. Will Bryant still had ten yards to go...

Five...

With Jimmy's help, he clambered aboard. The spear skimmed the stern and plunged into the water. The rowers heaved. Then the sea took command, sweeping the *Beauty* well away from the beach.

Soon the spears were falling short and the natives were struggling in the surf. More and more of the thwarted throng threw themselves into the waves. But in a short while their furious cries were far enough away to be drowned by the mocking ones of the gulls.

Sam Bird's own beady eyes glinted with hate as he spat over the side.

'Rot in 'ell, you black 'eathen scum!'

'Law, Sam!' panted John Butcher behind him, 'that was a close'un. I nigh had me beard shaved from me face by them ravening savages. What a din! What a damn belownder they made!'

'Praise the Lord for our deliverance again,' wheezed Old Bill, hoisting the foresail.

'Amen to that,' muttered Jimmy.

'Amen,' they chorused.

* * *

Nat Lilley's hair was shining like snow now as the morning sun's brightness intensified, and he was redder than ever, from the strain of rowing.

'What are we goen to do, boys?' he puffed. 'Everywhere we land, we get attacked by them black beggars. For all we know, the whole damn coast might be one long rabbit warren of 'em all the way up. As many plaguy blacks as we've got rabbits in Suffolk!'

Mary was standing with Charlotte in her arms, looking ahead.

'Hi! The whole damn coast might be but I can see something, way in the distance, that could be the answer to our prayers. See yonder?'

The rowers looked over their aching shoulders.

'Oi can't see nothing,' said Old Bill. 'But my eyes ain't what they used to be. And they've gotten worse these past days, what with straining them in all this bright sunlight, both direct and reflected from the water, like. I mind my dear Betsy once saying, that if – '

'Charlotte do see something!' shrilled the child, wriggling with excitement, 'Charlotte d'see it!'

'Yes, my sweet'art,' smiled Mary, kissing her, 'it's a little island.'

'Yes, I can see it now,' said Will. 'It's several mile yet, though, so put your backs into it, my billies. We should reach it before noon.'

Sam spat into the waves. 'If this bloody leaky tub don't sink first.'

* * *

The gently sloping white sand in the sheltered cove had given them an easy landing. Mercifully there was no sign of natives. So after enjoying pork and rice, washed down with thirst-quenching hot sweet tea, Will and his crew turned over the boat and payed her seams with beeswax and rosin. With no fresh water on this tiny island, Mary had had to ration the tea to half a tin mug per person. She would also have to go carefully when she boiled the 'cabbage' for the evening meal as there were no cabbage tree palms either.

But at least there were the coastal banksias, low trees with trunks bent lower than old Dorothy Handland's, and it was paradise to lie here under one with the sleeping children. What a blissful change from the searing sun and tossing waves. She was determined to make the most of it, for tonight there would be precious little sleep when they were all sweating together in the remaining tent: sliddering over each other like a seineful of plaguy pilchards.

* * *

After two days' rest, they bade farewell to this pleasant spot and briefly visited the mainland to restock with water and 'cabbage'. They did see some canoes but, thankfully, the copper-coloured, shock-haired natives kept their distance.

Then a sou'westerly breeze filled the *Beauty's* sails and carried her ever northward up the surf-dashed coast. During the night, though, the wind veered westerly and drove the gallant little vessel out into the forbidding ocean.

CHAPTER 35

'Mummy, Charlotte be thirsty-thirsty,' croaked the little girl, her grey eyes looking up appealingly.

It was the Friday of the following week and everyone had taken a turn for the worse. Agonizing cramps and stomach pains kept them awake each night, and when morning came they could scarcely move because of a terrible weakness and stiffness and this horrible dizziness. And oh how bloated their legs. As for the hideous salt sores from sitting in soaking clothes and being rubbed raw with the boat's endless tossing, they were driving everyone crazy with pain. Nobody could bear to touch, or lean against, anything or anyone. Mary could not even hold her children now, for she and they were in such agonies from the open, swollen sores, which were constantly bleeding. Armpits, crotch and back of the knees, all were covered with the things. The three-inch ones on the buttocks were the worst, welding rumps and seats together in sticky scabs. Each time salt water washed along the seats, the hapless victims cried out, their eyes filling with tears.

'Mummy, Mummy!'

'I know, I know, my lover. So's Mummy. So are our poor men, resting a little bit from their hard rowing in this blistering sun. But Mummy's got to measure out a *ration*, as I keep telling you, dear. You know how quick all the pork went, even though I rationed that. Mummy's only letting us have a tiny li'l dwinky every three hour, because we ain't got much water left. It's Friday afternoon now and it was Wednesday night when we last managed to put a little rainwater in the breakers. You know how rough the sea's been, breaking over us all the while for more than a week, so even though we had that terrible heavy rain all the time till Wednesday night, we couldn't manage to catch much.'

Crimson with rage, Charlotte Bryant spun round to glare at Will.

'Why don' you leave us go on the beach over there, like what us did on t'other beach long time agone?'

'Because,' growled the Cornishman, 'because that pounding white surf would smash the old gal to splinters – and a certain *young* gal, too! Ten day of dang surfs! I tell you all, those raging surfs are far higher than those monster ones that time when that French ship was wrecked on our Cornish rocks and we had the best Christmas present of our lives: barrels and barrels of lovely brandy!'

'Chrismiss...' Charlotte's black-rimmed eyes were glazed when she turned them back to her mother. 'Chrismiss... Jimmy did say us'll see this Chrismiss, Mummy.'

'I mind well he did say it,' said Mary, who, despite the unbearable pain, just had to stroke this darling child's salt-thick hair. 'And we will, my lovely,' she winced. 'We will see it!'

Sam looked at Will despairingly. 'For Gaw'sake,' he said hoarsely, 'for Gaw'sake, how many days 'ave we been looking at bloody surfs? I've lorst track.'

Poor devil, his mind had been wandering, like everyone else's these days; he obviously hadn't been listening.

'Ten,' said Jimmy grimly. 'Ten long days and nine long nights and no place where we could land safely. And *eight* days and nights the heavens stayed open and soaked us to our shivering skins. And the waves threw in their million gallonsworth!'

John Butcher was tearing at his beard so furiously that he would surely pull out a tuft in a minute.

'Yes,' he said, 'and no wood or coal left to make a tidy little fire on the boat to warm ourselves at night. Law, what I wouldna give for a drop of Mary's sweet tea... We'll be *dead* in another ten if it goes on like this, look you, Sam.'

Mary just had to brighten for Charlotte's sake.

'Aw, stow your moaning, all of you! The surf must end soon; nothing goes on for ever.'

'Charlotte's thirsty-thirsty do, Mummy,' said the child, in the merest whisper. 'For ever: past Chrismiss.'

'Aw come on... think of something nice, my beauty. It'll take your mind off your dry throat.'

'Charlotte can't fink of nuffink nice. Charlotte do keep finkin' of they dingo bones on the beach a while agone: they *bleached* dingo bones.'

Jimmy forced a grin. 'Och, Charlotte, 'tis glad I am ye've remembered the word "bleached" that I taught ye, but I don't like ye dwelling on such things. Whist now while I tell ye a wee story. Aye, let us pretend that I'm a *seanachie*, an Irish village storyteller. *Ye* can listen, too, Mary darlin', for 'tis about the yarrow plant that ye told me once ye used boil to rid the dear da of his indigestion.

'As ye know, Charlotte, I come from that magical place called the Nine Glens of Antrim, in the north of Ireland. My glen – my valley – is Glenariff, Ploughman's Glen, the greenest and grandest of them all. Well, on May Day Eve there – just two weeks from now – let's pretend there's a pretty girl with long golden-brown curls and grey eyes and she's called Charlotte – er – Charlotte O'Shaughnessy. Now, she's getting on in years – let's say fourteen – and wants to know who'll be her future husband.

'Well, on May Eve, after the sun sets behind the dear Antrim hills and mountains, Charlotte sneaks out of her wee cabin. She lives by the shell-covered, red-tinted sands of the lovely Red Bay. She *swishes* her sally wattle, a branch from the fairy-thorn hedge, to keep away the Pooka, the Bogyman. And she goes up the long, long riverside track to the part of Glenariff we call the Fairy Glen, where there are beautiful waterfalls and where the yarrow grows thickly on the bank. She looks round to see that she hasn't been followed. But nobody has seen her except the animals, the badgers and foxes, and those strange birds, owls, with great big eyes that can see in the dark. Then while she's picking *nine* sprigs of the yarrow – one for each of the Nine Glens – she says these magic words:

Good morrow, good morrow, fair yarrow;
And thrice good morrow to thee;
Come tell me before tomorrow
Who my true love shall be.

'Then she takes the sprigs back to the cabin and stows them in the foot of her right stocking, which she then puts under her pillow. During the night, she'll dream of the lucky fella that she's going to marry. There's one wee thing can go wrong, though! She must not say another word from the time she's said the magic words till the time she goes to sleep, or 'twill break the charm. Somehow, I think that Charlotte *Bryant* would find *that* part the most difficult – Charlotte?...'

'Charlotte Bryant's asleep, Mr Story-teller,' murmured Mary. 'Brayvo! Please God she stays asleep till the next ration. She's a tough gal and my Emanuel's tough, too, but, dear life, they can't last much longer without regular water!'

CHAPTER 36

'Another *ten* days, you said, John Butcher?' croaked the skeletal Bill Morton, urging one last drop from the second breaker into his mug. 'Well, we've survived eleven, lad.'

'Ten... eleven... 'tis all the same to dying men,' said John, his faint words almost lost on the wind as he glanced over his shoulder at the navigator. 'It metna have been the end of the world when we finished the bread yesterday, because we still had the rice. But 'tis now, now that the water's gone. Man canna exist on rice alone. Come tomorrowday, we'll be dead. As for you, Bill, you dunna look as if you'll last another hour till noon, look you.'

John's rowing-mate, James Cox, wheezed, 'And still that damn s-s-surf... keeps crashing itself on the shore as far as the eye can see.'

'Hi, look'ee over yonder!' exclaimed Will. 'The surf ain't so high over on that side of the bay.'

Old Bill Allen peered at him through salty lashes. 'We'd still be swamped, boy; we'd–'

'I know that but if two of us could *swim* through it, with the breakers acting as floats in front of us. And then when we've filled the breakers and gathered some firewood, we tied it to 'em...'

'I'll do it,' murmured John. 'I canna abear this molten-hot sun no more. 'Tis Devil-sent!'

'I'll go, too,' said Jimmy weakly.

'No, Jimmy!' gasped Mary.

'And why not?'

Despite the heat already in her cheeks, they burnt even brighter.

'Because... because Charlotte's sinking fast, that's why. If... if you tell her another one of your stories, it maybe might – it might help her.'

'*I'll* go,' muttered Sam Bird, much to everyone's astonishment. 'If

I'm going to die, wot better way is there to meet me Maker than wiv me best mate, John Butcher, Sam Broom, by me side?'

Minutes later, as the two men slipped painfully, wearily, over the side, Mary whispered to Will, 'Pray God there ain't no sharks.'

'Amen to that, gal.'

Mary Bryant's salt-sore eyes blinked against the sun as they strained to watch those brave mortals. Sam Bird, of all folk! Well, you never could tell. Where did the exhausted pair find the strength? True, she herself had found surprising reserves of it during these past weeks. Perhaps she would not have been so strong, though, if she'd had only Mary Bryant to fret about, but to save these poor little mites, she'd sail this boat by herself all those thousands of miles to England.

'How are they doen, Mary?' asked Old Bill. 'My eyesight's failing fast, with all these days of glare from the sea.'

'Slow, Bill, slow. But no sign of sharks yet,' she breathed.

'Oh, pray the Almighty,' he murmured, 'pray the Almighty, there won't be.'

James Cox shuddered.

Her ragged hem was being tugged.

'Is them gonna be swimmed after by sharks, Mummy?'

This amazing child! Back from death's door!

'Naw, my precious,' Mary choked, gently hugging her, despite their mutual pain, 'Lord Jesus will guard them.'

'They're winning,' said Nat, 'they're winning their foight against the waves!'

'Oh no,' groaned Jimmy. 'Oh no!'

'What's amiss, Jimmy?' asked Will. 'What you seen, for pity's sake?'

'Over in the trees along on the right there. Hey, Sam! Hey, John! There's a battalion of barbarians waiting to skewer ye! Hey, fellas, turn back! Sam! John!'

But Jimmy's parched throat was losing its own fight with the waves – the weaker his voice grew, the louder seemed the surf – and the swimmers gave no sign of hearing.

'Mummy... Mummy,' said the child feebly, 'be they *bad* blacks a-goin' to kill *nice* Unca John an' *'orrible* Unca Sam?... An' them won't want no rice tomorrer?... Or for *Chrismiss*?... Or for *ever*?'

'Whist, child, whist!'

'How are they doen now, Mary?' asked Old Bill.

'They're through the surf now... Yes – yes, they're ashore!... They're on their feet, and... They've left the breakers on the sand for the moment and they're heading for the trees at the back there on the left, to pick up some dead wood.'

Jimmy raised his musket, which he had just loaded after taking from the box.

'No, you dang buffle'ead,' hissed Will, 'no, that'll sign their death warrants for sure! Row, boys,' he cried hoarsely, sitting down in Sam's place and grasping the oar, 'row as near to the surf as you dare.'

As the boat drew close, the red-smeared natives thrust the bushes aside and a madly barking dingo ran towards Sam and John. Both sprang into action: Sam like a bird startled while taking twigs for a nest, John a farm hand caught stealing. Clutching their small bundles of wood, they hurtled back down the beach.

'Run, John!' shrieked Mary. 'Run, Sam! *Run*!'

Reaching the shore, the panicking pair hurled the wood as far as they could towards the *Beauty*, grabbed the breakers and plunged in. The first spears were piercing the surf, like harpoons. The next deadly shower would pierce the struggling swimmers.

'Closer still,' grunted Will, frenziedly pulling his oar. 'Look out, John!'

The swimmer ducked beneath a wave and a barbed spear struck the prow, just below Old Bill's hand. Moments later John broke water and Jimmy stretched over and grasped an arm. A second spear thudded into the gunwale as, with James's help, the Irishman dragged this spluttering hero and his breaker aboard. Will, meanwhile, grabbed Sam's tattered collar and hauled him and his keg into the stern. Like a scraggy, half-drowned fowl, he sprawled in the straw, his long black hair in streaks down his quivering bearded face.

Will snatched up Jimmy's musket and fired at the dingo, barking by the waterside. It spun in the air and fell dead in the sand. Pincher's big brown, appealing eyes flashed in Mary's brain.

The shot had done the trick and the savages fled hollering.

'Hark at their din,' laughed the Cornishman, settling back at the tiller. 'They'll be kicking up a rare ol' dido for the next half hour as sure as my name be William Bryant.'

The firewood was floating swiftly by but they managed to catch some before it was swept out of reach. Just enough to start a blaze – if they'd had any water to boil.

'Sorry – sorry about the – about the water, Will,' coughed the dripping John, back on the seat, his head between his bony knees.

'Yes, so am I,' muttered his captain.

CHAPTER 37

Mary caught her breath. 'Aw *no*, Will, the *Beauty*'s leaking mortal bad again!'

The Cornishman sighed.

Sam pulled himself up onto the seat and tore at the sodden strands of hair dangling from his forehead to the twitching tip of his raw nose.

'Curse the bloody boat!' he snarled. 'Gaw'sake, how much more punishment can we take? *We* can't get no water and the boat's getting too much. The Devil's playing games wiv us to see how soon we'll crack!'

Jimmy gulped. 'Talking of cracks, Samuel, this one by me foot's getting wider by the second!'

'We'll head for t'other side of the bay,' said Will. 'We *might* find a place to land: in a creek or cove. Put your backs into it, my billies! *Heave* away!'

'We'll never get there,' groaned Sam, looking over his shoulder at that far-too-distant shore.

'I th-th-think you're right,' stuttered James Cox, his eyes, widening with fear, staring from his terribly sunburnt face. 'S-s-somehow I know, I just know, it's my fate to end up in the belly of a razor-toothed sh-sh-shark... Jimmy,' he puffed, addressing the back of the only person, apart from Mary, who ever listened when he was voicing such morbid thoughts. 'Jimmy, I f-f-felt strong... I felt so *strong* when I was with my S-S-Sarah... In *her* eyes, I was a *man*... It was her what gave me the strength to go on this mad journey - even though she didn't know I was going, poor gel... Lord 'elp me' – he was almost crying – 'I wish I'd stayed back at the colony with my darlin'.'

'Och, James, m'lad, ye're crazed an' weak with thirst and ye're... ye're tortured by sores and this devilish sunburn, so you are. Sure, yer poor auld bleeding cheeks look like a wounded gum tree with red rosin oozing from it! Aye, 'tis making yer mind all fuddled... 'Tisn't like ye to talk this way. Ack, ye'll be yer auld self when we've landed and ye've guzzled a gulletful of God's grand water.' Somehow Jimmy forced his own frail, tortured body to swing round so that James could see the special smile that rarely failed to cheer.

The Londoner's anguished eyes looked into the Irishman's twinkling ones.

'Jimmy Martin,' he choked, 'you're a good'un and no lie... You never change, do you?'

'Jimmy be Charlotte's besterest friend,' beamed the small girl. But her freckled white face was suddenly crimson as her dry throat suffered a coughing fit.

The Irish eyes moistened.

Just minutes later, Mary shrieked, 'Lord-a-mussy, the boat *is* sinking this time!' She sprang to her feet, then gasped as agonizing pains shot through her. 'The water's up to my ankles!'

'I always knew I'd end up with the snarks,' gulped James. 'I always knew it, I always *knew* it!'

'Never fear!' roared Mary Broad from Fowey, snatching Jimmy's hat from his head. 'Rot you, *cussed* sea, you ain't a-goin' to give us to no sharks!' she yelled, bending to scoop up a hatful of water and throwing it over the side. Swiftly filling the hat again, she panted, 'Will, give me one of the cooking pots in the box under your feet... I'll pass along another for Old Bill... and you take the last'un.'

'Wot's the use?' said Sam, groaning again. 'You can't bail as quick as the bloody water pours in, canya?'

'She's right, damn you!' raged Will, flinging open the box. 'The rest of you pull those oars as if Old Scratch is trying to sclum your eyes out if you don't keep out of his reach. We'll *still* head for t'other side of the bay.'

'You're both mad!' cried Sam. 'Better to take our chance wiv the surf an' the savages – if they're still about. Even if the boat capsizes, we can swim through the surf, like wot me an' John done.'

'And what about the rest of us?' demanded Mary, passing along Old Bill's pot. 'What about Charlotte an – ?'

'Keep bailing, woman,' rasped Will. 'Pull for t'other shore, my billies, pull for t'other shore. Pull!...

'Pull!...

'*Harder*, damn you!... Pull!...

'*Pull!...*'

Jimmy's hat was floating amid the straw, and Charlotte grabbed this sloppy, floppy thing and began copying her mother. The little girl got it half full but when she threw the water, the hat went, too, flying away on the wind. Undaunted, the fishergirl's daughter picked up her mug, filled it and had another try. The water blew in her face; she was far too short to throw the dang stuff over the side. Furiously, she scooped up some more.

'Rot you, *cussed* sea,' blazed Charlotte Bryant, 'you ain't a-goin' to give us to no sharks!' The mug shot up and over. Still undeterred, she fumbled around Jimmy's bare feet and produced his mug.

'Quick, my lover,' puffed Mary, hurling another potful, 'the water's licking poor Mummy's legs now! *Aw, God bless the child*, she thought, while the water again splashed into this brave, determined little face. Her help was useless, but anything to take her mind off this nightmare.

'It's 'opeless,' sighed James Cox, several minutes later, slumping ever lower over his oar. 'The sh-sh-sharks'll be swarmin' 'ere any second.'

'Stow your whining!' cried Mary.

'Faugh, it's all very well for *you* to be brave, Mary... You was brought up to the sea... bein' as how you're a fisherman's daughter... I'm scared of it and I can't do nothin' to help that.'

'My *life*,' she panted, 'don't you think *I'm* scared of it? All fisherwomen *hate* the bloody sea... We've lost too many of our menfolk... Goddammit, man, if Charlotte can keep fighting, so can... so can *you*... Just look at her... she's dead on her little raw feet... but she's still goin', bless her.'

James bowed his head even lower to hide his shame. He put more effort into this stroke. And yet more into the next.

'Mummy... Charlotte can't go... can't go... no fasterer,' gasped the mite, her long, salt-caked curls blinding her as, at last, she successfully threw a mugful. 'Charlotte can't go– '

'Keep goin', my sweet'art,' said her mother, gulping for air herself. 'The men'll get us to shore just as soon as they can – Lor', look at Jimmy... I've never seen him row so hard... Ha, he'll be as strong as Mummy if... if he goes on like this.'

Jimmy Martin was too jaded to respond.

Bailing like a madman, Will puffed, 'There... there's a little river over there where we're 'eaded. An' no surf... If we can... if we can only manage to keep this cussed water out for just two more minute... we should be safe.'

'We'll never do it,' wheezed Sam, surely about to collapse? 'It's risin' so fast... we'll be flooded in *one* minute.'

'Stow *your* whining, too, Sam Bird!' shrilled the Cornish girl, feeling the water lapping her knees. 'Stow it, I say!'

Charlotte staggered, clutching at her mother's frock. The poor child, too, was on the point of collapse.

Mary Broad from Fowey suddenly saw red and screamed inwardly, *Rot it if I'll let my daughter die! This beautiful golden-curled child was born to live, to soar like a singing lark. Not to die, to drown like a squealing rat! And as for my poor little Emanuel –*

'We're in calmer water now,' panted Will.

Sam hawked, and spat into the water swirling round his torn black trousers.

'Yeah but it's still coming through the seams, ain' it?'

'Aw stow it!' Mary screeched. 'Stow it!'

''Tis a blessed miracle,' huffed Old Bill, hurling another potful. 'We're nearly there. By 'eaven, oi never thought the ol' gal would... would 'ang on.'

Jimmy turned and grinned. 'Och, she may be a veteran of the seas, like yerself, Auld William... but you auld'uns still have a few... a few fights left in ye, don't ye?'

The Cornish girl looked past the old man's strained sunburnt face. Amazingly – truly miraculously – they had reached the river's mouth. If they could just... if they could only just row another twenty yards, they would be safe on its muddy bank.

'Don't you give up now, Sam,' she begged the exhausted cockney. 'We're only twenty yard from shore... Don't you give up now, old comrade.'

He squinted through his curtain of wet hair and caught her eye. His bearded jaw set determinedly. He pulled as he'd never pulled before, and, as if the word 'comrade' had inspired them, too, so did his fellow rowers.

Charlotte fell groaning into her mother's arms but the brave little girl's efforts were no longer needed, because, moments later, the cutter was sliding onto the bank.

'Brayvo, my *Beauty*! Well done, m'dears,' beamed Will. 'It's a grand fish supper we're going to have tonight. Yes, it's our lucky day, I tell you. We'll have fish and we'll have shellfish: we'll have all the produce of King Neptune's garden, as sure as my name be William Bryant.'

* * *

'I don't think much of auld Neptune's garden,' mumbled Jimmy, three hours later, chewing some 'cabbage'. 'We never even got one fish to bite our hooks. If his Marine Majesty ain't even got a few wee sprats in this part of his garden, then no wonder there're no natives in this neck of the woods.'

Mary glanced round nervously. 'How do you know there ain't no blacks here, Jimmy?' Her eyes sparked. 'Why, a spear might have the *impudence* to come a-*whooshing* through the cabbage trees and skewer James Martin, Esquire, to the ground before he could say "*Damèeli*!"'

'Ah sure, and if it did, wouldn't this gentleman farmer from the

County Antrim die a happy fella if his last sight on God's earth was yer pretty sparkling grey eyes, darlin'?'

She blushed and Will grunted. His joints cracked as he rose painfully.

'It's time to pay the *Beauty*'s seams with a deal of soap, being as how we used up all the beeswax and rosin. One thing's certain. We can't stop here for long, because even though we scared those savages, I suspicion they'll want revenge for us killing their dingo and invading their territory.'

'Ye're right there,' muttered Jimmy, squashing a huge mosquito which had had the impudence to land on the wrist, the territory, of James Martin, Esquire. 'Jeez!'

He wiped away the blood.

CHAPTER 38

After two days of vainly trying to catch some fish, they decided to sail farther round the bay in the hope of finding something to eat apart from 'cabbage'. On discovering that the land hereabouts looked as unfruitful as the hated Botany Bay itself, they headed out to sea again.

'Devil's horns, the waves are high this morning!' exclaimed the master seiner as hurled by this sudden fiendish wind, green water poured over the sides.

'Mercy!' gulped Mary. 'It's covering my ankles already! It's coming over too fast to bail! It's –' A wave slapped her face and broke over Emanuel and Charlotte.

The baby screeched and the spluttering Charlotte grabbed him and held him to her.

'Law,' gasped John, 'what a sea! 'Tis Satan hisself ravenin' an' roarin' with anger at us. What're we a-goin' to do, Will? We'll be drownded this time, look you.'

'We'll have to–'

'We'll have to make us lighter by throwing away all the clothing,' cried Mary, wrenching open the clothes box.

Five thick blankets she tossed into the waves. Six heavy greatcoats followed. Then she toppled the box and its remaining clothes over the gunwale.

'Right,' she panted, 'that should – Mercy!' She dived to the boards and fought with this monster of a wave for possession of her children. 'Help me, Will, help me!'

'My son, my son!' The Cornishman snatched his darling boy from Charlotte as Mary flung her arms round the girl.

Old Bill had his pot and was bailing like a man possessed, while Mary, huddling here, with the water lapping her legs, could do nothing but watch him. The rowers shipped their oars to follow his example. Jimmy grabbed his own pot and the others swiftly untied their hats.

'Eeh my!' cried Bill Morton, clutching his seat to foil a massive wave's attempt to sweep his skeletal frame overboard. 'Eight miles off the Northumberland coast can be a right tattery place, with thirty-foot-high waves, when the wind's blowing from the east but this is worse!'

James Cox had swallowed a mouthful and was 'glug-glugging' like a drowning man, poor mortal.

'Charlotte d'feel sick, Mummy!' wailed the child, burying her face in her mother's soaking lap.

'I know, my lover, aw I know. Mummy feels sick, too. Be brave, my sweet, be brave.'

'The *Beauty* ain't getting no lower in the water,' said Will. 'I do believe we've saved the old gal yet again.'

'Aw, thank the Lord,' spluttered Mary. 'Thank the good Lord!'

Nat was combing his spindly fingers through his shock of white hair.

'And saved ourselves, boy, and saved ourselves.'

'Jeez,' breathed Jimmy, 'methought for a wee minute there that auld Neptune was wreaking vengeance on me for insulting his garden. Faith, I nearly saw the place for meself – and yer man, too!'

James looked at Will imploringly.

'Can't we *land* s-s-somewhere, Will? Can't we land somewhere, for pity's sake? I feel so *sick*.'

'And where d'you suggest we land?' was the sarcastic reply. 'Look at those surfs all along that distant shore. We'd smash her to bits and ourselves, too. We're over the worst for the moment. The only thing we can do is start rowing again and pray to God there's a break in the surf further on.'

CHAPTER 39

They had anchored in a bay at dusk. Now, in the middle of this windy night, they were being swept towards these glistening, surf-dashed rocks in the corner here.

'The grappling's broke!' cried Nat, the lookout.

In the eerie light of the quarter moon was a silvery-white, leaning skeleton of a ghost gum, with strips of bark like rotting flesh dangling from its knotted joints. It was waving, welcoming them: sighing Death beckoning. The *Beauty* was about to be staved to bits in Satan's hissing cauldron. There'd be a sickening splintering and snapping of wood – and bones. This cruel, creamy, crashing surf would smash their bodies onto the rocks and Mary Bryant and her children would be nothing but bloody lumps of meat. The rowers scrambled onto their seats. No one spoke, or screamed; as if they were spectators and this were happening to some other poor mortals. A gigantic white-topped wave hurtled down upon the boat, sweeping her towards a massive rock. The rowers heaved as they had never heaved before and the larboard bow scraped the rock, Old Bill whipping away his hand a fraction before.

'More rocks!' roared Will. 'Avast there! More rocks to starboard!'

Another murderous monster of a white-crested wave was curling towards them.

'Ship oars, there's more rocks to *lar*board!'

'Dear life!' gasped Mary, crouching over her screaming children. The *Beauty* was too wide to squeeze through. 'Lord preserve –'

The last thing she saw before another wave mounted and swelled over the vessel was Bill Morton's death's-head. Then everything was a screaming, tumbling, jumbling blur of arms, ropes, legs, boxes, oars, water and sand. *I'm drownding! Oh, Lord, I'm drownding!* Lungs bursting, agony of agonies. A terrific roaring and rushing. *Breath! Breath! Must get... breath!* 'Ahh!... Ahhhh!... *Ahhhhh! Thank God!* Oh no, the undertow was pulling her back! *Boat! Must grab boat! Here she is! Got her! Faith, the surf's way back there! Thrown us all this way! But – praise be – I'm alive! And – and I'm walking! I'm pushing the boat, with my screaming children still mercifully inside! My knee hurts, my elbow hurts like fury, the salt's stinging my grazed face and body, but I'm alive, I'm alive! And Jimmy and Will are here, too, Bill Morton makes three, Nat four, all pushing the old gal. And Old Bill five, John six, Sam seven, hauling her along by the rope. And James?... Drownded?... No, praise be, struggling for his breath, over here. Aw, merciful God, we're all safe. Thank Thee, oh, thank Thee!*

* * *

It did not take Will long to find that his precious boat had herself miraculously escaped with just a few scratches.

Jimmy patted his friend's arm.

'*Beauty* nigh unblemished, eh, William? Just a few wee marks.'

'Except f-f-for my broken oar-blade,'stammered James Cox. 'I'm s-s-sorry, Will; believe me, I'm very sorry.'

John Butcher put his arm round James's shuddering shoulders.

'Law, dunna take on about it,' he murmured.

'Don't take on?' blazed Will. 'Faugh, you can trust a plaguy pig-pinching Shropshire landlubber to say that. Satan's horns, the worst of the journey's yet to come; we've still got near two thousand mile to go! Dang me, Cox, why didn't you ship your oar like everyone else, you chuckle'eaded beggar? A damaged oar's mortal serious.'

Mary was rocking her shivering little Emanuel.

'Well,' she said, 'it's betterer than a damaged man, woman – or child!'

'Mummy, Mummy, Charlotte's c-c-cold,' shivered the mite, burying her face in Mary's sodden frock.

'We'll light a fire, my sweet'art, and Mummy'll make some sweet tea. That'll warm you.'

Sam had been fumbling with the flint-and-steel and suddenly spat. 'That's easier said than done, that is. The bloody canvas covering the box has got split, so the tinder's wet and so's the firewood. And we ain't even got *blankets* to warm us now.'

Will sighed. 'Well, we'll just have to do what those dang savages do. We'll get a reed, shave one side flat, make a small hole, to reach the pith, shove in a stick and turn the stick round and round between our hands as fast as we can, till there's a flame... Right. Jimmy, Sam, Nat, let's go and look for some wood and reeds.'

Within half an hour, they were all huddled round a roaring fire, their shaking hands clutching mugs of steaming sweet tea. Emanuel was finally asleep and Charlotte was nodding off beside the crib, and Mary relaxed at last.

'Aw, Will, let's rest here for a couple o' day. The little ones are proper exhausted, and I'm fair davered myself. And it'll give our terrible salt sores time to heal a mite and the rowers' bleeding blisters.'

He gripped her wrist tightly. 'If we find fish or shellfish here in the morning, we shall. But if not, we'll be off again as soon as we've mended cussed Cox's oar.'

CHAPTER 40

They had found shellfish and, mercifully, water. Now, after the best meal of their lives, they lay on the white sand and let the mid-morning sun ease their paining bodies. Emanuel and James were in the tent.

'Ah, this is the life,' yawned Jimmy, stretching his arms and screwing up his tired eyes against the glare. 'Hey, leave me toes alone, Charlotte O'Shaughnessy! Stow yer tickling, ye wee devil!'

'Charlotte bean't not tickling Jimmy's – aaahhh! A crab, a great big crab!'

'Yeeoww!' Leaping to his feet, the Irishman frantically shook his swollen right leg to hurl away this fearsome monster, whose orange shell was covered with blood-red spots. But it had clamped its claws to his big toe and had a look of 'till death us do part' in its stalky eyes.

'Yeeowww!' He raced to the trees and kicked the nearest. '*Yeeowww!*' But the brute held on.

'Jimmy!'

Mary's shriek made him look up, despite this torture. A score and more of armed natives were pushing aside the undergrowth twenty paces farther on, with Jimmy Martin their obvious target. Crab or no crab, this was no time to kick trees. He turned and began running back down the beach, knowing that, any second, an agonizing pain would sear him between the shoulder blades and he'd lie impaled in the sand.

Will aimed the musket and fired over the savages' woolly heads. They scattered like screeching blackbirds, and two white cockatoos in the trees squalled a chorus and joined the flight.

The panting Irishman slithered to a halt beside Mary and looked at his foot.

'Merciful Jesus, the Devil's pincered kinsman's scuttled off, too.'

She ruffled his mop of long black hair. 'Aw, you killjoy, Jimmy Martin. I was going to boil that big old crab for our supper, but it's somewhere in the surf now and all we're left with is the teasing thought of what might have been...'

'Mummy,' whispered Charlotte, tugging Mary's frock, 'Mummy, will they *bad* blacks come back an' eat Charlotte for *their* supper?'

Jimmy laughed piercingly, releasing his own tension but causing Mary's shattered nerves to twitch. 'Of course not, darlin',' he said. 'There ain't enough meat on ye. Faith, there ain't enough on any of us. Aye, now that they've seen us close to, they know that they'll be better off chasing 'roos. No, Charlotte, they won't be back. Take auld Jimmy's word for it.'

'Mummy, is Jimmy being a silly ol' buffle'ead?'

Mary caught a warning in the Irishman's blue eyes. She squatted in front of this bright girl, held her at arm's length and looked into these serious grey ones. But it was no use: the mother couldn't lie to her child.

'What do *you* think, my beauty?'

A long pause. Will grunted with impatience.

Charlotte fingered her swollen, blistered lips. 'Charlotte d'fink Jimmy's being a silly ol' buffle'ead an' them will come back.'

CHAPTER 41

The escaped convicts stayed another day and night, though, without further threats from savages – or crabs. Then on the morning of Saturday 30 April, they returned to sea. Soon the *Beauty* was being lashed by more huge waves, so Mary and Old Bill were again forced to bail like demons.

* * *

By the early evening of Monday 2 May, 'Captain' William Bryant had succeeded in steering his brave *Beauty* through even higher surf and they landed on another white beach. They were in a vast, shallow bay, sheltered by a crescent of islands strewn with sandhills, one of which was so enormous that it must have been nearly a thousand feet high.

As the weary voyagers clambered stiffly and painfully ashore, they noticed two native 'oven' huts by some small coastal banksia trees farther on. Each hut was nothing more than two long, wide, curved sheets of gum tree bark, laid together lengthways: like the shape of a baker's deep oven and closed at one end, and no higher than Charlotte.

'Mummy, Mummy, look'ee, look'ee! Li'l *gals* – like Charlotte!'

Two native women and two small girls scuddled behind the huts and crouched down. One of the women was holding a brand, having been about to light a fire.

'Mary,' grunted Will, 'leave my Emanuel with me and take Charlotte and show those black bitches that we want to borrow their torch to light a fire for ourselves.'

Her swollen legs swaying as if she were still on the *Beauty*, the Cornish girl handed over her little boy and, taking Charlotte's hand, stumbled along this plaguy hot sand.

The women and children were peeping out, and, as Mary reached them, she pointed at the brand and then back at John and Sam. They had just begun gathering dead wood from a clump of trees near the boat. She held out her hand and waited.

Their bowed shoulders scarred with tribal marks, the native women jabbered nervously for about half a minute and seemed ready to turn and run. Suddenly Charlotte broke free, and before Mary or the natives knew what was happening, the child was hugging the smaller girl – about her own age – and kissing the filthy, fish-oiled, fly-covered cheek.

'My name be Charlotte Bryant. What be yourn?'

The black child frowned.

Mary prodded Charlotte's bare chest. 'Charlotte. Char-lotte.' Then she pointed at the little black girl's panting one. 'Your name?'

'Mìlba,' she said, giggling and touching her lower lip with the little finger of her left hand. This was a finger which would doubtless be shortened to the first joint in some hideous tribal ceremony one of these days, for the two women had been thus mutilated.

'Hi, Mìlba,' grinned Charlotte.

'Hi – hi, Tar - Tar-lot,' beamed Mìlba.

The woman with the brand, who was surely Mìlba's mother, smiled, too, and handed it to Mary.

'Thank you kindly, ma'am,' she said gaily. 'I'll bring it back in a minute. Don't you go away now. Come on, Tarlot.'

The native women and children waited behind the huts as Mary and Charlotte rejoined the others. Once the fire was crackling merrily, mother and child returned the brand to its owner. Uttering a strange cry, the black woman snatched the thing and her reluctant daughter and fled with the other pair into the trees.

'Thank ye!' yelled Jimmy. 'Thank ye, ladies! 'Twas mighty good of ye, leaving us two huts to shelter our poor fleshless auld bodies from this cursed wind. Ack,' he winced, 'the sand itself's stinging worse than a plague of sandflies! Aye, James Cox, I've had about enough as

I can stand of eleven of us being squashed together in one tent and having your teeth grinding anxiously in me ear every night we're ashore.'

* * *

Two hours later Mary, Will, Charlotte and Emanuel were snuggled together in the smaller hut.

'Aw, Will, this is a million times betterer than shiverin' an' pukin' on that tossing boat. And, thank God, the wind seems to be keeping the mosquitoes away.'

'Yes, it's certainly better than the boat,' he yawned, putting an arm round her bony shoulders. *How spindly his arms these days!* she thought. 'It's certainly better than that, gal. But it's well that ol' Jimmy's sitting in the entrance here, keeping both eyes open to see if those black bitches bring back their black-hearted sweethearts to roast *our* hearts for a midnight feast.'

Jimmy's shadowy form turned to address them. 'Ye're right there, William. Ye don't have to fret about your hearts, for I'll guard them, so I will. Aye, while there's the smallest wee flutter in this Irish heart, ye can sleep the sleep of the just.'

Charlotte yawned loudly. 'An' you *will* save Charlotte from the snakes, Jimmy, like what you did say once?...'

'I'll do that, me darlin'. James Martin, Esquire, of the County Antrim is no *chicken*-heart. Why, he'll – *he'll* strangle *them* like chickens, with his bare hands. Never fear while *Jimmy's* here!'

Charlotte put her lips to Mary's ear, giving her the tickling shivers. 'Mummy,' she whispered, 'Charlotte d'like Jimmy much *much* betterer than Will. Couldn' Jimmy be Charlotte's father?'

Smothering a sob, Mary Broad of Fowey pressed her own lips to this tiny ear. 'Whist, child! Mercy me, don't you ever say that again!'

CHAPTER 42

It was a snake- and savage-free night and the exhausted escapers slept far into Tuesday morning. Mary lay and stretched and yawned. Then catching her breath in pain, she dragged her stiff body and bawling baby out into the dazzling, scorching sun.

James Cox had relieved Jimmy at sunrise, while she'd been briefly awake feeding Emanuel his mashed shellfish. She saw that the Irishman was still sleeping in the other hut, which he now had to himself. By the smile on his thin, bearded face, he was dreaming of blue-eyed Irish girls far, far away. Over by the boat, Will was mending his net and she staggered across, with Charlotte at her heels.

No sooner had the Cornish girl reached her husband than there was a cry from the huts.

'Will!' It was James, with levelled musket. 'Those b-b-black bitches have brought their menfolk!'

Thirty or forty armed savages were emerging from the trees.

'Come along with me, boys,' muttered Will, grabbing his own loaded gun and turning to Bill Morton and the others, who had been soaping the *Beauty*'s seams. 'No dang savage is going to send William Bryant scuddling into the sea like a crab ever again!'

When the two groups were about twenty paces apart, Will took aim, then fired over the natives' heads. Squawking with fear, the blacks turned tail and careered back into the woods, some falling over each other in their panic. Much as if they were chickens terrified of being strangled by Jimmy Martin, thought Mary.

'That's it, you fly-encrusted, black-bottomed buggers,' roared Will. 'Run like Old Scratch, your father. Run, damn you, run! You won't see *me* running. Will Bryant'll leave this bay when he's ready, and not one second before.'

* * *

Will was ready by late Wednesday afternoon, and Charlotte gazed wistfully at the huts as the *Beauty* left the white beach behind.

'Mummy, will Charlotte not never see Mìlba again? Be Mìlba gone for *ever*?'

'Yes, my lover, for ever,' she murmured, thinking, *Thank the good Lord for that!*

By nightfall, Will was steering away from the coast, because the surf was running so high that, again, there was a serious risk of staving the *Beauty*. But no sooner had the little cutter left the land's protection than this fiendish gale and strong current were doing their damndest to drive her far out to sea.

'Yes, my billies, she's being swept out into the ocean,' their captain bellowed, trying to make himself heard above the roaring wind. 'The only thing to do is keep her under a close-reefed mainsail, because, at this rate, the ol' gal will soon be at the *bottom* of the danged ocean.'

CHAPTER 43

When Thursday dawned, New Holland had disappeared and it seemed that the entire Pacific Ocean was sweeping down upon the flimsy craft. They were surrounded by mountainous green seas, the like of which even fisherman Will had never seen.

By the time the sun's rays had turned the colour of the waves to sparkling silver, low black clouds were gathering: curling and glowering like the Devil's very eyebrows. Howling, mocking winds from Satan's throat were scornfully sweeping the tiny vessel along a valley a hundred yards wide, with thirty-foot sides.

'Lord 'elp us!' gasped James Cox, 'the b-b-boat'll be capsized for sure this time!'

'Mummy, hold *on* to Charlotte!' shrieked the child. 'Charlotte be a-goin' to be drownded into the water!'

With one arm round Emanuel in the apron pouch and the other gripping Charlotte, Mary would have no means of stopping Mummy herself being swept overboard. Gabbling a prayer, she wedged herself sideways. No one could help her; every man jack was desperately struggling to save himself.

'Dear life!' The screeching gale smashed into the cutter with such fury that the breath was forced back down Mary's throat and she was flung onto her children. She stayed here as a massive, roaring wave struck the stern, lashing her face with stinging, blinding spray. 'O Lord, *help* us!'

The Lord's reply was to hide the sun and burst the clouds. Gone were the sparkling-silver waves: dark-grey whitecaps now, attacking the *Beauty* unmercifully. Gone, too, was the blood from Charlotte's face, leaving her freckled cheeks like speckled white eggs.

'Mercy on us,' groaned Mary, 'I feel so *sick*!' Her racing heart skipped a beat, then another: the wild waters were so high, they were breaking over the sides and swelling round her ankles. Any moment now the vessel would be swamped and that would be the end of the world. The stern rose and the quivering *Beauty* shot down the face of the wave into a trough, making Mary's teeth rattle and tumbling Charlotte between Jimmy's legs. Never had the mother seen such terror in her child's grey eyes. Quieter down here in the blackness – loud roars again now up on the crest! Up here it was like being on a Cornish hill with every other hill moving around you. The *Beauty* tottered, shivered, then plunged again. Mary felt so ill, she must pull herself up and lean over the side. *If I can somehow find the strength...* She took a deep, shuddering breath, making her feel even worse, and she was on one wobbly knee, her head swimming horribly. *Mercy, the roaring's inside it now! Maybe I'll feel betterer if I shut my eyes... Yes, a mite betterer.* On both knees now. *Steady, gal... Steady!... Yes... Done it!* She was on her feet, with the screeching Emanuel squeezed under her left arm. Hanging on for blessed life, she forced her head over and was sick.

Slithering round, she saw, through a mist, that she was almost nose to nose with a green-faced, glazed-eyed Jimmy. A sudden hellish squalling! Something big and white swooped on him. A gull.

'Ack, get away from me, ye squawking scavenger ye... Away with ye, or, by me blistered palms... I– I'll strangle ye... Like a chicken...' he finished weakly.

No feeble threat from a helpless human could frighten away this greedy gull, whose beady eyes were glinting at a fish head protruding from the box under Jimmy and Sam's seat.

'Ack, fly off out of it! Jeez, can't ye see I'm nearly dead? Hey, I said get *away* from me! Get *away*!' shivered the Irishman, aiming a pathetic punch, which merely made the bird swerve just out of range. Needless to say, no sooner had Jimmy collapsed with the effort than his attacker dived again and succeeded in snatching the prize. Then, as Jimmy, too, vomited over the side, the gull veered away with mocking cries.

Seeing Jimmy spewing the meagre contents of his stomach, immediately made Mary sick again.

'Aww! Awww!' *Oh, God! Please, please let this nightmare end!* She was shivering so violently that her jaws were aching, and her poor head was throbbing fit to split.

The world heaved, as surely the most monstrous wave that the *Beauty* had ever met surged under her bows. She spun crazily on the creamy crest. Then, with her timbers groaning in mortal protest, and her passengers and crew groaning in mortal distress, she pitched into the whirling trough. She soared again and another dark-grey monster, even mightier than the last, slammed into her. Again she spun. Again she was hurled down into a fleetingly black, silent world.

Yet the defiant *Beauty* was refusing to surrender, marvelled Mary, still leaning over with Emanuel under her arm.

'Get *down* with my boy, woman!' thundered Will. 'Get *down*! You'll both be swept overboard! For God's *sake*! A fisherman's daughter should know better than to lean over the gunnel! What's wrong with being sick in the straw? Dang me, what's gotten into your head? Have the waves dashed all your brains out? Get *down* with my boy, you stupid bitch! Jimmy, for mercy's *sake*, man, *grab* her, will you? I daren't leave go the tiller, because without steering, we're doomed, as sure as my name be...'

Shivering loudly, Jimmy slid from his seat and clutched her sodden waist. He held her with difficulty, his fingers stiff and claw-like from all the rowing they'd done while wet.

'Get *away* from me! Get *away*!'

'Ack, Mary,' he cried, gasping for breath, 'ye're clingin' to the side like a... like a bloody limpet... Now, don't be... don't be stupid, lass... Get yerself and the wee fella back *down*.'

'Get *away*, I said! Get *away*!' Mary Broad of Fowey was determined that nothing and no one would make her let go, because she knew that if she budged just one tiny inch, she'd again be horribly, agonizingly sick. Oh, torture of terrible tortures! Those bouts of morning sickness when she'd been with child were as nothing compared with this. God, it was even worse than being back on the *Charlotte* in the Southern Ocean. 'Aw, help me, Lord!' she screamed.

The wind shrieked derisively through the rigging and the Old Lady of the Seas groaned even more piteously. A lady in agony... Mary's thoughts turned to a real lady in agony: poor Agnes Lakeman. Divine punishment, Mary Broad!

In truth, the *Beauty* was in her death agony. The gale and the waves had had enough play-acting and were now intent on destroying her without more ado. Waves even higher. Coming ever faster. No sooner had she been plunged into a trough than she was instantly hurled up again with merciless ferocity.

'Save us!' The same cry from two straining, paining throats as Mary and Jimmy saw the terror in each other's sickly face. Who would be the first to be cast into Satan's hissing cauldron?

The *Beauty* had once more hurtled into a trough. Judging his moment, Jimmy pulled Mary and they sprawled in the straw, Emanuel tumbling into Charlotte's arms. The Irishman crawled back onto his seat as the boat rose, spun, and plunged yet again. *Dear life, how much longer?* Mary wondered. *How much longer before we're all borne down into the icy black depths, where Ghastly Death's waiting to welcome us to Eternal Agony?*

* * *

In the bows, Old Bill had kept bailing until he collapsed. But the sea never tires, so, scarcely knowing what she was doing, Mary floated Emanuel in his crib and wedged it under Will's legs, then took a pot from the box. Her limbs and back were so stiff but she knew that if she did not bail twice as fast as the old man, the water would soon submerge Charlotte, who was oh so frighteningly still, lying here slumped against Jimmy's legs.

* * *

Only the Lord knew how long Mary had been bailing, when suddenly she saw Jimmy's face spinning before her. She was enveloped in a strange muzziness. Wind and waves were silenced as darkness fell.

CHAPTER 44

Dear life, I'm drownding! She was gulping for air but the sea was flooding down her throat! Father was crying, 'Mary's leaving us, too.' Dolly was screeching, 'First Mother leaves us and now you! You're selfish.

'Selfish!

'*Selfish!*

'Shellfish, Mummy?'

'Ack, have some shellfish, Mary darlin'.' Jimmy from far away. 'Sure, 'twill give ye some strength back. Jeez, ye bailed like a dozen Jack tars today. No wonder ye exhausted yerself. Aye, no wonder ye're done.'

'Aw, Jimmy... W-what's happening? It's mortal dark!'

''Tis night, lass, and 'tis raining hard.' His voice a mite closer. The 'flooding' was only rainwater. 'Ye collapsed like Auld Bill.' Closer still. 'But the good Lord has seen fit to bring both of ye back to us... We're taking it in turns to do the bailing now, two at a time. Nat and Bill Morton are bailing at the moment... And Will's towing a hooped canvas bag behind the boat, to stop her turning so that a great big wave don't hit her on the side and knock her over.'

Fully conscious now, she managed to gasp, 'It's called... it's called a "drogue", Jimmy, it's–'

'Yes,' muttered the captain, 'we've come to, under a drogue, to keep the *Beauty*'s head to the sea, so's to stop her broaching to. Because there's still a fierce gale a-blowin', as you can well feel!' He pulled his wife up into a sitting position against the side, and the salt sores stabbed her back and bottom. 'Now, get this little bit of shellfish down you. It's impossible to light a fire, so the rest of us have made do with a little raw rice. It was by common consent that the last of the shellfish should be given to you and your daughter, who's her old self again now,' he grunted.

'Yeah, Mary,' sniffed Sam, 'doncha go an' sick it up, gel, 'cos I meself could've done wiv some luverly shellfish, instead of that bloody rice – hey-ho, 'ere comes another bloody whitecap!...'

* * *

Only the Lord knew how; they were still alive when, at last, Friday slowly dawned. Mighty slowly. Emerging from night's terrifying blackness was another vast nothingness, of grey.

It took an hour before it was fully light. Whitecap after plaguy whitecap. Still no sign of land.

Will peered at everyone through salty eyelashes. 'With the gale still raging,' he yelled, 'we must needs keep under this close-reefed mainsail. With every dang thing so wet, we won't get a fire started today either, so we'll just have to have some more raw rice. Mary, open the chest and dish us all a sparing ration, will you?'

Jimmy looked at him in utter disbelief. 'Jeez, Will, the poor wee girl can scarce open her *mouth*, leave alone the bloody chest! Look at her, for goodness' sake, man!'

Mary tried to get up on one elbow but to her horror could barely raise her hand from the straw.

The Irishman's tired, pitying eyes looked down at her and she smiled weakly. 'Och, Mary,' he murmured, 'I'll get the rice, darlin'. Rest yer pretty wee head a wee while longer.'

* * *

Another night came without their sighting land. The waves were as high as ever and Mary's stomach was empty, remaining as turbulent as the sea. How she had managed to keep down that shellfish yesterday, she'd never know; she could face nothing now.

Charlotte and Emanuel rolled with the boat but were otherwise motionless, only an occasional cry telling the distraught mother that her mites were alive. Would they still be on Saturday morning?

CHAPTER 45

'Land ho to nor'ard!' gasped Mary. She had been scanning the horizon as a bright Saturday dawned.

Oh Lord, these mites look so mortal ill!

'It's land, Charlotte! It's land, Emanuel! You'll soon be betterer now, both of you. Aw, praise be! Praise be!'

'Yes,' breathed Will, 'it's a fair distance but the wind's veered to the nor'ard now, so I reckon we'll get there by eight o'clock sun.'

James Cox's sunburnt face creased into a tortured smile.

'Praise Gawd,' he winced. 'If we hadn't sighted that, we'd have been drownded before much longer, because no boat can keep taking such a battering as this. Inside me head, I could already hear the sh-sh-sharks gnashing their teeth. Gawd 'elp me, I could.'

Jimmy grinned weakly. 'Ah, so *that's* why yer own teeth gnash at night and drive me crazy, is it? Inside yer head ye're having nightmares of *sharks'* teeth... Ack, 'tis when ye hear them gnashing *outside* yer head that 'tis time to fret, 'cos we'll all be hearing them then. Aye, that'll be the time to fret, James, me auld darlin'... Mind ye, though, there could be other nasty craturs lying in wait for ye, on this bit of land we're heading for: monster spiders and slimy black snakes, who'll all make straight for yer wee toes as soon as ye set them ashore, and whose bites will kill ye within a few minutes. But even before that, don't forget the great big jellyfishes who'll sting ye to death before ye've even had the chance to put yer toes on dry land. Gnashings inside yer head, indeed!'

'Oh go and *boil your* head, you bloody Irishman,' muttered James, pretending annoyance.

'Boil me *head*? Sure, everything's so wet, we can't even light a fire to boil the blasted rice!'

* * *

An hour later, Old Bill at the prow suddenly came to life.

''Tis an island!' he croaked. 'A little old island... But – woe's me old bones – there's nothing but reefs all the way round it, if these dangblasted eyes of mine ain't deceiving me. And the surf's mighty high, too. So, Lor' knows how we're goen to land... Still, 'tis better to take a chance than–'

'Of course it is, Bill!' Mary cried, with feeling. 'It's betterer to take a chance, because it's certain that every soul aboard will perish if we stay out here much longer. My – my poor babbies are sinking fast,' she sobbed.

'I agree,' said Nat weakly, his normally red face drained nigh as white as his hair and fast-growing beard. ''Tis our only hope.'

'So do I,' growled Will. 'We ain't got no choice.'

Mary looked longingly at the island. 'Aw, please God there'll be fresh water there, because this dang *gallon* won't keep us alive for very long. And after all that rain we had, too. If only we'd had something to catch it all in. Aw, my poor, poor babbies.'

'Yeah,' muttered Sam Bird, 'we ain't got no future out at sea, that's for sure. Either dying of thirst to give these 'ere screeching gulls a treat, waiting to peck out our eyes. Or being capsized and giving James's sharks a treat – oh, dammit, fings is bad when I ain' got no spit left to spit!'

* * *

Providence! Tucked away among all these sharp reefs was a tiny beach.

The surf tossed the *Beauty* as if she were no more than driftwood but the sand gave her a soft landing.

'Right,' grunted Will, jumping out, then gasping as the stiffness caught him. 'Let's haul the ol' gal up out of the way of the surf... And straightway get some wood for a fire; because we're so dang weak from hunger and sickness, we soon won't have the strength to lift the bowls of boiled rice to our blistered lips... Sam and John, you gather some wood. James and you, Jimmy, you go and look for some water – and, by God, you'd better find some. This little island's only about a mile round, so drag your skinny carcasses all the way round it till you find the cool, fresh Water of Heaven.'

* * *

'No Water of Heaven, I'm sorry to say, Will,' panted Jimmy, when he and James tottered back to camp after an hour's exhausting search. Their paining legs were more swollen than ever. 'Not even a pool... not even a small wee pool from Thursday's deluge!'

'It's as I feared,' groaned Will, staring at the fire. 'Aw, Lord, it's as I feared.'

''Tis sorry we are, all of ye,' said the Irishman, seeing the anxiety in everyone's eyes. 'James and I looked everywhere but there was no liquid nowhere. Sure, we didn't even see a mosquito with his leg cocked up a tree – ah, thanks, Mary.' He gave her a weary smile as she handed him his bowl of boiled rice.

Will was gazing at the waves now. 'The tide's ebbing. Pray God we can find some shellfish, because *I* need more than bloody rice to keep *me* alive, I tell you. If we don't find none round the rocks, we'll look on that long reef over there.' It jutted a mile and a half into the sea. 'It'll be safe to walk along at low water.'

* * *

'Hey, Mary!' exclaimed Jimmy. 'Look along there! Just *look* along there!'

The pair had left their exhausted companions behind and, despite painfully bloated legs, were searching along the reef. Mercifully, the children had taken a turn for the better, now that they were ashore, and were sleeping under the palms back there. As for the little Irishman, his strength had astonished Mary, for hadn't he walked round the danged island just an hour ago?

'Where, for goodness' sake?'

'Along there, left by the tide and basking in the sun: twenty or more great big turtles! *They'll* keep us alive for a wee while, won't they? We'll need some help turning them over and dragging them back to the beach. Because even James Martin ain't that strong.'

'Yiss,' she breathed, 'we'll need help and we'll need some rope. The *Beauty*'s mooring rope will do the trick, I'm a-thinking.'

'Right, darlin',' he yawned, 'ye stay here while *I* drag me poor auld legs back.'

'No, Jimmy, I'll go!'

'No, lass, I'll be fine. Mind ye don't try sitting on a turtle's back, though, as soon as *my* back's turned, and do some basking of yer own. You look jaded enough to fall asleep. With ye aboard snoring yer pretty head off, the cratur might get it into its *wrinkled* auld head to crawl back into the water. And with *ye* gone, I'll have to be mammy as well as "unca" to them brats of yours.'

'And a mighty fine job you'd make of it, too, Jimmy Martin.'

* * *

Keeping well away from the thrashing clawed flippers and the snapping beaks set in powerful jaws, Will, Mary and the others used the rope to turn five of these five-foot-long olive-green turtles onto their dark-brown, heart-shaped shells. How helpless now, these wildly lashing limbs. How vulnerable these white underparts. Then Will, Mary and the whole panting lot of them hauled the reptiles, one at a time, back to the camp. The Cornishman reckoned that they weighed 'five hundred plaguy pounds each'.

Looking into their protruding eyes, Mary herself had felt pity for the doomed creatures. Dear life, the turtles had tried and tried but they'd been unable to retract their heads and necks fully, to hide from their attackers. Pity, yes, but, as with that sheep in Farmer Tregenna's field, 'needs must when hunger drives'.

Will and the others tied the turtles to a palm tree, having finally got all the creatures upright again. All, that is, except the chosen one, which the Cornishman proceeded to stab deeply in its leathery neck, into its very spine. Later, at the evening meal, as the weary band sat contentedly round the campfire, a well-bloodied Will Bryant smiled for the first time in ages.

'Dang me, this here turtle and her eggs are delicious!' he said, dribbling over a chunk of flipper and one of the hundred eggs which, in the cool of the evening, the turtle would have laid, and buried more than two-feet deep in the warm sand. 'Here, Mary, try some limb. It's the best of all: beautiful, *beautiful*! It's a terrible pity we can't take the craturs aboard the *Beauty* and kill 'em when we need 'em. Because there are enough turtles here to last for a good few meals, ain't there? But when we're ready to set sail again, we'll bleed them to death so the meat lasts longer and doesn't go all dark. We'll just have to dry some of it over the fire and take that as a poor substitute.'

He frowned and sighed. 'We can't survive on food alone, though, can we? This ol' turtle's spurting blood has been red wine from Heaven, and wasn't at all salty, was it, but being as it starts going thick within a minute, we can't save any to take on the *Beauty*, can we? We'll kill another tomorrow but if we go back to sea without first finding water, we'll all be dead in a couple o' day.'

CHAPTER 46

'Mummy, Mummy, Charlotte be thirsty-thirsty.' It was the middle of the night and, in the big tent, the child had been tossing and turning since her mother had laid her down.

'Aw, so's Mummy, my lover, but we mustn't have no more till morning. That's cap'n's orders,' she whispered, while Will snored in her other ear, and everyone else snored in everyone else's ear.

'I hate him, I hate him, I *hate* him! Why can't Jimmy be Charlotte's father? Jimmy would leave Charlotte have some water!'

'Oh no I wouldn't, darlin',' murmured the sentry swatting mosquitoes outside the closed flap. 'If I'd given ye water every time ye wanted it since we left Sydney Cove, bless me blisters we'd have all been dead from thirst days ago.'

'But, Jimmy,' protested the child, 'won't you let Charlotte have just a widdle dwink? *He* wouldn' see...'

'No.'

'Charlotte won't like you no more if you don't.'

'Well, 'tis sorry I am about that, young lady, but that's just one more cross that poor auld Jimmy will have to bear in this cruel life. Talking of crosses: if ye pray to Lord Jesus and ask Him to fill the mainsail, which we've spread out here for rain, why, who knows, He may oblige ye. Say "please", though... Go on, Charlotte. Put yer wee hands together.'

'P-p-please, Lor' J-J-Jesus, can Charlotte her have some rain? 'Cos her be so thirsty-thirsty. An' so be Mummy, an' Emanuel – an'... an' Charlotte's *friend*, Jimmy.'

But five minutes later, the only sounds were the snores, the ceaseless pounding of the surf and, of course, the frogs' chorus and the shrill chirping of a million plaguy cicadas.

And after another five minutes, nothing had changed.

'Jimmy,' whispered Charlotte, 'how long will it be before Lor' Jesus *oblige* Charlotte?'

'Ah sure, He might not have heard ye, chick. He's mighty busy, ye know. Pray again.'

The little girl did.

* * *

It must have been an hour later when Mary became really anxious about Charlotte, for the precious mite was gasping so pitifully. Dear life, it reminded the Fowey fishergirl of her poor darling mother's last night on God's earth – *Lord, is that –?*

'Rain! *Rain!*' Jimmy's cries, as he opened the flap, woke everyone, and Charlotte rallied, clutching her mother excitedly.

'Praise the Lord,' sobbed the Irishman. 'Oh, praise the Lord! 'Tis filling the mainsail. 'Tis filling the breakers and pots. We're saved, we're saved! Oh, praise the Lord! Bless ye, Charlotte. Oh, bless ye, darlin' – no, stay there, little one; I'll fill a mug and bring ye some. Now, how do those verses from St Mark go?... Jesus said, "Whosoever shall give a cup of water to drink because ye belong to Christ, verily I say unto ye, he shall not lose his reward. And," *mark* this, William Bryant, "whosoever shall offend one of these *little* ones that believe in me, it is better for him that a millstone were hanged about his neck and he were cast into the sea."'

Mary snorted. 'Aw, brayvo, Jimmy, brayvo!'

'Devil fly away with you on this sou'easter, Martin,' growled the Cornishman. 'Dammit, we're all as thirsty as hell; hurry and bring us *all* some dang water, you Irish swab.'

CHAPTER 47

They remained on the island for another five days. In this time, they'd killed eleven more turtles, and had picked a tasty fruit which resembled that of the bell pepper and which, so far at least, had had no ill effects. They had dried some of the turtle meat to take with them and had payed the *Beauty*'s seams with soap and turtle fat. The remaining fat had been collected in a pot and Mary had later used some of the resulting golden oil to rub into everyone's sore parts. The men had been too damn sore to enjoy the experience – even Jimmy.

On the morning of Thursday 12 May, at about eight o'clock by the sun, they set sail on a mercifully calm sea, Will steering them ever northward.

Everyone had eaten too much of the fruit. As the sun's midday rays beat down on her head, it was Mary's turn to perch on the starboard gunwale, her salt-sore backside bared to the sea. She was holding on to the rope tied along the larboard side. Her bottom was below the level of the gunwale, so she was private. Even so, Jimmy and the other rowers had closed their eyes as usual, bless them.

Will and Old Bill were looking out for sharks but what she was most terrified of were those lightning-quick squirmers of tropical waters, sea snakes. Captain Smit had warned Will that the yellow-headed devils could suddenly squiggle up from the depths when you were least expecting it and inject enough venom to kill three men.

Aw, Dolly, if only you could see your big sister now. Would you be laughing or crying, I wonder? I never had to face this problem when I was on the Jenny, *did I – face it ain't the word, is it? No, I never had to fret whether a snake was suddenly going to bite my –*

'Ahhhh!' Something had touched her and she flung herself at Jimmy's feet.

'Dear life!' she shrieked. 'Dear *life*!'

'What's wrong?' gasped the Irishman, blinking open his puffed eyes.

'Something got me!'

Will was roaring with laughter. 'It was only a bottle-nosed dolphin having a little nuzzle. Look, there it goes, over there.' The shiny grey mammal was leaping in and out of the water with a grin on its face, the saucy beggar. 'It's a good omen, boys, when they come alongside like this: a promise of fair weather. It's bad luck to harm 'em.'

Everyone else was laughing now, including Charlotte.

'*Harm* 'em?' shivered Mary. 'I could *kill* him, the way he scared me. Mercy,' she gasped, 'I thought it was the end of me.'

Jimmy grinned, adjusting her frock. '*'Twas* the "end" of ye, darlin'.'

James Cox gulped. 'It'll be the end of all of us in a minute. Look! A shark! Look, over there!'

The large, white-tipped triangular fin was about fifty yards off, but heading this way.

'Ship your oars,' breathed Will.

'Mummy, Mummy!' screamed Charlotte as Mary scrambled to her knees and hugged her.

Soon the ten-foot flesh-eater, with its pilot fish attendants above, was circling the *Beauty* and drawing closer by the second. Suddenly the creature turned towards them, its small allies in a perfect arrowhead, in line with the quivering James Cox. Then it slid under the keel. They held their breath.

The shark stayed under them, and a minute later was still there.

Mary whispered, 'It's not bothered about us; it's only sheltering from the noon sun.'

'Right, boys,' muttered Will, 'back to work. And that means you, too, James Cox. This old shark ain't interested in *your* skinny carcass. He's a cratur after your own heart: *he* don't like the sun either. He's just coming along with us for a while.'

The shark made use of them for a good half-hour and then swam off.

The day proved to be otherwise uneventful. As evening fell, they rowed the *Beauty* through a gentle surf and landed on a small mainland beach.

CHAPTER 48

They were back at sea early on Friday. In the succeeding days, they called at numerous small islands in a vain search for more turtles. If it had not been for the dried turtle meat and for pots and pots of barely edible shellfish, the voyagers would have starved. All the rice had now gone and they'd had no luck with the fishing.

But at least their prayers that they might find plenty of fresh water were answered at almost every palm-fringed beach on the main where they landed. For there were many rivers flowing down from the forested mountain ranges all along here.

Mary could not help believing that Lord Jesus was particularly listening to Charlotte. 'Suffer little children, and forbid them not, to come unto me.'

* * *

God was good, because, at last, in the early morning of Thursday 26 May, they reached wild Cape York, the continent's northern tip.

The triumphant Will's only comment: 'Ha! Corporal Anderson and his whiskers and his cat are well over two thousand mile away now, rot an' perish 'em!'

Once past the point, they sailed westward through high swells, through the perilous, largely uncharted waters of the Endeavour Straits, leading to the 400-mile-wide Gulf of Carpentaria. Bill Morton used 'dead reckoning', estimating the *Beauty*'s position: from the distance sailed, by the log, and the courses steered, by the compass, making corrections for leeway and current.

They were safely delivered through the straits but, with the water again running low, the westward crossing of the gulf would have to wait. So, looking for a fresh supply, they sailed southward instead and after about ten miles came upon several small islands.

'We'll head for the one on the far right,' said Will excitedly.

At the *Beauty*'s approach, a large, screeching flock of tropical birds with dazzling feathers flew above the trees.

Mary caught her breath. 'Will,' she gulped, 'it ain't *us* that's disturbed 'em. It's *them*, look: armed blacks in two canoes!'

'Where, for God's sake?'

'Yonder: landing on that little beach on the right there.'

'Yes... yes, I see 'em, the pesty varmints!'

Sam Bird's swollen beady eyes flickered nervously. 'Why not turn away and 'ead for that other island over on the far left? Gawd'sake, they've got bows an' bloody arrers!'

'No. Will Bryant ain't going to let a gang of frizzly-heads think he's scared of 'em. Be danged he ain't. There's only a dozen of 'em, Sam.'

No sooner had the natives alighted than they noticed the intruders. One man frantically reboarded his canoe, then a second savage scrambled into the other and the pair began paddling feverishly towards the rear of the island.

'They're going to hide their canoes,' muttered Will. 'Well, we don't want their plaguy vessels. But we do want their water if they've got some!'

James Cox was shaking. 'Let's do what S-S-Sam said. For mercy's sake, they've got the most devilish black skins of any savages we've seen!'

'No, James,' said Will, taking his loaded musket from the chest. 'Rot it if I'll scuddle away from a handful of bloated blacks. Look, they're all fat, puffed-up pigs. If they're that fat, there's good food on this 'ere island, as sure as my name be William Bryant. One warning shot'll send 'em rolling into that stinking swamp behind them faster than barrels of Rusco brandy down John Copinger's plank!'

Sam glared at him. 'Good food? Good bloody food? The good food'll be us! I'll wager they're cussed cannonballs; that's why they're so fat.'

When the *Beauty* was twenty yards off, the savages raised their bows and arrows. Will aimed the musket at the tall palm behind them and fired over their frizzly heads. The 'puffed-up pigs' replied with a torrent of abuse and arrows.

'Och, William,' grunted Jimmy, as everyone dived for cover, ''tis thinking I am that ye'll have to swallow *your* puffed-up pride and find another island.'

With the arrows spattering in the water all around the boat, Will flung down the gun and started hoisting the mainsail.

'And the foresail, too, Bill!' he gulped, as an arrow *tzicked* between his head and the sail. 'Heave *'way*! Row like the Devil, me billies. But for goodness' sake keep your heads low.'

As the *Beauty* sailed out of range, Will spat over the side.

'Rot them!' he fumed. 'Satan's horns, I wish I'd fired instead at that hog of a chief there with the shells round his shoulders. Yes, a musket ball in the shoulder would have stopped *him* shooting his arrows. By heaven, it would. Aw well, we'll just have to sail a little further south and land at some place on the main. Rot an' perish that fat swine!'

* * *

'There's a small river yonder by the woods!' cried Mary, kissing Emanuel, as Will and Jimmy led the jaded band up the mainland beach late in the afternoon.

'Avast!' hissed Will, raising his musket. 'There's a village among the trees. It looks deserted, though. And there ain't no canoes here, so the *men*, at least, probably ain't here. Yes, I reckon we're safe – for the moment. But keep your musket ready, Jimmy, just in case.'

Jimmy needed no telling. On reaching the grass-roofed bark huts, he murmured, 'Jeez, there's a good twenty dwellings here. They're far better built than the primitive ones we've come across before; why, six or seven natives could *stand* in each one.'

'Gawd,' shuddered Sam, 'that makes a deal of savages, don't it?'

'Mummy, be there li'l gals like Mìlba here?'

'No, my beauty, there's no other mortals here save ourselves. Thank the Lord,' she said.

Nat stooped by the ashes of a campfire. As the stiffness pains did their worst, he winced, sucking in his breath, his red face turning crimson. 'This fire's been out for hours,' he muttered.

James Cox was darting nervous glances over both shoulders. 'Well, that's maybe s-s-so, but them black beggars might come at any time, so we'd best get the breakers filled and sail off before they do.'

'He's right, bonny lad,' said Bill Morton, wiping his glistening skull.

'Yes, I know, Bill,' murmured Will, handing him the musket and contemplating the river: little more than a stream trickling along its wide white sand bed. 'Give me a breaker, John, will you? Mary, take the children back to the boat. And hurry! I've got a feeling in my bones, and 'tain't the stiffness I'm talking about neither!'

Within four or five minutes everyone was aboard again.

'No one wants a night ashore more than me,' panted Will, hoisting the mainsail, 'but we daren't stay. We'll drop our killock three or four mile off shore and return tomorrow to fill up with more water and gather some firewood. Yes, judging by the number of huts, I suspicion there could be forty warriors paddling their cussed canoes somewhere hereabouts.'

CHAPTER 49

As dawn broke, they sailed back towards the mainland. But with less than a hundred yards to go, Mary gasped, 'Rot the black lot of 'em! Look! Look, to larboard! Coming round the point there!'

Just a couple of hundred strokes away were two huge white canoes, heading their way.

'They're like sh-sh-sharks,' stammered James Cox. 'They're like bloody sharks!'

'Jeez,' breathed Jimmy. 'Jeez, will ye look at the *size* of 'em! And, look, they've got fighting-stages on 'em. Holy Mother, there's thirty or forty warriors in *each*! Hold. The leading canoe's stopped, waiting for the other to catch up.'

As the *Beauty*'s horrified company watched, the second canoe drew alongside the first, whose crew were hoisting her sails. Now, the other lot were following suit.

'The sails seem to be made of matting,' said the Cornishman. 'Well, we ain't hanging about to see if they are. Here come the buggers now. We'll just have to put the old gal in stays,' he grunted. 'Yes, we'll turn her head to the wind and keep tacking about. With a good old Cornish freetrader's trick like this, those savages will be left far behind, like the revenue men! We'll just have to manage with what water we have. Come on, my *Beauty*,' he murmured. 'Show those heathens what a Cornishman's boat can do, gal, because if they catch up, we'll end our days in their fat bellies. No more pussivanting; 'tis straight across the Gulf of Carpentaria we're going!'

Mary and everyone stared in horror at their captain.

Sam's beady eyes narrowed with hatred. 'The Gulf? You're out of yer bloody mind, Bryant. It's four 'undred mile across! Why didya let us keep drinking the water last night, damnya? We'll never make it last now. We're going to die. All of us.'

'For pity's s-s-sake, Will,' shuddered James Cox, fear flickering in his wide blue eyes, 'it's certain death!'

Will's dark-brown eyes challenged them all. 'It's certain death if we don't.'

'They're catching up!' cried Mary, as Charlotte's fingers dug into her Mummy's wrist. 'O Lord preserve us, *Lord preserve us*!'

'Mummy, be Charlotte a-goin' to die? Bean't her a-goin' to see Chrismiss, Lor' Jesus's birthday? Nor the next Chrismiss? Nor the next?...'

Mary looked at Jimmy beseechingly. What could she say?

A shower of arrows darkened the rising sun. One thudded into the mast, another into the food chest, an inch from Mary's left leg.

'Ack, don't fret yerself, Charlotte,' said Jimmy, forcing his split, swollen lips into a smile, making them bleed. 'The Auld Lady of the Seas is more than a match for any upstart native tubs, is she not, bless her stays!'

'Iss... iss, Jimmy,' she said, doubtfully, studying his eyes. 'Iss... Charlotte s'pose so...'

'Law, James!' gulped John Butcher, gripping his rowing mate's bony arm, 'they're gaining on us, look you! I can see the whites of their ravening black eyes now!'

Nat turned to his own partner. 'Can we do it, Bill?'

The navigator sighed, rolled his sunken eyes to heaven and said nothing.

'Eek!' An arrow pinned Charlotte's tattered skirt to the boards and blood was seeping through the coarse linen.

'Aw, my *precious*!' shrieked Mary.

The child had gone as white as a shroud. She just sat there, though, biting her lip, neither screaming nor crying.

'Unca' Jimmy slid from his seat, grasped the arrow, and forcefully, but carefully, pulled it out, dropping it like a snake. The trembling mother lifted the garment...

Just a graze. Sobbing with relief, she looked up at an equally relieved Jimmy.

His own blood-drained face broke into a smile. 'Och, Mary, she's fine. God be praised! Ye're not hurt bad, chick. Sure, 'tis only a wee scratch; 'tas torn yer skin, that's all. Ye may be a Cornish girl, Charlotte Bryant, but ye have the luck of an Irish one: a Charlotte O'Shaughnessy. The luck of the Irish must have rubbed off from me to ye.'

What had happened to her had suddenly sunk in and the poor mite squalled, bringing the colour back to her cheeks.

But, brave little girl, the squall was soon over. ''Iss, Charlotte's got the luck o' the Iwish,' she sniffed, ''cos you're her friend, Jimmy.'

'Aw, Mr Irishman,' murmured Mary, shaking violently, 'pray God you give us *all* some, to escape from those murdering savages; they're catching up even more.'

Jimmy's luck held, because after ten minutes of tacking about, the gap between them and their pursuers had finally widened.

Will grinned broadly. 'Ha, I knew she'd do it. There's life in my old *Beauty* yet. Dang me, she's outrunning 'em like as if she's a healthy young maid scuddling from a bunch of bosky ravishers at Badment Fair!'

After another ten minutes, the natives gave up.

Will Bryant spat in their direction. 'That'll learn you to chase a Cornish fisherman, ye black beggars. I knew if I sailed into the wind, I'd beat you.

'Right, now all we've got to do is survive for four hundred mile, under a tropic sun, with bare enough water to give pussy to drink.'

CHAPTER 50

'Well, the last drop's drunk, John, mate,' croaked Sam Bird four days later. His once glinting eyes were glazed like a dying crow's. 'All we can do is lie down and meet our Maker.'

'Four day,' groaned John Butcher, slumped over his oar. 'Four day we've been... frizzlin' an' fryin' and tossin' an' plungin' in this... in this God-damn gulf... We should've seen somethin' by now, Bill Morton, if you're doin' your job right... Law, I canna abear it no longer... I'll be dead afore... afore tomorrowday, look you.'

'Hi, ain't *that* land?' gasped Mary, limply pointing ahead. It was danged difficult to speak, her tongue being so swollen. 'I can see *something* on the horizon there...' She turned to her husband, who seemed not to have heard. 'Hi, Will, shake yourself, man. Look yonder. It's land, I'm thinking!'

Their captain roused himself from his stupor.

'You're right, gal! By heaven, you're right! Aw, thank God,' he said weakly, 'thank God! It'll be somewhere along the north coast of New Holland, if me and Bill... if me and Bill have got it right... Yes, it's nearer *five* hundred mile we've come. Love us all, by midday we'll be drinking beautiful cool water again... Brayvo, my billies, brayvo! And God bless my old *Beauty*. God bless you, old gal... Cool, fresh water!'

* * *

'There ain't no bloody water 'ere,' raged Sam, almost crying. 'And the sun's so *'ot!*... Gaw'sake... Gaw'sake, it's like the Devil's breath burnin' me por ol' back... Yeah... yeah, laughin' at me 'e is... Sayin'... sayin' to 'isself, "'Ere's ol' Sam Bird from Whitechapel way... A bit delirious, like... a bit touched from the sun is Sam... Finks he'll find water, but there ain't none 'ere... There's plenty in me cauldron, though, hee-hee-hee."'

It was not just Sam; they were all bordering on delirium. Mary herself kept seeing water ahead in that endless, flat yellow sand but the glorious liquid had always vanished by the time they'd staggered to the spot. They had scoured the luxuriant woods fringing this wide mainland beach and stocked up with fuel, but there was no river, no stream, not even a tiny pool.

'Back into the boat,' said the Cornishman, his words slurring, his body swaying. 'We'll search... we'll search further westward along the shore.'

Sam looked at him askance, then the curved, black fingernails dug into the big man's wrist.

'We'll be dead before we find some,' wheezed the cockney as they staggered back towards the water's edge. 'We won't see the end of... we won't see the end of this day, I'm tellin'ya... we won't see the end of this day.'

Returning to the tent, where her children were sheltering from the searing sun, the Cornish girl told herself that the 'Whiner' was right for once. This time their luck had run out, even that of 'Mr Irishman'. Yes, even Jimmy Martin looked defeated for the first time since she had known him. One thing was sure: the Lord was so busy at the moment that He was no longer listening to their prayers, not even Charlotte's.

CHAPTER 51

Evening was falling when their prayers were answered. 'A river.' Mary's cry was so feeble that only Jimmy raised his muzzy head from his oar. 'Over there,' she gasped, struggling to find the strength to direct her shaking forefinger. Twinkling across those interminable, squiggly tidal flats was a silver stream. 'Aw, merciful God! We're saved, Charlotte!... Your prayers are answered, my beauty... Your prayers to Lord Jesus are answered –Charlotte?... Charlotte!' She lifted the child's head.

Lifeless.

'Mary, is – is she–?' Jimmy's eyes were filled with a horror reflecting her own.

'Charlotte!' She shook her darling, her angel, the joy of her wretched life. The puffed, horribly white lips were spread wide, revealing the tiny milk teeth and swollen tongue; the salty eyelids were tightly shut.

Jimmy groaned, flung aside the oar and tore the child from her mother. Frantically he rubbed the stilled little heart. He didn't know what he was doing, but somehow – somehow – he must force precious life back into this dear wee mite. Helplessly he looked at Mary, who could feel that her own face had gone as deathly white as her darling's. He looked at Will, who was so exhausted that he was slumped here with a lifeless expression himself. He looked at Sam, but there was no reassurance in the glazed eyes. He looked at Charlotte again – and her eyes were open.

But... but they were not dulled in death; they were sparkling in expectation.

The white lips moved. 'Why be *you* a-holdin' Charlotte?... Be it bedtime? Be you a-goin' to tell Charlotte 'nother story?'

'Oh, Charlotte,' he choked, kissing this sweating, blistered brow – as puckered as an old woman's. 'Oh, me darlin' chile. Auld Jimmy, the *seanachie*, has got a million stories to tell ye and ye've got a lifetime ahead of ye to listen to them. Here, Mary, for goodness' sake take yer daughter back before I drown her with me tears.'

* * *

Having quenched their thirst and refilled the breakers, the starving voyagers were overjoyed to catch and eat the juiciest, fleshiest fishes of their entire lives. The tree-lined creek was full of them. Other creatures inhabited it, too, though. Several huge saltwater crocodiles were basking along the opposite bank, farther on, one monster being sixteen or seventeen feet long. So the meal had been eaten under the trees, well back from the bank. 'Otherwise,' the Cornishman had grunted, '*they'll* make a meal of *us*.'

Afterwards a revived Will said that, although it was mighty tempting to rest their paining bodies on soft sand for the night, he felt the pull of Timor. For it was now only about five hundred miles away, to the north-west. So to the accompaniment of crocodile screams – like those of old cows – they put out to sea late in the evening. They hoped to make one last watering call on the mainland sometime on Wednesday, 1 June, before entering the wide, and wild, Timor Sea.

* * *

Late on Wednesday afternoon, they hoisted the sails to hasten the *Beauty* back to the main. But the vessel was soon being flung about by a heavy swell. So Will decided to abandon this dangerous attempt and they never even sighted land. Thus, with Mary cursing herself for grossly exceeding the ration the past twenty-four hours, they had to rely on what little water remained, and, speeding before the south-east wind, shaped a course for Timor.

CHAPTER 52

'Land ho,' croaked Old Bill as a hazy Friday dawned. Scorning her salt sores, the ecstatic Cornish girl hugged Emanuel and Charlotte, whose own skins were healing quicker. Then, despite this horrible weakness and these searingly painful legs, with both mites under her arms she staggered to her feet. Blinking open her smarting eyes, she sucked in her breath in wonder. Out of this magical mist, lush green, heavy-scented Timor was rising like Paradise itself.

The low shore was covered with woods whose palm leaves spread like Mary Johnson's fan. Here and there were wide stretches of the prettiest, greenest lawns that the Fowey girl had ever seen. And behind all that was a beautiful range of misty mountains. The whole scene was like the painted backcloth of a play that she and Dolly had watched with their mother at the May Fair in Fowey, the year before the cursed consumption had struck that poor woman. *Aw, Mother... Mother!*

'Aw, you've done it,' she sobbed, turning to Will. Like everyone else's, his swollen face, lips and tongue and barely open eyes showed how close to death he'd been. 'You clever old Cornishman, you clever old beggar.'

'Yes,' he murmured, enclosing the children as he gripped her bony shoulders, 'when William Bryant says he'll do something, he'll dang well do it.'

Abruptly releasing her, he looked along the boat, and every eye was upon him. Especially Emanuel's here.

'Give me my brave little fighter, woman,' choked the proud father, his lower lip trembling. 'Give me my son – hi, careful now, for God's sake! Don't drop him over the gunnel, after all he's been through.'

With Emanuel in his arms, Captain William Bryant of the *Beauty* addressed his crew.

'Well done, every one of you. Well done!' His voice was cracked with thirst and thick with emotion.

'Now... now, there's no hope of calling hereabouts for fresh water, because of the high surf, as you can well see. But Cap'n Smit told me that, further west, there are some tidy bays where we can land. It'll be sometime tomorrow before we reach 'em, though. We'll see some native settlements – *friendly* natives – but we won't reach the Dutch port of Coupang till Sunday.'

Sunday: 5 June. Their journey of 3,254 miles would have taken nine weeks and six days.

'I misdoubts if we'll see any Dutch vessels in the meanwhile. Howsoever if we do, we'll tell the cap'ns the same as we're going to tell the Dutch guv'nor. We'll say that we're the only survivors of an English whaling ship that was wrecked a long way south of Timor on her homeward journey from New South Wales. Those cheese-wormy Dutch would never dream that we're convicts who've sailed our *little boat* all this way from there.

'Yes, we'll get ol' Jimmy to tell a convincing tale. His swollen Irish tongue will blarney a way for us to be treated as poor suffering wretches washed up by the sea. Which, in truth, is what we are, for goodness' sake!'

CHAPTER 53

'So, as I was saying, yer Excellency, we were aboard a whaling ship, like,' said Jimmy, on this pleasant Sunday afternoon.

The whole boatload of them were luxuriating in the wonderful softness of the green-silk-cushioned sofas in Governor Timotheus Wanjon's beautiful white, sandalwood-scented house.

Sitting on the next sofa, Mary studied the blue-eyed Irishman. *Mercy, what a difference!* True, he was a hollow-eyed, skin-and-bone spectre at the moment, and would have scared out of her own skin any woman who did not know the cause of this blistered, brown-scurfed countenance and the festering salt sores on his limbs. But his swellings had gone down, he'd given himself a shave and a good soaping, and, for the first time since the Fowey fishergirl had known him, he was wearing fine clothes. The white cotton shirt and bottle-green knee breeches had been presented by the sarong-clad Malay manservant, with His Excellency's compliments. The betel-chewing Timor wenches had better watch out.

Jimmy frowned. 'No word of a lie, sir, the ship was hit by a hurricane from hell! 'Tis mortal sad but we were the only survivors.

'Sir,' he went on, 'we're mighty grateful to ye for giving us *two* sets of clothing each. 'Twas most Christian of ye. Lashed for days by such Devil-sent wind and rain, our own clothes were falling from our backs by the time we got here, so they were. As ye well know, of course. Aye, most Christian of ye.'

Humbly, the Irishman lowered his heavy-lidded eyes. 'We're all Christian, God-loving folk and will work hard in Coupang in return for *your* Christian hospitality.'

Behind his shiny, reddish-brown, gold-trimmed desk, the handsome Dutchman in the navy-blue suit, with its own gold trimmings, smiled. He smiled with his light-blue eyes. He was flaxen-haired and in his early middle years.

'My poor fellow, I can see that you are honest people, and I know that you are hard workers, by the hard skin – among all the blisters – when we shook hands. There is here much work. For we are a busy port and we have – forgive me, my English is not good – no *intention* of letting the English take over our trade and – er – *influence* in this part of the world. We do not mind using – er – *employing* English people to help us, though,' he laughed, giving Mary a look which showed that he thought her a desirable woman.

She blushed and stared at her blistered bare feet, with their puffy ankles.

The Governor went on, 'Two years ago, when I was what you would call "Deputy" Governor, I had the great honour to help Captain William Bligh. You will, of course, know all about him and the mutiny on the *Bounty*.'

'Aye, sir,' smiled Jimmy. "'Twas on everyone's lips for *months* in the col– in the country. Sure, folk were talking about it all over England. Jeez, more than three thousand miles! How did them brave folk ever do it? Can ye imagine going more than three thousand miles in an open boat?'

Mary's heart thudded and her brain screamed, *Don't overdo it, Jimmy, lad, or he'll know we're liards. Lord, the Guv'nor's looking at me real peculiar, like: reading my thoughts!*

'I see, mistress, that my wife's maid has found you a pretty yellow frock to – how do you say – *do justice* to your beauty. I see a blush on your poor pale cheeks, but it is the truth, for I can see beauty in your grey eyes. Once you have had a month of good food and, also, of Coupang's healthy climate, you will have all my soldiers in the fort looking at you.'

He turned to Will, who was deliberately keeping quiet, in case, in his exhausted state, he said something that would betray them.

'You are a fortunate man, sir, to have such a wife.'

'Yes, sir, Mr Vanion, sir,' he grunted. 'I know it. It's fortunate I am.'

'*Ja*, mistress, you will find the air – what was the strange word that

Captain Bligh used – salu–*salubrious.* Coupang is the favourite resort for invalids from Batavia and elsewhere. The flowers are – the word is "*luxuriant*". You, especially, will love them. As for the scenery, it is truly *magnificent*!'

His blue eyes suddenly clouded and he glanced at Charlotte in her mother's lap and the sleeping Emanuel in Will's.

'There are only two things to beware of. There is a – what is the word – *contagious* skin disease among the natives. There, also, are many snakes – whose poison is fatal.'

Mary bit her tongue. She'd almost blurted out, *In all those three year at Sydney Cove, we never had much trouble from poisonous snakes. But I'll never forget that officer's little old terrier that had a fight with a black'un and swelled and died in mortal agony, poor cratur.*

'Now, dear friends, my servant here will take you to your huts. There are two empty ones by the waterside. They were the–' he cleared his throat and briefly looked away. 'They were the homes of two native families but, unfortunately, the – er – the poor wretches no longer have need of them.'

Will Bryant sat bolt upright, looked at him sharply, then down at Emanuel. 'You – you don't mean?...'

'Do not fear, my good fellow. The insides have been smoked, cleaned, limewashed, then sponged with oil of tar. I can assure you that you will suffer no sickness from living there.'

He cleared his throat again. 'Now, there is the little matter of keeping ourselves alive. Food, I mean. You have had one meal…'

'Yes, sir,' said Mary, 'and that native honey were proper soothing for our sore throats, I can tell you, and all those lovely juicy fruits proper quenched our thirsts, and the fish were delicious.'

He beamed. 'Good, good… *Ja*, you have had one meal, which, of *course*, was with my compliments, but your future needs cannot be – how do you say – a drain on the public purse.'

Will smiled. 'Aw, don't you fret about that, your Excellency. We'll draw bills on the *British* Government – that is, till we get sorted, like.'

Timotheus Wanjon smiled back. 'And why not? Why not, indeed? But as for the kind of *work* that you can do… You were on a whaling ship… Could you not, um...'

'Yes, sir,' said the master seiner grinning. 'Some of us can help your busy settlement by doing a bit of fishing for you.' He turned to his companions, all of whom had suddenly looked away. 'Would anyone of you brave billies like to join Cap'n William Bryant on a little ol' fishing trip out on the pretty blue sea? I'll give you a present at Christmas, whoever does…'

Charlotte's tired eyes lit up at the word but not even she took the bait.

CHAPTER 54

Within a week, though, all the men except James Cox had decided to join the hard-working Will. James himself had already found plenty of ship's-carpentry jobs.

It wasn't just to ease their consciences. Hunger pangs would never be relieved on the pittance that the Dutch paid Will as a solo fisherman.

Even so, their joint income proved insufficient for their needs. All those weeks at sea, preceded by the years of near starvation, had left them with a hunger that was not easily satisfied.

And a thirst.

'We'll just have to keep drawin' bills on the British Government,' said a drunken Will to a barely sober Jimmy as they sat with Mary round the table in the Bryants' hut. It was Sunday evening, two weeks after Wanjon's welcome.

Jimmy grinned. 'Sure, 'tis only what they owe us after depriving us of our livelihood and liberty all these years.'

'Yes,' hiccupped the Cornishman, 'fishin' never did pay for the necessies – necessaries o' life. Like swacks o' this,' he scowled, tapping the empty rum bottle.

'Rum! *Rum!*' Mary flared at him. 'That's all you ever think of: bloody spirits! Some bloody Methody *you* be!'

The glazed eyes tried to focus on her.

'Stow yer clack, woman!' he thundered.

'I will not!' she shrilled. 'If it wasn't for smuggling spirits – *and* being drunk on the stuff – you wouldn't have been taken in that fight with the revenue men in Cornwall and you wouldn't be here now!'

'An' *you* wouldn' be screechin' in my ear like Ol' Scratch's daughter!'

Jimmy looked at the squalling children, woken from their sleep on the mattress.

They were under a beautiful woven blanket, vegetable-dyed in the earthy colours of yellow, orange, rust and red. The folks back at the Belfast dyeworks would have been delighted with it, he told himself. Made from cotton threads bound with vegetable fibres, it was the natives' warp *ikat*, where the decoration had been applied to vertical warp threads. It had been made, and lent to Mary, by the manservant's pretty little wife, who by gestures had explained the traditional motifs. The crocodiles symbolized the underworld, the birds the upper world and the tree of life the afterlife. Sure, they could have done without the bloody crocodiles.

Emanuel kicked himself free from the blanket.

'And Emanuel Bryant would never have been born,' murmured Jimmy.

This sobered Will enough for him to cast a knowing eye at his friend.

'So thank the good God for spirits, James Martin, Esquire. *She* got bosky on gin and snatched an old gal's bonnet and got transported, too, didn' she? Yiss, wi'out 'eaven-sent spirits, li'l ol' Emanuel would never ha' gi'en William Bryant immor – immor – immortality.'

He stumbled over to Emanuel and snatched him up. Mary was close behind and picked up her howling daughter. Then they returned with the children to the table and sat glaring at each other.

'Och well, gentle folk, 'tis time that auld Jimmy bade ye goodnight,' said the Irishman softly, easing open the door. Jeez, talk about a bickering couple, talk about 'chawing the rag', 'twould have required a braver man than Jimmy Martin to wish these two 'Sweet dreams'.

CHAPTER 55

Through July and August, Will's mood grew blacker as his rum intake increased.

'It's the on'y thing that keeps me sane in this heathen hellhole of an island,' he roared drunkenly, on this stormy Friday evening in late August. He seemed determined to make more noise than the Devil's thunder itself.

'Calm yerself, man…' breathed Jimmy, seated next to him at the Bryants' table.

It was just the three of them yet again. Fishing excepted, these days the others avoided this irascible Cornishman like the plague.

'… Sure, ye're louder than the Devil's dunner.'

The trembling Cornish girl clasped her friend's own shaking hands.

'You're wasting your breath, Jimmy. He won't be happy till the thunder scuddles off defeated.'

'Bitch,' rasped her husband. 'Will Bryant won't be happy till he's out o' this stinkin', suffocatin' part o' the world an' breathin' the sweet air of 'is beloved Cornish coast. He's 'ad a bellyful o' natives an' cheese-wormy Dutchmen. Those ign'rant *natives* are the worst; they never gi'e their jawin' tacks a rest. Save on'y for this storm, they'd be makin' a rare ol' caprouse outside the windey now. Satan's 'orns, they're *drowndin'* me wi' their chitter-chatter palaverin'! I'm up to 'ere wi' it, I tell 'ee!'

'Yes,' she muttered, 'we can see that, Will Bryant. Up to here with it, you sure are. Bloody spirits!'

Hurling the table aside, he raised his big hairy fist. Charlotte screamed and rushed to her mother's side. Jimmy leapt between Mary and Will.

'Out o' my way, Jimmy!' roared the Cornishman.

'No.'

'Out o' my bloody way! The bitch 'as got it comin' to her. She *dotes* on this Charlotte: another man's brat!'

Mary's bottom lip quivered. 'You *loved* Charlotte once: enough to marry me.'

'I never loved her. 'Twas *you* I wanted, Mary Broad, but I've always been made to feel in second place in your love.'

'Yes, you were always jealous of my Charlotte, weren't you? Jealous of a poor little *mite*, for mercy's sake! Oh, I've known for a brave long time that you only wanted me for one thing, Will Bryant. That first night ashore at Sydney Cove, I suspicioned that you were with some other woman, when you should've been looking after me. Jimmy may be able to blarney Mr Vanion, but I knew Jimmy too well and I never really believed him that you'd been put in one of the other tents at t'other side of the stream. But it was your words after the marriage ceremony that pierced my heart like as if they were native spears, and have never left me for a single dang minute since. "I don't regard a marriage in this plaguy place as legally binding, because the banns weren't read." Yes, once we've got back to Cornwall, you'll be wenching again. The Lelant trulls must be missing proper terrible your brandy breath filling their flared nostrils.'

Jimmy caught Will's right arm as his fist flew. Mary grabbed his left. Charlotte kicked his left ankle. Then the right. Too fuddled to resist, he was propelled to the door. Jimmy opened it and flung him outside, where he fell face down into the mud. The Irishman darted back in, slamming then bolting the door.

'Rot an' perish you both!' bellowed Will, while the lightning flashed. 'I won't waste my strength on smashin' it down 'cos you ain' worth it, but you'll be sorry for what you've said an' done to William Bryant. You'll be sorry; just you wait an' see.'

The thunder boomed its agreement.

CHAPTER 56

An hour later Mary, Charlotte and Jimmy nearly choked on their bread and cheese. 'Open this door!' The voice was not Will's. The thud of a musket butt caused the door – and the three eaters – to shake.

'Open this door, James Martin!'

Jimmy looked at Mary fearfully and gulped down the half-chewed mouthful. Easing out his chair, he slowly rose. Charlotte's tiny knuckles were white in the candlelight as she gripped her mother's yellow sleeve.

He slid open the bolt.

A stern young officer stood here in the gloom with two armed privates. The fellow was blond, handsome and strong looking and he towered over the little Irishman.

'James Martin, you are under arrest. Mary Bryant, you, also, are under arrest. Your friends have already been arrested.'

'W–what for?' spluttered Jimmy, the breadcrumbs catching him.

Mary's heart raced. Charlotte followed her as she got up from the table and stood behind the Irishman.

'In the name of God, why?' asked the Cornish girl, partly hidden by Jimmy. 'What's he talking about, Jimmy?'

'Only the good Lord knows, darlin'. Pray explain, sir.'

'Your countryman, William Bryant, who is now a prisoner in the fort, has told us everything.'

Mary's heart fluttered.

'Everything about what?' demanded James Martin, Esquire. 'Be plain, sir. 'Tis double Dutch ye're talking.'

The blue eyes hardened. 'Do not play games with me, Martin. Your drunk friend has told us everything about your escape from the British colony. You have deceived His Excellency and abused his hospitality.'

Mary squeezed in front of Jimmy, and the Dutchman saw her clearly for the first time, and her tight yellow frock.

'We'm worked damned hard since we'm been here! My life, all them fishin' nets I've mended for 'ee! We'm done no wrong against *Dutch* law.'

The steely eyes softened, even holding the hint of a smile.

'I find it a little difficult to understand your particular kind of English, Mistress Bryant. Your voyage to Timor was an epic one, in the finest traditions of your nation. Your own and your companions' bravery is an example to us all. Because of that, His Excellency does not intend to treat you people as common criminals. He will, therefore, let you go out of the fort, for exercise, two at a time for one day, and another two the next day, and so it will continue until he decides what to do with you. Now, get your baby and follow me, please.'

CHAPTER 57

On this steamy Monday morning in mid-September Mary, Will and family, and Jimmy and the rest, were escorted to the commander's office. An English naval captain had arrived at Coupang and wished to see them.

Mary and Will were still living together, in a small room in the fort, but 'dammit' if she'd ever let him make love to her again. At least he had no money for drink, now that he was no longer working. They rarely spoke, for what was there to talk about? Their marriage was over. She was Mary Broad again.

The convict girl's stomach shrank as she looked down at this black-haired, crimson-faced, thick-necked officer sitting with the fat commander at the desk. The Englishman, who was about fifty, had the Devil's own coal-black eyes, and her right cheek started twitching madly as if one of Old Scratch's imps had suddenly sneaked inside it.

'I am Captain Edward Edwards,' he growled, thrusting two fingers down the collar of his tight shirt in a vain attempt to ease the discomfort. 'I came from England in the frigate HMS *Pandora* to search for the *Bounty* pirates and to take them home in chains to undergo the punishment due to their demerits. I arrived at Tahiti on the twenty-third of March. There I succeeded in arresting fourteen of the sixteen piratical dogs that had remained, after Fletcher Christian – damn his eyes – and his eight cronies had left six months earlier.

'Unfortunately, after dark on the evening of the twenty-eighth of August, south of New Guinea, while trying to get through the Labyrinth, that great barrier of New Holland reefs, my poor *Pandora* had her bottom torn from her. Ten of the prisoners survived and helped row me and my surviving crew to Coupang. Including the pirates, there were ninety-nine of us in a longboat, pinnace and two yawls.

'Now as for you scoundrels, I've heard the commanding officer's side of the story; what is yours?'

Jimmy Martin stepped forward smartly, the disgraced Will no longer having the others' trust to speak on their behalf. The Irishman nervously cleared his throat but looked Edwards in the eye.

'If you plaise, sor.' The accent was exaggerated. 'We're after escapin' from Sydney Cove in the dear Guv'nor's eighteen-foot, six-oared cutter and survivin' a journey near as long – and every bit as dangerous – as Cap'n Bligh's when dat poor gentleman was turned off into the *Bounty*'s great big *twenty-tree*-foot launch and himself sailed to Timor. I'm tellin' you, sor, our achievement was almost as heroic as yer man's. We –'

Captain Edwards's crimson face turned purple. 'You damn deserting bilge rats! How dare you compare your despicable selves with an officer of His Britannic Majesty's navy!'

Jimmy stole a glance over his shoulder and Mary caught the twinkle in his bright-blue eyes.

'Sure, we would never *dream* of doin' such a terrible ting, sor. The poor misfortunate soul has had enough blows to his pride, without havin' the achievement that's enabled him to hold his head high agin – one of the grandest-ever feats of navigation – rivalled by a motley crew like us! Perish such a terrible tawt! You were too quick, sor. I said "*almost* as heroic".'

Mary and the rest of the 'motley crew' sniggered.

'Dammit, *silence*, you insolent villains! By God, I'll wipe the grins from your faces. To cap it all, you had the infernal impudence to draw bills on His Majesty's Government and were supplied with every "necessary" – including rum!

'Well,' he said, 'you are now *my* prisoners. I'll leave you in the fort until I'm able to charter a vessel to Batavia and take you and the pirates with me, but you'll no longer be permitted to go for walks. And, once aboard, you won't be going for walks on deck either, because your ankles will be shackled. Aye, 'tis the bilboes for you, you *scum*! God damn your blood!'

CHAPTER 58

'Lord help us if this small sh-sh-ship sinks like the plaguy *Pandora*,' shuddered James Cox, miserably contemplating his shackled ankles.

With the last prisoner secured to the long iron bar, old Will Moulter, bosun's mate, locked it to the lower deck boards of the *Rembamg* brig, which Edwards had hired from the Dutch East India Company.

' You can say that again, lad,' grunted this grey-haired little fellow, struggling up beside the convict girl, standing with the children in her arms. 'Cap'n Edwards is a mortal hard man. After our *Pandora* struck that spiky reef and was in her death throes, some of your fellow passengers 'ere was still in "Pandora's Box", a closed-in wooden coffin of a lockup on the quarterdeck, and the sea was pouring in it. If it hadn't been for me doing my Methodist Christian duty and risking my life by unbolting the scuttle in the roof – lifting the lid off "Pandora's Box" – when I should've been leaping overboard, they wouldn't have been saved.

'*Would* you, Mr Midshipman Heywood from the Isle of Man? Aye, this Three-Legs-of-Man tattoo that the Tahitian islanders did on your right leg nearly made an interesting picture for the fishes to puzzle over, didn't it, boy? An interesting picture before it disappeared past the spiky teeth of a shark, who'd have ripped your prison open!'

James shuddered even more and Mary studied this brown-eyed, baby-faced midshipman with the long light-brown hair who was shackled beside the other mutineers at the far end of the bar.

'No, I wouldn't have been saved, Mr Moulter,' croaked Heywood, 'and I thank you yet again. But if the court-martial decides against me, then it'll be a matter of merely exchanging one form of suffocation for another: a hanging *above* the water instead of a drowning *in* the water.'

'Well, lad, you shouldn't have joined in the mutiny, should you? 'Twill be the Lord's judgement if you *are* hung: giving in to the temptations of the flesh, the lure of them Pacific island maidens, instead of fulfilling your duties to your king and country.'

'I swear on the life of my ever-honoured and dearest mother that I had nothing to do with the mutiny! It is a gross aspersion! I'm a friend of both Captain Bligh and his wife and they've been very good to me. Peter Heywood is not that vile wretch, void of all gratitude, which the world has the unkindness to think of him. He's a young man of strict honour who, at the tender age of sixteen years, had the misfortune to...' His voice trailed off with exhaustion.

Moulter turned to Mary and stroked Charlotte's curls, then tickled Emanuel's bare belly. Both mites smiled up at his friendly hazel eyes.

'Mistress Bryant, if calamity strikes the *Rembang*, too, God willing I'll rush down 'ere and help you and your children and mates to escape.'

'God bless you, Mr Moulter,' murmured Mary, kissing his grey stubble and saying a silent prayer of thanks that she was to stay unchained, but fretting herself silly about these dear, darling men with whom she had been through so much. *Yes, even you, Will, damn you. Even you, Will Bryant!*

The stormy season had started early, and tomorrow, Thursday 6 October, the *Rembang* was setting sail across more than a thousand miles of tempestuous seas to Batavia, Java. True, Dutchmen were good sailors, and this was a ship, not a six-oared cutter like the *Beauty* – Lord bless and preserve her at Coupang. But at least in the *Beauty*, 'Captain' William Bryant and the experienced sailors in his crew had been able to use all the seafaring skills that God had given them and saved themselves. With their feet in shackles, England's 'epic voyagers' would be as helpless as the gurgling Emanuel here as he and they gurgled away their lives.

CHAPTER 59

'Mummy, Mummy, Charlotte can't stand up!' screamed the terrified child, falling onto her mother's face. Mary herself was sitting wedged between the ship's larboard side and the bulkhead.

The *Rembang* was well on her way to Batavia but would surely never make it there.

'Damn the world!' raged the bearded Cornishman. 'We're being smashed by a dang tempest! Every sail will be shivered to pieces!'

Water was pouring in through the gaps in the hatch and spurting through the sides.

'Mercy on us!' shrieked James Cox, 'the bilge water's coming up through the boards! We'll go to the bottom this time and drown like rats. Edwards called us "b-b-bilge rats" and that's just what we are now. Will Moulter! *Will Moulter!* Cap'n Edwards! Please tell Moulter to come down an' unlock us, for mercy's s-s-sake!'

John Butcher laughed scornfully. 'You're a-wasting your breath, look you. Moulter be under orders, and Edwards canna even hear us with all this ravenin' an' roarin' thunder. Law, what a belownder!'

Sam spat into the swirling water. 'Even if bloody Edwards could 'ear us, he's got other fings on 'is mind; same as when he left Heywood and 'is mates in *Pandora*'s bloody box.'

'Mummy, the water's wetting Charlotte's leggies... 'Tis wetting Charlotte's *knees*! 'Tis *drowndin*' 'em!'

'Don't you fret, my sweet'art. After all those wet weeks on the *Beauty*, you should be used to it by now.'

Jimmy stretched across and patted Charlotte's curls.

'Mary,' he grunted, 'Will Moulter said just a wee while ago that we were only seven miles from the shore of a beautiful island called Flores: The Isle of Flowers. Sure, it sounds like a place after yer own heart, darlin'. Captain Edwards won't have any trouble in putting in there until the storm's over.'

'Won't have any trouble?' snorted Will. 'Won't have any *trouble*? Dang me, you bufflehead, I thought you knew a bit more about the sea these days, after all we've been through together. Didn't you hear what else Moulter said? There're high surfs. It's a lee shore and she's driving down on it so fast, it's as if she can't wait to destroy herself, and us with her!'

'Yes,' shuddered Mary, 'and it's a devilish place. Did you all hear what else Will Moulter said…'

She clapped her hands over Charlotte's ears.

'… That the islanders sacrifice children there? When a house is being built, they kill a poor little mite and bury it under a corner post, for good luck!'

'Will Moulter, help us!' croaked James Cox. 'Help us, for pity's – hey, look!'

The hatch had been flung open and the gloom was brightened by a flash of lightning. It was soon followed by an almighty explosion of thunder: so loud that Mary's eardrums must surely burst. A man was hurrying down. Moulter? Lightning flashed again, to reveal not the grey hairs of old Will but the blond ones of a terror-crazed young Dutch sailor.

More panicking Dutchmen came, until there were a dozen huddled down here.

'Get back *up*, you cowardly curs,' rasped Will. 'The poor ol' gal can't save her*self.* Get back up and help our British tars, you Dutch cheese-worms. Scared of a little thunder an' lightning, are you? Satan's horns, the Dutch are supposed to be a great nation of seafardingers like us. Lord knows how old Tasman would have managed if he'd had *you* aboard. Rot me, Charlotte here's braver than you, you big gals!'

Another flash lit up the terrified blue eyes of a seaman of about seventeen who certainly looked even more frightened than Charlotte. But fear is as contagious as plague and, seeing such terror in the eyes of a grown up, the child screamed hysterically, burying her face in Mummy's skirt.

'Aw, dear God,' groaned the convict girl, 'how much more? Ain't we suffered enough?'

'Och, be of stout heart, me darlin',' said Jimmy, whose pinched, and again bearded, face had been briefly illuminated as a sickly green. 'Don't listen to Will. Our Captain Bryant's getting to be a real fretting-belly in his auld age. 'Tis the wearisome, lonesome pressures of command: being a nursemaid to us lot all these months, like poor auld Tasman. Sure, the *Rembang* won't sink or be wrecked. We've weathered worse storms in the *Beauty*, ain't we? The Lord's brought us *this* far, first in the Brave *Beauty* and now aboard the Resolute *Rembang*, and He won't desert us now. Aye, in a week or three, we'll be safe in Bonny Batavia.'

There was sarcasm in his voice as he went on, "Tis a grand place, so the dear Captain Tench told me. He recalled that Captain Cook, Lord rest his soul, once wrote that he believed the unwholesome air of that city-on-a-swamp caused the deaths of more Europeans than any other place of the same extent on this earth. Och, 'tis a veritable graveyard for Europeans: the Batavian Boneyard. So the story goes, the whole sickly-faced Dutch settlement is buried and gone after every five years and must needs be replaced by a new bunch of fresh-faced fools, who'll end up as grinning skulls, too, in due time.

'And mind well, that Lieutenant Ball of the *Supply* was ill himself, and lost many of his crew, from Batavian fever, and also had to leave several others in the hospital there, who all eventually died, except Mr Midshipman Ormsby. And, later, when Captain Smit of the *Waaksamheyd* reached Sydney Cove from Batavia, he told us *he'd* had to bury sixteen of his own Malay crew at sea, who'd caught the fever. Jeez, d'ye remember the ravaged scarecrow figure of young Ormsby, who Smit'd brought back? D'ye remember him staggering from the wharf to the Governor's house? Ormsby had once been such a strong, handsome lad: the very picture of virility, bless his boils. The poor misfortunate–'

'Oh, stow it, Jimmy!' everyone yelled.

CRASH!

'That's part of a mast gone,' muttered Will. 'And these dang leaks are gaining fast, look. It's too much for the pumps to cope with. Choked they are, choked and useless. Dear *Christ*! I wish I was up there helping our tars!"

'What good would that do?' groaned James Cox. 'We're doomed this time, we're doomed.'

'Will Bryant, I'm coming for you!' Moulter was swaying by the hatch. 'We'll need every man jack to get these pumps working again, so Cap'n Edwards has ordered me to free you all, including the mutineers.'

'Praise be,' sighed the Cornishman, 'praise be.'

* * *

They took their turn at the pumps and, on collapsing with exhaustion, were put in leg-irons on a sail soaked with the drainings of a pigsty, under which it was spread. Even before the strength had returned to these tortured arms, the shackles were removed and the prisoners resumed their seemingly impossible task.

But this day, Will Bryant and his fellows helped the British tars save the *Rembang* from destruction.

CHAPTER 60

'Oh, me por swollen an' bleedin' ol' ankles!' Sam Bird sucked in his breath as Will Moulter unlocked the shackles on arrival at Batavia.

Yes, Batavia… Batavia. The convict girl still could not believe it. *Safe,* she told herself, *safe at anchor in Batavia roadstead. Jimmy was right about the passage, bless his blisters. Saved by the British tars!*

'You won't get no release from pain 'ere, mate,' grunted Moulter, helping the cockney to his shaky feet. 'These ankles will stay purple and bleeding, I'm afraid, because Cap'n Edwards is having you all stowed in a Dutch guard-ship lying in the roadstead, until he can find a vessel bound for Europe. Because of them terrible storms, we've arrived 'ere too late to catch the October fleet to Europe, it being the seventh of pesty November now. And just to cheer you even more, the west monsoon is due, and such a wind will cause the guard-ship to curvet about like a mare with a thorn under her saddle!'

'Damn his black eyes!' hissed Will as his own shackles were undone.

'Don't let him hear you say that, brother Methodist,' murmured Moulter, 'or that murderous devil will shut yours for ever!'

* * *

'My babby's not well, Will,' sobbed Mary, waking from a fitful sleep on the guard-ship's lower deck, in the early hours of this first day in December. 'Will, wake up! It's so suffocating that the poor little boy can't get his life's breath!'

Even with this fiendish wind and the endless monsoon rain, the air here in Batavia stank to heaven. The violently swaying lantern cast a ghastly glow onto the shackled men's skull-like faces.

'Just look at the poor mite; he's shivering proper terrible but the sweat's pouring from him. And… and… *Jesus God!* He's going blue!'

'What's that you say, woman?' gasped Will, fully awake now and wrenching at the fetters, like a lunatic. 'Give me my boy!' he cried, thrusting out his shaking bony hands. 'Give him to me!'

Gently, oh so gently, she crawled across from her corner and handed him this precious little twenty-month-old mortal, whose tiny Cornish heart had resisted everything that the ingeniously cruel sea and sky could think to hurl at him. Yes, all that long, exhausting way from Sydney Cove, this frail, starved baby, who'd only had his mother's milk for the first two months of life, had come through healthier than any of them. When they'd reached Timor, she and Will had marvelled at their son and said that, if he survived to adulthood, what a strong and handsome man he would be.

Terrible groans filled the deck as the Cornishman rocked his beloved Emanuel. 'Aw no, merciful God, no! Don't leave my boy die. He's my future. My immortality! Through him I shall live far into the nineteenth century, and through *his* sons an' grandsons an' great-grandsons I'll go on into the twentieth and beyond. Every night of this cussed existence I've dreamed of the day when I'll learn him to sail an' fish. O God, don't You leave my Emanuel die! Don't leave him die!'

'Will Moulter!' yelled Jimmy. 'Come down, will ye? Hurry, for the love of Jesus! The baby's took bad! The baby's mighty sick! We've been down here for more'n three weeks now and the poor wee chile's dying in this stifling stench, d'ye hear me? He's dying in this stinking hole! Moulter! *Moulter!* Hurry, for Christ's sake! Moulter!'

Mary and everyone else joined in, and, at last, the tired old seaman's brown feet slowly descended the creaking steps.

'What's the matter, for goodness' sake?' he puffed. 'The cap'n will have my guts for sausage skins if you carry on like this. He told me that you'd feel the cat if you got mutinous, like.'

'My poor b-b-babby's dyin',' wailed Mary, scarcely able to breathe herself. 'Take a… look at the poor li'l mite an' you'll see. His…his poor li'l face's goin' all blue an' bloated... There's an 'orspital in Batavia. Can you take him there, for pity's sake? You're a Christian man. Help me!'

Moulter took the lantern from the slimy beam, then eased his old bones onto the boards. He shone the light close to Emanuel's shrivelled face. The shivering had stopped. This tiny mouth was wide open now; so were the eyes, these unblinking dark-brown eyes.

The old mariner looked along the line of prisoners at Bill Allen, a man of his own age, and their weary eyes stayed on each other's.

'Did you hear me?' screeched Mary, pummelling Moulter's stringy arm. 'Did you hear what I said?'

Old Bill turned from shaking his head sadly at Moulter to giving 'Unca' Jimmy a meaningful glance. Jimmy Martin understood.

So did Mary.

'No! *No!*'

'I'm so very sorry, my poor, poor love,' said Will Moulter, kneading her shoulder. 'He's not quite gone yet, but I've lost six babies of my own, so I know this little lad's beyond any mortal's help. He'll soon be with the Lord Jesus, my poor dear. I'm so very sorry, Bryant... I'll ask the cap'n to let you take Emanuel to hospital, Mary, but it'll do no good.'

The lantern was swinging crazily, thought Mary. Or was it the deck swaying? Everything was swimming and swirling and the lantern went out.

CHAPTER 61

Mary had wanted to curl up in the corner, against the bulkhead, and die, to be with her little fellow for all eternity. Never to see those beautiful dark-brown eyes again. Never to see that lovely smile. Never to hear his delighted gurgling when she'd tickled his belly. Never to have him grip her finger, using his little man's strength. Never to see his character develop from those funny baby ways of his. It was impossible to believe that she would never see any of this again. Impossible to believe that his dear little head had now joined the 'grinning skulls' in 'the Batavian Boneyard'.

Yes, she had wanted to curl up and die, and surely would have done but for Jimmy. And Charlotte. This truly amazing child seemed to have found even more hidden strength. Though pining for her brother and praying for Lord Jesus to send him back soon, she had become a little mother to Mary, bringing food and water and holding her limp hands. At first Mary had only sipped the water and left the food. But with the persistent encouragement of Charlotte and Jimmy, after two – or was it three – days she managed a few mouthfuls of bread and honey.

As for Will. He'd already aged ten years since leaving England, the boat journey had stripped the remaining flesh away, and this new imprisonment, made unbearable by Emanuel's passing, was turning her husband into a wizened old man.

And now, the ravings had increased and he was shivering, though the sweat was pouring from him. Despite her own despair, Mary crawled over and wiped his throbbing temples with the sleeves of her filthy yellow frock. Then she pressed the tin mug to his white, quivering lips, but he would not – indeed, could not – drink.

'Will Moulter!' Jimmy shouted hoarsely. '*Will Moulter!* Will Bryant's mortal sick down here with the Batavian fever. Tell Captain

Edwards the poor man needs the hospital or, be Jasus, we'll have another corpse for the boneyard!'

* * *

Mary had discovered that she, like her daughter, had hidden strength. Leaving Charlotte in Jimmy's arms, the convict girl, with Will Moulter and two English tars, carried Will in a wagon the short distance to the Dutch East India Company's hospital, where Emanuel had breathed his last tiny breath.

This hospital was in an unhealthy part. The bustling, walled city was delightful to the *eye*, the imposing Dutch buildings forming straight, tree-lined streets with canals running through most of them. Delightful to the eye but offensive to the nose. More so when, as now, the tide was low in these mosquito-breeding canals.

Moulter had wanted to take the Cornishman to the large, airy country hospital for seamen, four miles away. But though the old mariner had pleaded passionately with Edwards, the captain had refused to seek the Governor-General's leave to lodge the patient where he would have a far better chance of recovery.

* * *

In spite of the tireless efforts of Mr Aansorp, the head surgeon, and his staff, Will Bryant died eighteen days later, on Thursday 22 December. After breaking the news to Mary aboard ship, Will Moulter returned her to the hospital to say farewell to the dead master seiner on his final voyage.

An hour later, back at the spice warehouses along the harbour, as Will Moulter helped her down from the wagon, Mary suddenly realized that she still hadn't cried. She couldn't, because she had shed all her tears for her dearest Emanuel. Perhaps she would have shed none in any case… And yet… yet this man whose heart was silenced for ever had once held her to a wildly pounding one, when he'd comforted her on the *Dunkirk* after that animal's ravishment. This poor dead Cornishman had given her the beautiful Emanuel. This clever ol' mariner had fulfilled his promise of bringing them all safely across more than three thousand miles of ocean and sea. She could not love the man and yet neither could she hate him. She had no feelings; she was utterly drained of everything. So numb, oh so numb.

Charlotte and Jimmy kissed her on her return to the lower deck. Jimmy Martin said nothing, knowing her too well. She crawled between the shackled James and Jimmy and rested her head on the Irishman's bare, bony chest. He put an arm round her, and Charlotte snuggled in with them.

'Don' be sad, Mummy; Jimmy says 'tis Chrismiss on Sunday.'

CHAPTER 62

On the afternoon of New Year's Eve, old Will Moulter told Mary that she was to be denied even Jimmy's comfort. He was to be put aboard the Dutch East Indiaman *Hoornwey*, with Nat, John, Sam and Bill Morton. Mary, Charlotte and Old Bill would be sailing on the *Horssen*. Poor James Cox would be with Captain Edwards and the *Bounty* mutineers on the *Vreedenberg*. And where would Will Moulter himself be in this small Cape-bound fleet? On the *Horssen*, too, was his pleasing reply.

* * *

At dusk, as this endless – pitiless – monsoon rain danced wildly on the guard-ship's rail, mother and daughter said their tearful goodbyes to the temporarily unfettered bearded Irishman. He was about to start his torturous climb down to the tossing longboat.

'So, Jimmy, we're bound for the Cape of Good Hope. The Cape of No Hope's a betterer name, I'm a-thinking.'

'Ah, whist, Mary,' he smiled, giving her cheek a tender kiss, then winced as he stooped to pick up Charlotte and give her one, too. 'Hush now. 'Tis not like ye to talk like this.'

'She's right,' muttered Sam Bird, squinting through the long, greasy black hair plastered over his own bearded face. 'Wot 'ope is there for us when we get back 'ome? There won't be no pretty gels putting garlands of flowers round *our* necks to welcome us, like wot Fletcher Christian an' 'is *Bounty* mutineers got on Tahiti. As escaped convicts, Jack Ketch's halter's the only fing we'll get round our necks when we get back to Ol' England. 'Appy New Year, 1792!'

'If we even get that f-f-far,' stammered James Cox, gaping at the rain-lashed waves flinging the longboat against the ship's side. 'Jack Ketch's halter? Davy Jones's locker might still get us f-f-first.'

* * *

'What's all the shouting about, Bill?' asked the drenched convict girl on this New Year's Day evening as the *Horssen* followed the *Vreedenberg* through the Straits of Sunda. They were sailing along the channel between the Thwartway Island coral reefs and the Java coast. Though the monsoon rain was still gushing from the black sky, Will Moulter was carrying out Captain Edwards's order: that the convicts should be freed from their shackles and exercised without fail for the half-hour before nightfall.

'Heaven only knows, love,' replied Old Bill.

Almost everyone on deck was tottering towards the stern rail. Despite this shrieking sou'wester's blowing the stinging torrent into their faces, Mary and Old Bill, clutching the staggering Charlotte between them, struggled to join the throng.

Will Moulter was already here.

'Will!' yelled Mary. The wind snatched away the word and he did not hear. '*Will!*' she bellowed, gripping the rail with her left hand. 'What's all the shouting about?'

He grabbed her dripping sleeve. 'Look! Thirty yards astern. Some poor mortal's fallen overboard from the *Vreedenberg*, but the sea's too rough for her to launch a boat to rescue him. And *we* can't get no closer because of the coral rocks.'

'Where is he?' asked Old Bill. 'Where is he, for the Lor's sake? With this monsoon rain and it being almost dark, oi can't see nothing. My eyes are a mite better but they ain't what they used to be.'

Will Moulter pointed. 'Just over there: about to be swamped by that huge whitecap! See?... Oh goodness... I do believe...'

Mary had seen him now: a sandy-haired fellow.

'Dear life! Aw, dear life!' She gripped the rail even tighter. 'James,' she choked. 'James!'

'Lor' Christ!' gasped Old Bill. 'Close your eyes, Mary, gal, and bury Charlotte's face in your skirt. Poor James is drowning!'

'Mummy!... *Mummy!* Be James really a-drowndin'? Be nice Unca James really a-*drowndin*?'

'Aw, my dear love, you mustn't look.' She covered the child's face, then pressed her own against Bill's heaving wet chest and said a silent prayer. *Not James, Lord. Not poor James. He's been with us right from the very start, back on the* Dunkirk. *Please don't let him die! He always knew he'd die this way. He always said he'd– O Lord, help him! Help him, for mercy's sake!*

Even with the wind's howling and the rain's rattling, they could hear his terrible screams, which made Bill's hammering heart race hers. Almost as soon as they'd heard them, though, the screams stopped. The carpenter and *his* heart would never hammer again.

In a daze, she realized that she was descending the lower deck steps, Bill following with the now-shrieking Charlotte in his arms.

'Aw, Bill. He must have *fallen* overboard, because he surely wouldn't have jumped, being as how he is – was – so mortal scared of the sea. He *must* have fallen...'

At the bottom, Bill laid Charlotte on the boards, then held Mary at arm's length, and here the shivering pair stood, lurching against the slimy side.

Sadly he gazed into her streaming eyes and sniffed loudly.

'Mary love... Poor James knew that, as he'd escaped from his lawful punishment in New South Wales, he could expect no mercy in England. No more'n you nor I can. He'd already cheated the gallows twice, first for stealing cotton stockings and thread lace, then for the *Mercury* mutiny. He knew he wouldn't cheat it a third toime. Of course, it could be that nobody aboard the *Vreedenberg* actually *saw* him go overboard, and then we'll never know for *certain* whether he fell because of this mighty monsoon wind or whether he deliberately took his own loife. But he's had that ghastly haunted look ever since Will told Vanion that we were escaped convicts. Yes,' sighed the old man, 'somehow oi think he took his own loife, poor boy.' He whispered, 'The sharks'll hev him now, sure enough.'

She shuddered violently. 'Thank the Lord poor Sarah ain't here… Aw, Bill, we're all going, one by one, ain't we? We were all so full of hope once.'

'Yes, gal,' he sighed again. 'Oh, James, James! Why did yew do it, boy? Why did yew do it? While there's loife there's hope.'

Savagely she wiped her eyes with her clenched fist.

'Jesus *God*! How many more of us'll die before we reach Old England? How many more?'

CHAPTER 63

The young Dutch officer was at the starboard rail. He'd just supervised the latest sea burial: the latest of the many men who had died from the Batavian fever, now rampant in all three ships. Mary and Charlotte staggered across and stood swaying next to him.

He pushed his fair hair from a troubled brow.

'Ah, Bryant, I have news for you from the *Hoornwey*...'

His soft brown eyes looked away.

'... Bad, I am sorry to say...'

Her heart froze.

He swallowed, stuck out his strong chin, then faced her again.

'... Two more of your friends also have died.'

Her skin crawled and her belly shrivelled to a tight knot. She clutched his blue sleeve.

'J-Jimmy? Not – not Jimmy?'

'Jimmy? What is his other name? I do not know their first names.'

'J-Jimmy Martin?...'

'Martin? Martin. *Ja*, I –'

The words were like punches to her heart. She couldn't breathe. She looked at Charlotte. Did the child understand what was being said? Jimmy... *Aw, no, not dear Jimmy... This really is the end. This –*

'*Nee*, Bryant.' The Dutchman pressed her icy hand. '*Nee*, I got it wrong. It is Morton, not Martin... *Ja*, Morton.' He smiled weakly, embarrassed. 'These English names are confusing, *nee*? The other man's name was Bird – an easy one to...'

Relief swept over her like a warm wind. Trembling, she swept up Charlotte and squeezed her.

'Mummy, be Jimmy fine?'

'Yes, my beauty, my sweet'art, Jimmy's mighty fine. 'Tain't Jimmy, thank the good Lord, it's –'

She checked herself, realizing that she was glad it was the skeletal Bill Morton – a terrible thing to be glad about! Poor Bill, he'd been their navigator: their guiding star. Without him, none of them might ever have reached Coupang. Poor, dear, quietly spoken 'bonny lad'…

And poor old Sam. He had been a miserable beggar, but a brave one, like all her comrades. He'd forever been grumbling and groaning, with his skinny face much miffled. But Jimmy had told her, with a grin, that it was 'just his way: part of the oul sceach's lovableness'. The Irishman would miss him. So would John Butcher, the other 'bloody foreigner'. Poor Sam.

CHAPTER 64

On Sunday 18 March, the ships anchored in Table Bay at the Cape of Good Hope. Up on deck for their evening exercise, Mary lifted Charlotte to show her the white mist rolling down the mountain at dusk.

'See? The white tablecloth's being spread over Table Mountain. Like the white linen one I told you about that dear Miss Hannah Treeby had in Plymouth, England – hey, I wonder whether Miss Treeby's cloth had been handled by Jimmy's family at the linen works in Ireland. Now, there's a thought. It's a beautiful tablecloth, ain't it?'

'Iss, Mummy, 'tis *bleached*, like they dingo bones lone agone.' The child smiled. ''Tis being laid for supper. Supper... Dang me, 'tis making me have belly grumbles!'

'Yes, I can hear 'em… You know, it's nearly four-an'-a-half year since you and me were here, my lover. We were up on the *Charlotte's* quarterdeck, and the Reverend Mr Johnson sprinkled your head with water and spoke your name so that everyone knew you were one of Lord Jesus's children.'

'Jesus d'love me, don' 'e, Mummy?'

'Yes, my sweet'art,' grunted Mary, setting her down.

Table Mountain, mused the convict girl, *misty and mystical mountain of no hope. You saw me sail off to New South Wales and now you're seeing me return to my doom in Old England.*

* * *

The noon sun of the following Friday saw Mary, Charlotte and Bill Allen being taken aboard the frigate HMS *Gorgon* which had arrived from New South Wales nearly a fortnight before.

Old Bill could barely lift one swollen, bleeding foot above the other but this proud Norfolk mariner was determined to climb the entryport steps himself and do so in an upright manner. Mary was struggling, too, behind him, Charlotte under her arm.

'Yes, woe's my old bones, Mary love, but damme if oi'll *crawl* before that swine Edwards, smirking up there on the quarterdeck,' he gasped, finally reaching the top.

'Bless you, ol' fella,' she panted, thankfully putting Charlotte down on the upper deck boards. 'Glory be, look'ee there! The deck's stowed to the rails with caged animals and birds! Look, Charlotte!'

'Iss, Mummy! There's a 'roo – an' over there's 'nother one! An', look'ee, there's possums! –an' cockies!…'

Bill wheezed. 'An' that ain't all, Mary. Look up on the quarterdeck. Ha, methinks surgeon John White had a deal to do with all o' this. Look, 'tis *full* o' shrubs an' plants.'

'Yes, a pretty picture,' she muttered, 'but spoiled by Edwards's scowling red mug among 'em. God, I wish that tight shirt that Vanion gave him would choke him, damn his black –'

Her heart skipped a beat.

'Dear life,' she gulped. 'Look over yonder, on *this* deck. Just look who's over there… among the party of marines!'

The old man followed her eyes. By the larboard rail were three marine officers exercising their jawing tackle.

'Good Lor', Mary! Good *Lor*! Sergeant Scott and –'

'Cap'n Watkin Tench,' she breathed. 'Have our fortunes changed at last, Bill? Aw, pray God they have… The other one's Lieutenant Ralph Clark,' she muttered, 'who I told you about.'

Clark was holding a crying baby and gave it to a young blonde woman, decently dressed in a cotton-check frock. A fretting little blond boy of three or four was clutching her hand.

Mary gasped. 'That's Mary Branham, one of the *Penhryn* women. That's her boy, William, by William Curtis, a *Penhryn* seaman. She went to Norfolk Island on the *Sirius* at the same time as Clark. Her term must have expired. Gor, she's had Clark's baby… Ralph, you dirty devil. And he always looked down his nose at us "damned bitches". Well, well, well… Well I'm damned… What will "dearest Betsey" say?'

Tench had seen them now and, breaking off the conversation, strode across. His friendly bright-blue eyes shone delightedly in the brilliant sunlight.

'Welcome aboard, Mary Bryant. By my stars, how this pretty Charlotte has grown – despite her ordeal!' He curled the child's matted hair round his long, womanish fingers. 'Welcome aboard, Allen.'

'Thank yew, sir,' beamed Bill, touching his grey forelock. 'Boo'ful day.'

'Yes, thank 'ee, sir,' smiled Mary, who had blushed as soon as she'd seen Watkin, dammit! 'Charlotte, you – you remember Cap'n Tench, don't you?'

''Iss, Mummy. He were a *good* man – not like that swine Edwards!'

'Hush, brat,' grinned Tench, tickling her chin, making her wriggle and giggle. 'The captain will clap you in irons – young as you are!'

'I don' care!' she screeched. 'Tis true, 'tis true! 'Tis *true*!'

He stroked her hair and lifted her quivering chin.

'I see you've lost none of your spirit, Charlotte. Takes after you, Mary Bryant, no doubt about it. By the way…'

His tone was gentle as he gripped Mary's shoulders. Her whole body thrilled strangely.

'… I was deeply saddened to hear about your stout-hearted husband and little Emanuel. Captain Edwards has given us a full report about you all. I was also saddened to hear of the deaths of your brave friends.'

'Th-thank 'ee, sir,' she mumbled, biting her trembling lip.

'May I say this to you people? I *pity* you. But I also *admire* you, for your astonishing achievement. You miscarried in a heroic struggle for liberty, after having combatted every hardship and conquered every difficulty. In truth, it is a strange combination of circumstances which has brought us together again. God's my life, it baffles human foresight and compounds human speculation!'

'It do, sir,' said Mary. 'That ain't no word of a lie... *Whatever* it means!'

He held her at arm's length and looked into her eyes.

'Mary Bryant, you have been starved of female company for a year – save your pretty daughter, of course. You know some of the wives of the marines, so please feel free to renew your acquaintance with them. They may be of some small comfort to you after your bereavements. You can let your feelings flow,' he said, releasing her.

'Th-thank 'ee, Cap'n Tench... Er, sir, when – when will the other prisoners be coming aboard?'

'Oh, I should think within the next few days.'

'Mummy, Mummy, there's 'nother li'l gal over there! Can I play with her? Aw, please say I can. *Please.*'

'Of course you can, my beauty. You, too, have been starved of company, of your own *age*, for a brave long time.'

Bill sighed. 'And now oi s'pose *oi'll* be flung below deck again to renew *my* acquaintance with the shackles. Old Bill o' the bilboes, that's me!'

'No, Allen,' smiled Tench, patting the old man's arm. 'Captain Parker of the *Gorgon* has ordered that you and the other male convict deserters will no longer be ironed, whereas the mutineers must still have one leg in irons, and you will spend the daylight hours on deck. And convicts and mutineers alike will receive full rations.'

Bill's greyish-blue eyes lit up.

'By heaven, Mary, you're right. It do seem as if our fortunes hev changed at last. Praise be to the Lord Almighty.'

* * *

On Monday 2 April, as the morning sun warmed the boards beneath their bare feet, Mary, Charlotte and Bill waited impatiently for Jimmy, John and Nat to finish hobbling up the entryport steps.

No sooner had the Irishman put one painful foot on deck than

Mary and Charlotte – now in her mother's arms – gave him the biggest hugs of his life.

'Jeez! Let me breathe!' he gasped. 'One at a time, wenches, one at a time!'

White-haired Nat squeezed in, kissing Mary's burning cheek.

'What's he loike, this Cap'n Parker, Mary love?'

'He's a kind man, Nat,' she said, still gazing into Jimmy's tired, yet still-twinkling, blue eyes. 'Cap'n Tench says that Cap'n Parker has ordered that none of you are to be shackled and we can spend all daylight hours on deck. Cap'n Parker said that, in the baking-hot African climate, we'd die, stowed below all day. And the mutineers are getting daily ex–'

'Captain Tench?' Jimmy freed himself from the females. 'Captain *Tench*, did ye say? By God, that's a blessed miracle! *He'll* see that we ain't roughly treated, won't he, Charlotte darlin'?'

''Iss,' she mumbled, averting her eyes, as Mary put her down.

Surprised at the tone, he squatted, fondled these spindly arms and looked into her troubled little grey eyes.

'Hey,' he said brightly, gently tweaking her nose, 'where's my Charlotte's great big smile?'

'I – I feel 'ot.'

'Ack, stop fretting about yerself,' he said. 'Go and play with the other childer.'

'I don' wanna, I don' *wanna*!' she shrilled, stamping her foot. 'I'm too 'ot, I'm too *'ot*!'

CHAPTER 65

On Friday 6 April, as dawn broke over the black and forbidding Table Mountain, the *Gorgon* set sail.

After two weeks, with the island of St Helena behind them and the equator threateningly near, the night-time heat on the deck beneath the lower gun-deck was unbearable. The prisoners were sharing this furnace with the marines' families.

'Mummy... I... I... can't breathe.'

'I know it's terrible, my beauty; Mummy feels bad, too... Lie *still*, you'll feel a mite betterer then.'

Children were crying all around.

God, thought Mary, *will any of our childer live to see the morning?*

* * *

Praise be, every child did see the morning.

But over a period of eleven more hellish nights five little hearts had ceased to beat. And Charlotte herself was sinking fast. At sunrise on Thursday 3 May, when Mary carried her all the way up on deck and sat her against the side, the child just slumped here, moaning and gasping.

Jimmy, who had rushed ahead up these interminable steps, knelt down and mopped the beads of sweat from Charlotte's brow with a rag plunged into a bucket of damnedly warm seawater. She showed no sign of recognition and Mary's breaking heart thudded. The Irishman's tears dropped into the bucket.

* * *

They kept Charlotte up here this Thursday night, but even at such a time, Mary had been denied Jimmy's comforting arms. Despite the heat, all the male convicts had still had to go below at sunset.

Black-curled little Lizzy Turner, the youngest child of Private John Turner and his wife Susannah, died up here during the night and the poor mother's breast-beating shrieks threatened to tear out Mary's own heart.

* * *

Mercifully no child died on Friday or Saturday.

* * *

In the terrifying darkness before Sunday's dawn not a star shone. Charlotte's breathing had grown so weak that Mary was straining to hear. Watkin Tench had finally persuaded Captain Parker to let Martin share the convict girl's vigil up here, and now Jimmy held her own sweating hand while together they clasped Charlotte's tiny fingers.

A sail suddenly flapped.

'The wind's getting up, Mary,' he murmured. ''Tis the Lord's Day and, at last, merciful God's giving the poor wee girl some air. And wasn't that a raindrop I felt then? Sure, the fresh air will bring life to her poor tortured lungs… Can't ye feel it, Charlotte darlin'? Lord Jesus is sending rain in answer to your prayers, just like those other times when ye prayed. Rain to cool yer poor wee perspiring brow. Wind to –'

Mary suddenly realized that the bigger hand had clenched. The smaller had slackened. She felt the side of this dear little neck… Nothing. She felt this dear, loving little heart…

'God's mercy's come too late!' screamed Mary Broad. 'Why, oh why, didn't He send the wind an' rain yesterday?'

CHAPTER 66

On the windy evening of Monday 18 June 1792, HMS *Gorgon* anchored in St Helen's Roads, Isle of Wight. By Thursday evening, the convicts were aboard a ship that would be sailing for the Thames within a week. The men were chained on the lower deck, where Mary herself was allowed to feed them.

* * *

On the morning of Saturday 30 June, Mary Broad put her first shaky foot on English soil in six years. In truth, she put it *in*: into the Essex marshes, for it was rainswept Purfleet that welcomed her. So much for her sunlit dreams of a panting Pincher swimming ahead of the Fowey fishing fleet that would take her home: to life. Brutal reality was a snarling bulldog, held back with much difficulty by Sir Sampson Wright's Bow Street officers, who were waiting to shackle her in the prisoners' coach that would take her the twenty miles to Newgate Prison: to her death.

* * *

'… And so, sir,' concluded the fettered convict girl, swaying at the Bow Street bar, as the big dusty clock on the wall behind ticked this precious life away, 'we would sooner suffer death than return to New South Wales.'

Beneath his grey bob wig, Nicholas Bond, looking more like a foxy thief-taker than a respectable justice, had opened his narrow green eyes wide. The story that Mary and her fellow prisoners had just told must surely have been the most amazing one that the magistrates' court had ever heard. As God's life-giving sun beamed through the circular skylight onto the cobwebbed chandelier, onto these dirty pale-blue walls and onto this greasy, grimy rail of the felon's box, the justice blinked those eyes of his. Then stared at her.

He sucked in his pinched, freckled cheeks and cleared his throat. But no amount of blowing would have cleared the passages of his pointed nose to rid him of this horrible nasal whine.

'I have never seen people who bore stronger marks of sincere repentance. Nevertheless, I have no alternative but to commit you all to Newgate. I must say, though, that I have never experienced so disagreeable a task. I hope that when you are put to the bar at the Sessions House, Old Bailey, your past sufferings may be considered as a sufficient expiation of your crimes. I assure you that, as far as it lies in my power, I shall assist you. Take them to the coach!'

The officers jerked them by their chains, from the felon's box and along the passage leading to the street door, outside which they would again have to push through the cheering, heaving, boiling throng of well-wishers.

'Assist us?' muttered Old Bill. 'What can *he* do?'

Jimmy smiled. 'Sure, the auld fox will probably put the rope round our skinny chicken-necks with his own freckly, clawed hands and assist us on an even longer journey than we had from the Cove to Coupang.'

Mary looked at Jimmy defiantly, some of her spirit having returned since their arrival in England.

'Whoever puts the rope round *my* neck to end *my* life will have more than freckles on his hands. I'll bite those hands so powerful hard that he'll carry Mary Broad's mark for the rest of *his* cussed life!'

CHAPTER 67

It was the following Saturday morning. From the grey-walled Old Bailey's large wooden dock, Mary Broad and friends watched the Crown Prosecutor's sausage fingers grip the top of his black gown. The last time the convict girl's knees had trembled like this when she'd been faced with a group of men deciding her fate was on that beach of the bleached dingo bones: as the thirty natives had advanced from the trees. Those frizzly-haired, savage young men on the beach had been naked and armed with spears and shields, while these frizzly-wigged, civilized old gentlemen on and below the bench were begowned and armed only with quills and books. Yet she was just as terrified now.

Unable to face them a moment longer, she turned her Newgate-dimmed eyes to the left and was dazzled by a ray of sunlight from the street. That end of the court was completely open, except for a low wall. Jimmy, on her right, had told her that the judge and 'his mates' wanted as much air as possible to reduce the stink, and the risk of infection from the gaol distemper. The Irishman had said that, about forty years ago, two judges and the Lord Mayor and other dignitaries had died after prisoners brought the fever from 'Hell above Ground', the adjoining Newgate. Because of that, Mary and the others had been scrubbed with vinegar before entering the court, which itself had been washed with the stuff and with wine. Herbs were burning on open braziers. Throughout the hearing, vinegar-soaked handkerchiefs had stayed firmly clutched to the mouth by the garlic-chewing judge and his mates, in the hope of preventing the pesty poor from destroying these human pillars of 'justice'.

Faugh, she scoffed, *so, too, might poor King Louis over the Channel protect his head from the guillotine's blade one of these days by keeping a kerchief round his neck!*

Screwing up her eyes, she looked longingly at those pretty nosegays of sweet-scented flowers that all the paying spectators in the gallery were pressing to their nostrils, for Fowey would be full of flowers now. Father's pink roses would be in full bloom…

'Prisoner Bryant, keep your insolent eyes on the court!' rasped the scraggy old judge, white with anger, his own nostrils flaring. The words repeated themselves because of the court's notorious echo. Behind His Lordship, the panelling was covered with ominous blood-red cloth and above him was a wooden canopy topped by the royal coat of arms. Suspended under the canopy was the gold-handled sword of justice.

Cursing her eyes for watering, she gripped the rail tightly and outglared the rat-eyed old varmint, with his long, full wig and his fancy scarlet robes edged with gold.

As for that black-gowned Crown Prosecutor, his black-eyed glower was Satan's own. He was finally about to speak.

Nat Lilley, rocking against her left arm, nervously brushed back his shock of white hair and murmured, 'And now here come the words what'll kill us. Look, the clerk's already fingering the black cap.'

Watching the bewigged little man stroking the small folded square of black silk as if it were a favourite cat, Mary let go of the rail and wrung her own, clammy hands. To purify the court against stinking diseased prisoners, the ledge of the dock had been strewn with posies of strong-smelling rue and rosemary. Rue symbolized repentance, whereas rosemary was for remembrance. She had long since repented her sin against Miss Lakeman but would remember for ever the Exeter court's sin against *her.* She forced these shaking fingers to break off two bare stalks of rosemary and make the Cross of Jesus. As the 'hanging mob' among the spectators roared expectantly, she looked up and outglared the Crown Prosecutor, she outglared that son of a bachelor.

Turning to the judge, he boomed, 'My Lord, representations have been made to me in this case. You see, my Lord – how shall I phrase it – it was an astonishing achievement to travel three-and-a-quarter thousand miles in a small open boat. They miscarried in a heroic struggle for liberty, after having combatted every hardship and conquered every difficulty…'

Mary's heart swelled. Captain Watkin Tench, bless him, had put those beautiful words into the Prosecutor's ugly fat mouth.

'… So, my Lord, in the light of the ordeal that the prisoners have suffered, and particularly in view of this gloriously inspirational example of the triumph of the human spirit over terrible dangers and in the most calamitous adversity, it is not the Crown's intention to demand the full legal penalty for an escape from transportation. However, the Crown submits, that to give any special favours or kindness, or to grant the prisoners liberty before their original sentences have ended, would only encourage others to try to escape…'

* * *

Minutes later, the judge looked at them sternly.

'Prisoners at the bar, you are to remain on your former sentences…'

Mary and Jimmy exchanged delighted glances. So, *they* would both be discharged in eight months, Old Bill in two years, Nat in two-and-a-half years and John in three.

Jimmy whispered in her ear, 'Sure, eight months in noisome, noisy Newgate is better than being one of Jack Ketch's customers.'

The judge had not finished. '… until you shall be discharged by due course of law.'

Gasps from the spectators.

'Due course of law?' murmured a beautiful young lady in a pink silk bonnet and a lovely white muslin gown with a pink sash round its high waist. 'Pray what does that mean, Charles dearest?'

'Egad, my dear Sophia!' exclaimed her companion, a handsome young brown-haired gentleman in a blue velvet suit and white ruffled shirt. 'Egad! It's an unfixed time, the *poor wretches*!'

'Yes…' grunted a white-wigged older gentleman in green velvet. He sniffed some snuff from the back of his hand. '… Yes, indeed. It could mean sometime or never!'

CHAPTER 68

'That's Mary Bryant, sir,' growled Ben Love, this bald, fat brute of a turnkey, rattling open the cell door. 'She's that bitch over at the back there in the yeller rags. 'Er wiv the long brown 'air an' the stubborn look of a mule on 'er mug.'

Cocking his pistol, Love made way for a short, plumpish, rather dark-complexioned, red-nosed gentleman in a beautiful blue suit with gold-wrought buttons. The pistol was needed because many of the hundred half-naked women and children in this large cell would have relieved the gentleman of his fine clothes in two shakes of his wig's queue.

The convict girl pushed and squeezed through the swearing, stinking rabble that she called 'The Cats' Chorus'. She was well aware that Mary Broad smelt no sweeter.

''Iss? That's me. But I call myself Broad again these days.'

Love spat on her left foot – which had just trodden in something, dang it!

'Say "Yes, sir" to 'is Nobleness. Not "'Iss", you higorant 'ussy!'

'Rot you!' she snarled, scraping the foot on the straw. 'If the gentleman weren't here, I'd spit in your ignorant ugly fat face, you son of a sow!'

'Mary *Broad*,' spluttered the visitor, thrusting a vinegared yellow silk handkerchief to his mouth and nose. 'My stars, the *stench* of this place gets worse every time I come here! For weeks after my last visit, my vinegar phial still reeked of this pestilential prison.' He coughed loudly and looked as if he was about to vomit down his double chin and double-breasted waistcoat.

'My name is James Boswell, my dear. I am a barrister, a lawyer, and I am also a writer. I have read all about "The Girl from Botany Bay" in the newspapers and I have come hotfoot from Mr Bond, the Bow Street justice. Neither of us is happy about you and your brave companions being flung into "Hell above Ground" after all you have suffered. I have been racking my barrister brains to try to think how to get you all out of here. I am going to visit your friends in the men's section in a minute,' he said, removing the handkerchief to smile at her.

Unable to stomach the stench for even a second, though, he changed the handkerchief to his left hand, covered his nose and mouth again, then shook her hand with his fat, clammy paw. Behind him, Love sneered, as if to say, 'Fancy a gen'leman shakin' 'ands wiv *that*!'

'It is indeed a pleasure to meet you, my dear,' wheezed Boswell, his beaming dark-brown eyes filling with tears as a choking fit caught him.

Mary was staring at him in disbelief. 'Do you really think there's a chance, sir?'

'Why not?' was the muffled reply. 'James Boswell is a fighting bulldog and once he gets his teeth into something, he will not let go! Now, my intention is to ask personally for a royal pardon.'

Mary's eyes popped and the women and girls nearest to her gasped at his words.

'What?' she gulped. 'From the King hisself? You know the *King*?' She gazed at him in awe, as if he were the archangel Gabriel bringing glad tidings from the Lord.

The plumpish man swelled with importance and the waistcoat's gold-wrought buttons threatened to fly.

'Oh, indeed... indeed, and *Her* Majesty, too. Why, I bought this very suit for an attendance at Court when the Queen held a prodigious drawing room, a reception, back in March '89, doncha know. I regret that I am getting a mite too fat for the suit these days, though. It is a little worn now, otherwise I would not have put it on to visit this noisome cesspool.'

He looked her in the eye.

'But to be truthful with you, my dear, for I respect you too much not to be completely honest with you: the person with whom I shall speak is not King George himself but His Majesty's Secretary of State for Home Affairs, the Right Honourable Henry Dundas. He is the gentleman ultimately responsible for your fate. I have known the Home Secretary since we were students at the University of Edinburgh, doncha know.

'So, take heart, my poor girl. Dammit, I can see that you are a *beautiful* creature beneath this filth, and these rags that seem to be falling from your slender young shoulders even as I speak, by God!'

She could see him licking his full red lips under the handkerchief.

'Aye,' he growled, 'a beautiful creature... and by all the Scottish blood that is pumping through my body, I vow to bring the roses back to your pale, emaciated cheeks as surely as you have brought the colour back to mine. I would fetch you a pretty frock now but 'twould be ruined in here; though, God grant, you will be wearing one soon.'

'Sir, why should an important gentleman like you, that knows King George and Queen Charlotte Sophia, want to do this for me: a girl who pinched a lady's bonnet to throw in the duckpond? *Me*, the daughter of a poor Cornish fisherman.'

'Pshaw! There is nothing to be ashamed of, being a fisherman's daughter. Fisherfolk are essential to the country, and 'tis a dangerous business – as your epic journey was.

'Aye, lass, I know what a bad sea is like. Faith, in '73, when I made a tour of the Hebrides with that great man the late Dr Samuel Johnson – whose "Life" I have written, doncha know – the seas were often exceedingly rough.

'So, you see, Mary, a gentleman like me admires a woman like ye with all his being. Fisherman's daughter, indeed! I shall tell you something, girl. You "pinched" a bonnet; well, even if you had been accused of stealing sheep, I should still exert myself to get you out of this pesty prison before they hanged you. Why, my first criminal case was that of poor John Reid, accused of sheep-stealing.' He sighed. 'God grant he is resting in peace.'

If only you knew, she thought. *If only you knew, Mr Boswell.*

'Mr Love,' he boomed, 'I have finished. Fare thee well, Mary Bryant – er – Broad. My heart bleeds for you. I shall speak with Mr Dundas as soon as it is humanly possible to do so. By God I will!'

He briefly removed the handkerchief to smile broadly, spluttered once more and was gone, to the accompaniment of The Cats' Chorus. Mary herself stood open-mouthed, her feet rooted in the slime-thick boards.

'Faugh!' Betty Driver, a skinny, redheaded pickpocket, spat at the door as it clanged shut. 'Ol' slobber-lips just comes in 'ere for the frill of bein' surrounded and rubbed against by por crazy gels wot's near naked. Everyone knows 'im, the leerin' ol' lecher. He'll tell all his cronies about it and get *them* all excited, like. Yeah, that's the last you'll see of Whoremonger Boswell.'

CHAPTER 69

He's forgotten me, Mary told herself for what must surely have been the millionth time. *July 1792 he came and it's now May 1793 and my old sentence ended six week ago.*

But at least I'm alive, not like poor Betty. Aw, gal, I'll never forget that day when they took you to the condemned cells. And that following Sunday when all of us went to the prison chapel and looked down at you, and the men, in the condemned pew, that ghastly, grim big black pen with a coffin in the middle that you all sat round and that fills my nightmares. And you, poor Betty, had to listen to prayers for your own soul and join in the responses for your own burial service! And then the next day, that terrible Monday morning, as the prison bell was tolling, they dragged you a-kickin' an' a screamin' across the Press Yard on your way to the scaffold outside the debtors' door. Aw, gal, I can still hear the deep, gloomy bell of St Sepulchre's tolling its eight "dooms" and the bosky mob's roars as you were launched into All Eternity. Poor darling. Poor –

The key rasped in the lock. The door rattled open and Ben Love entered, followed by...

'Glory be!' she cried. 'Mr Boswell! Mr *Boswell*!' She threw herself onto his shiny black buckled shoes and kissed them. 'Aw, sir, *sir*! You've come back, you've come back at last! I thought you'd forgotten poor Mary Broad.'

'Arise, brave fishergirl,' he mumbled, behind this inevitable vinegar-soaked yellow silk handkerchief. 'Arise.' He helped her, with his free hand. 'Forgive me, my dear, for not having come before but there was nothing that I could have told you, in any case. I shall not bore you with the reasons but, for much of the time these many months, I myself have been in low spirits and, even if I had come, would only have made *you* more downhearted.

'As promised, I made an appointment with Mr Dundas but he

failed to keep it, and, dammit, I had especially postponed a long-planned visit to Penryn in your native Cornwall. There then followed letters between us, but – well, anyhow, to cut a tedious story short, Mr Dundas has finally acceded to my request.'

'What does that mean, sir?'

'It means, my dear,' he breathed excitedly, fondling her bare right shoulder, 'it means that I asked him to be compassionate to you and your friends and he has at last agreed. In *your* case.'

'You – you mean...'

'I mean, my dear girl, that the fisherman's daughter is free. But her shipmates – or should I say *boat*mates – on that epic voyage will have to be patient a wee while longer.'

The grip on her shoulder tightened and she clutched at the rags to stop their falling.

'Mary Broad,' he murmured, 'listen to this.' Releasing her with obvious reluctance, he pulled a sheet of paper from his pocket. 'This is a copy of a document addressed to the Sheriff of Middlesex...'

Still holding the handkerchief, he read:

> Whereas Mary Bryant, alias Broad, now a prisoner in Newgate, stands charged with escaping from the persons having the legal custody of her before the expiration of the term for which she had been ordered to be transported. And whereas some favourable circumstances have been humbly presented unto us on her behalf, inducing us to extend our Grace and Mercy unto her and to *grant her our free pardon* for her said crime. Our Will and Pleasure, therefore, is that you cause the said Mary Bryant, alias Broad, to be forthwith discharged out of Custody and that she be inserted for her said crime in our first and next general pardon that shall come out for the poor convicts in Newgate, without any condition whatsoever. And for so doing, this shall be your warrant, given at our Court of Saint

James's, the Second Day of May, 1793, in the Thirty-third year of our reign.

By His Majesty's Command, Henry Dundas.

Her heart leapt and she gulped. 'Aw, thank you, sir,' she sobbed. 'Aw, thank you!'

After letting this sink in, Boswell looked at her intently.

'I trust that you will want to go to Fowey posthaste.'

'No...no, sir, I – I'm frightened about going back there.'

'*What?*'

'It's my kin, sir. I don't know if my old widowed father and my young sister Dolly are still alive but if they are, I don't think they'll treat me well. You see, when I left home to find work in Plymouth, they were a-rampin' an' a-ravin' at me, saying as how I was deserting them – deserting them, too, after my poor mother had died of a consumption... Dear life, I've *yearned* for them with every second that's gone by since, yearned with every part of me. But now that the time's come, I'm powerful scared. I know they *hate* me. And every mortal being in Fowey will hate me, too; they'll all point at me. In London, I can keep myself to myself. Because it's such a huge place, nobody knows me.'

'But, Mary, your poor old father!'

'Least of all can I face *him*!'

'But, lass, you have done nothing *wrong*!'

'That ain't what *they'll* say. I've thought long and hard about it while I've been in here and I've made up my mind.'

'Your *mind*? I fear that it has been *addled* by all these months in this noisome place.' This time he rested his hand on her bare upper arm. 'Well, we shall discuss this further, Mary... But let me help you. I know of a room in Little Titchfield Street, off Oxford Street...'

'Whoremonger!' screeched The Cats' Chorus. 'Whoremonger Boswell!'

Mary blushed and lowered her eyes from his own flushed face.

'… Aye!' he bellowed, pretending not to care, 'I know of a *woman* there that will take you in for a few pence a week. She is a neighbour of my brother David's.'

'But I ain't got no money, sir.'

'I shall pay your rent until you are able to work.'

'But why should *you* do that, Mr Boswell?'

'Because, my poor dear, you have been grossly maltreated and I should not rest easy in my warm, soft and safe bed, thinking of you sleeping on London's cold, hard and dangerous streets. You are a comely wench, Mary Broad,' he breathed, 'despite your lack of flesh because of your woeful tribulations. You would not last five minutes before some salivating *whoremonger* got his teeth into you!' he cried, glaring defiantly at The Cats.

'Sir, I couldn't take your –'

'Oh, hush, Mary. I am right. I should not rest easy abed thinking about your being prey to every Willy Wolf and Jack Jackal from Whitehall to Whitechapel. Your old father – if he's alive – would never forgive me if he knew that I had thrown you to them. *I* am a father, too, doncha know, and, [illegible] I, too, am a *lonely* widower, my dearest Margaret having died of a consumption herself four years ago. Two of my three daughters are only a few years younger than you. Veronica, Ve, is twenty years old and Euphemia, Phemie, will be nineteen in a fortnight. My stars, the thought of *them* sleeping on the streets… Do as I ask, Mary: accept my offer, I beseech you.'

The Cornish girl smiled nervously. 'Very well,' she said, looking into these rather sad dark-brown eyes. 'Thank you, sir. Aw, thank you, sir!'

He beamed behind the handkerchief and linked arms with her.

'Turnkey Love,' he boomed, 'Mistress Broad thanks you for your *love*ly hospitality but regrets that she cannot partake of it for a moment longer, because her carriage awaits. Pray open the door, sir.'

CHAPTER 70

Three raps at the door of her gloomy cellar room made Mary leap from the creaky wicker chair and drop the shirt that she had been sewing, on this Sunday morning in mid-August. The beautiful white muslin frock, which her benefactor had bought, silently brushed the wide hemp mat as she crossed the room barefoot.

Nervously she opened the rotting door.

Her heart fluttered, under the pink-silk sash of this high-waisted garment. The gentleman himself and a stocky, brown-haired middle-aged man were smiling at her. The stranger, with his rosy apple cheeks, red plum nose and easy manner, looked like someone from her part of the country. He certainly wasn't one of the pale, haunted hurriers of this sunless, airless city. She curtseyed out of respect for Mr Boswell.

'Mary, this is Mr Castel, a glazier, who lives in Cross Street, Carnaby Market, but who comes originally from Fowey. He says that he knows you.'

Her heart was racing now. 'Well, *I* don't know Mr Castel,' she said defensively.

The man clasped his wide-brimmed brown felt hat to the waistcoat of his three-piece canary-yellow suit.

'Well, mistress, *you* might not remember *me* but I sure do mind *your* pretty face, my beauty, ever since you was a tiny tacker of a tomboy, knee-high to a pisky. You'm gotten an older sister what be married to Edward Puckey, the fisherman, bain't 'ee? Well, Edward Puckey did write to me to get your address from Mr Boswell so that I might come and see you and let your kin know how you be. Edward Puckey also asked me to tell your younger sister, Dolly, where you be a-livin' so that she can come and visit 'ee. She's in London, in service; she's –'

'Dolly's alive? She's *alive*? She's *here*?' Mary Broad staggered back and they entered. Scarcely knowing what she was doing, she flopped into the chair and stared at them.

'Dolly's *here*? In *London*? Merciful God, I can't believe it, I can't *believe* it!'

With much grunting and puffing, Boswell lowered his fat self onto the only other seat: the cracket, a three-legged stool.

'Sir, f-f-forgive me,' she stammered, struggling to rise.

'No, Mary, stay where you are. Pshaw, you should know by now that there is no standing on ceremony with James Boswell. Aye, Mr Castel says that Dolly is a cook in Charlotte Street, not far from here.'

'Dear life...'

'And,' said the grinning glazier, 'I have more good news. A large sum of money's been left to be shared between your feyther and three or four other folk: three hundred thousand pound in total amount. 'Tis what be called "a legacy".'

Father's alive... She felt giddy. *Aw, please God, I ain't a-goin' to faint in front of Mr Boswell, am I? Aw, please God, no...*

'D-D-Dolly's here, you said?...'

Castel was gawking at her. 'Mary, what's amiss with 'ee? Didn't you hear what I did say: about all that money? Your feyther's been left thousands of pound!'

'What colour's her hair?'

'What?'

'What colour's Dolly's hair?'

'Well, 'tis... 'tis always under a mob-cap these days...'

'If you know her, you'll know the colour of her hair. I've only got *your* word for it that you know her, ain't I?'

His red cheeks glowed like a Cornish sunset.

'Faugh, don't say you don't trust me. Don't you want to hear a mite more about that three hundred thousand–'

'A pox on the three hundred thousand pound! I want you to tell me the colour of my Dolly's hair. I *don't* trust you and that's the truth. You've read about me in the newspapers. You ain't one of those journalist craturs, are you? You ain't one of those liards that's writing rude things about me and good Mr Boswell here?'

Castel roared with laughter and held his waistcoat sides.

'Good Lor' no! I ain't edycated enough for that, Mary dear.'

'Don't you "dear" me. You tell me the colour of my sister's hair. Even if you ain't a journalist, I suspicion you could still be an impostor of some sort. I've known enough rogues these past few year, I can tell you.'

'You'm serious, ain't 'ee?' His own expression became so.

'Yiss.'

He looked her straight in the eye.

'I'm a Cornishman. And from one Cornish person to another, 'tis the truth I'm a-tellin' 'ee. I do know your sister Dolly.'

'And,' she demanded, 'her hair colour be…'

'Sandy – but a yallerish-red sand, not like the sand at Readymoney Cove at the seaward end of Fowey.'

She was still unsure of him. She caught Boswell's eye and saw a warning. Yes, she'd treat this fellow as Boswell would: in a refined manner. She'd adopt an air of quiet calm and try to keep the impatience and excitement from her voice – ha, she'd put on a voice to suit her fine frock!

'When would be a good time to see her, pray?'

'I can bring her round this evenin', after she be finished cookin'. Now, about the money…'

'Pray forget the money for the moment. It is my dear *sister* that I am concerned about, Mr Castel.'

CHAPTER 71

'Dear life, Dolly, how you'm growed! Aw, come *in*, my sweet'art. And you, too, Mr Castel. Goodness, I scarce recognized 'ee, gal!'

'I was only thirteen year when you left us, Mary dear,' sobbed this slender young creature in the white mob cap. Quite the young lady she was, in her plaid shawl, square-necked cotton-check frock and buckled brown leather shoes.

Mary hugged her, kissing her on both pockmarked cheeks. 'How – how's poor Father?'

'He's fine, but he's got terrible old a-frettin' about you. He still fishes for those ol' pilchards, though, bless his heart.'

'And – and Pincher? How's my dear old dog? He – he ain't–'

'*Naw*, he's fine, too, but, like Father, he's got real old waiting for you. Father says that Pincher's been going to the gate every night for the past seven-and-a-half year to see if you're coming home down the hill.'

Neither sister wanted to let go of the other so they just stood here in the middle of the room, their tears veritable floods now. The glazier was shuffling his hobnailed boots on the mat.

Mary sniffed. 'Sit you down, Mr Castel. Sit you down, Dolly dear.'

'No,' said Dolly, 'you sit down.'

'No, *you*.'

He prised them apart. 'Sit you both down. Good Lor', you'm both so weak-kneed, you'll *fall* down in a minute,' he grunted, helping Mary into the chair while Dolly sank onto the cracket.

'So, Dolly,' said Mary, 'you're a cook.'

''Iss,' she said, wiping her green eyes with the palms of her thin white freckled hands. 'I've been a-doing cookin' for near a year now. I came to London six year ago and got a position as scullery maid. Then, after about a year, they gave me the chambermaid's job, being as how that poor mortal was dying of a consumption. Now, I'm the cook at Mr Morgan's great big house in Charlotte Street, Bedford Square. 'Tis powerful hard toil, I tell you, 'cos 'tis a big household.' She squeezed Mary's hand. 'I can't stay with you long, Mary, 'cos I've got to get their suppers.'

'Yes, Dolly, cooking is hard toil and you're still only a skinny young thing, ain't you? Cooks are usually fat and old.'

''Iss,' she chuckled. 'Father says he's proper proud of me… Mary, when will you be going home?'

Mary Broad sniffed furiously. 'I – I *want* to go, of course… But I… but I'm afeard an' affrighted what they're all going to say to me in Fowey, being as how I deserted you both.'

'Don't be stupid! They'll be as pleased as pussies with dishes of cream to see their famous "Girl from Botany Bay".' Dolly suddenly frowned and there were lines on her poor pitted brow that had not been there seven-and-a-half years ago. 'How are you going to get money to get back all that way to Cornwall, though? I don't know nothing about your circumstances, save only that Mr Boswell, the writer and lawyer man, got you this little room. How are you managing to pay the rent for this place? Have you got a job as a lady's maid or something? And *howsoever* did you get this *beautiful* frock? Lord, 'tis such thin stuff that 'tis well you've got a bodice and petticoat underneath, 'cos Mr Castel here would have an eyeful!'

'I wouldn't *blink* an eye,' grinned the glazier but he was noticeably redder. 'I've knawed Mary when she were a tiny tacker.'

Both girls laughed derisively.

Abruptly Mary returned to the subject in hand. 'No, Dolly, I ain't got a job like that but I'm doing sewing: making shirts and things. It's only a pittance I'm getting, though. Dear Mr Boswell was the one that bought me this lovely frock and he is paying the rent, bless him.'

She bent down. 'And see under the chair? A beautiful pair of pink kid-leather shoes, that's got very pointed toes, and a pink silk bonnet… It's crazy, ain't it? I've had to go to the bottom of the world and back to get a pink bonnet. If I'd had a pink bonnet that night in

Plymouth, I'd never have had to take poor old Miss Lakeman's. I was so happy getting a job, and so bosky, I'd have just thrown mine into the duckpond and that would have been the end of the story…'

She went on, 'Mr Boswell's got his rich friends to pay – what's the word – sub- subscriptions to what he calls "The Mary Broad Fund". Ha, he even got someone called Lord Thurlow, that was once – what d'you call it – Lord Chancellor, to pay something. Mr Boswell said that, first of all, Lord Thurlow had said, "Damn her blood, let her go and do a day's work!" But when Mr Boswell told His Lordship about my "hardships and heroism", as he called it, Lord Thurlow said that Mr Boswell was a good lawyer man for me, painting such a good picture of me, like, and he *did* give something.

'And Mr Boswell had got a reverend gentleman friend of his in Cornwall to help, too: the Reverend William Temple, who's also a friend of the Reverend John Baron. Yes, Mr Boswell had asked the Reverend Mr Temple to collect money for The Mary Broad Fund. But the Reverend Mr Temple wrote back the other week, saying that whacks of rich folk down there wouldn't pay a brass farthing because Farmer Tregenna had said the Broads were sheep-stealers!' She turned to Mr Castel. 'What a terrible thing to say about us, just because *our* dog beat *his* dog!' She grinned impishly at Dolly. 'I didn't dare ask if the reverend gentleman had called on Farmer Tregenna!

'And Mr Boswell's even bought me a beautiful prayer book, saying that the Puckeys must learn me to read words of writing. Aw, Dolly, Mr Boswell's a warm-hearted man and I *love* him for it.'

Dolly's white face coloured. 'You – you mean he's been doing all this in – in return for your favours?'

'Dolly Broad! You know me betterer than that! Whatever must Mr Castel think!'

Dolly stammered, 'Well, I –'

'Mr Boswell's just a good, kind widow gentleman. Not once has he touched me – well, save only for a few fatherly pecks on the cheek.' She'd better not mention the shoulder-fondling.

'I'm sorry, Mary,' murmured Dolly, 'I – I just thought –'

'Aw, dear Dolly, I don't blame you for thinking the same things that all those snaky strangers have been thinking and saying and writing words about. Mercy's sake, it's been such a brave long time, *we're* almost strangers ourselves.'

'Naw, you and me will never be strangers. I know one thing, though: I'd like to meet this handsome stranger of yourn, Mr James Boswell. I want to thank him for his kindnesses to you: getting you this place and getting you out of that hell's kitchen. And being as how he's proper good at getting folk in and out of places, maybe he can get me out of Mr Morgan's *slaves'* kitchen and into an easier place of work.

'Goodness, Mary, there's so much to talk about and I've got to go in a minute. Mr Morgan's read to me what the *newspapers* have been saying about your terrible sufferings but now I'd like to hear it from you.'

'Well –'

'Er, excuse me, ladies.' Mr Castel rubbed his red nose with his brown hat. 'What about us talkin' about the *money* first?'

'Aw,' scoffed the 'sensible' Dolly, ''tis only a rumour that Edward heard. That a distant relative of ours had died, who, being an elderly bachelor man, had no one else but Father and three or four other folk to leave his fortune to. Maybe Mr Boswell, him being a lawyer man, could sort it out for us.'

'Yiss,' murmured Mary, 'it would pay for my wagon ride back to Fowey, wouldn't it?'

CHAPTER 72

'So you will soon be sailing for Fowey, Mary,' said James Boswell, 'now that Mrs Puckey's written to me to say that you'll be kindly received....'

This following Sunday evening, her benefactor was sitting in the wicker chair – though whether he'd manage to get out of it was another matter, being much fatter these days. Mary was on the cracket, with Dolly sitting at her feet, on a cushion. All three were drinking the delicious claret, which Mr Boswell had brought.

'... And you, young Dolly, God granting, will soon be in a far easier job. I resolve to exert myself to get you a place more suitable for someone so young – so *slender*...' His voice trembled on the word.

Dolly burst into tears and held Mary's hand. 'Thank you again, sir, from the bottom of my heart for your kindnesses to us both. No price can be put on what you've done for our Mary but if the rumour is true and us Broads do get the money, I swear before the Lord that I'll give you a thousand pound of it.'

'Bless you, my dear.' His eyes twinkled. 'Perhaps *my* fortunes are changing for the better, too.'

Mary felt herself blushing. 'Sir, about my four dear companions. Is – is there any more news?'

Dolly glanced at her, concerned, for Mary had told the girl all about Jimmy Martin, of course.

James Boswell sighed, wriggled and had a long drink.

'I am afraid not. For *your* information, Dolly, this is what I have tried so far. A few days after Mary's release, I wrote to Mr Dundas's new wife, Lady Hope Dundas. "Lady *No* Hope Dundas", Mary calls her, and with justification. I had thought that Her Ladyship might have helped. After all, I did take the trouble to go to their confounded wedding in April! But she wrote back saying that she had a golden rule about never even mentioning to "dear Henry" matters concerning his governmental duties. At the same time, I wrote to Evan Nepean, the Under-Secretary, and, as a result, discussed the matter with him. Soon after, I spoke with Mary's "old friend" Governor Phillip, who had just arrived home from New South Wales.

'Then came the night of the fifth of June, a date imprinted on my brain for ever more: by the boots of footpads. After drinking too much, I was knocked down and robbed by those foot-scamperers in this very street and left close to death's door – well, in truth, close to Mary's door, though she did not know it at the time. Aye, I was left unconscious with a fearful head wound and was confined to my bed, with a fever and great pain. But within nine days, while still on my sickbed, I was writing to Nepean again, begging him that nothing should be done to the Newgate Four until I could have another talk with him and Governor Phillip.'

He had another long swallow.

'And just six days ago, I visited the poor fellows in Newgate and assured them that I was doing all in my power for them. That is where we stand at the moment, Mary. But, never fear, Bulldog Boswell shall not let go!

'Oh, by the by, my dear, John Butcher has finally given me a copy of the letter that *he* wrote to "dear Henry" back in January.' Boswell puffed and blew as he put his empty glass on the mat and fumbled in his coat pocket.

'Aye, here it is,' he grunted. 'I shall read it to you.

> May it please your Honour,
>
> It ill becomes a person in the low spheres I move in to address a person of your exalted character, nor should I have presumed to have taken the liberty but for the following reasons:
>
> Having been brought up in the thorough knowledge of all kinds of land and capable of bringing indifferent lands to perfection, I had an offer some time ago of

going to Botany Bay to endeavour to make that land more fertile than it has ever appeared to be.

I submit the following list to your Honour's perusal of what is necessary seed and what has been tried and found not to answer the expectations found of them: Two sorts of English wheat; barley, rye and beans, one sort; grass is a good production, as, likewise, Indian corn; and some of the land will produce tobacco and all sorts of garden stuff, with proper instructions.

But, according to the manner in which they till the ground at present, they will bring nothing to perfection, owing to the different sorts of land in the island, which they are entirely ignorant of. And I flatter myself, from what I have seen of the island, that I could render it a great deal more productive, and, in a few years, could save the Governor a great expense in provisions for the colony.

Although I have suffered a great deal in going and coming back from Botany Bay, yet I am willing to go back again on proper terms, as I am very certain I can be of great service to the island in what I profess. And if your Honour should think me worthy of the situation I am willing to place myself in, I will be bound to perform everything I undertake, or expect nothing for my trouble.

I should be humbly thankful to your Honour if you would condescend to indulge me with an answer, that I may know what I am to expect. You will give great ease to the anxious mind of, honourable Sir,

Yours, etc., John Butcher.

'Dear life,' groaned Mary. 'Every time you mention John's letter, I want to scream. Stow me, after all we went through to get away from that cussed place! You once said to me that *my* brain was addled, sir. Well, his certainly is! I've always thought he was a mite crack-brained: him and his "look you"! Yes, he's a buffle'ead, look you!'

'But, Mary,' protested Dolly, 'maybe the poor wretched man thinks he'll never get out of Newgate otherwise. It didn't work but 'twas worth a try. I'll lay a curse that if *you* were still in there, you'd try a trick like that.'

'Never! Dear Christ, didn't I suffer enough, down at the "stinking backside of the world", as poor Will called it. Catch Nat or Old Bill doing something like that. Faugh, catch ol' Jimmy doing it!'

Having refilled his glass, Boswell turned his glazed eyes on her.

'It was your Irish friend who put the idea into Butcher's head, and, judging by some of the phrases in the letter, there is a "wee" bit of "yer man's" blarney in it, too. So Martin is the true bufflehead, I am thinking.'

'Yiss,' sighed Mary, studying her empty glass, 'and that's why I love him so…'

CHAPTER 73

As early evening brought even more October gloom to this lonely cellar room, Mary heard the rattling of a hackney coach.

Within half a minute, Mr Boswell and his blushing fifteen-year-old younger son, Jamie, were at her door. Within another half-minute, the boy had taken up her clothes box and she and Boswell had joined him by the coach. She was wearing the green woollen frock and plaid shawl which Boswell had bought her for the sea passage.

The writer, himself flushing now, took her elbow and helped her up inside and she felt the warmth in her own cheeks.

'Ooh, sir, you'm treating me like a proper lady.'

'And why not, Mary Broad? As a barrister, and a judge's son, it is the very least I can do to repay you for all the hurt that the justice system has inflicted upon you!

'Now, my dear,' he said, 'when we get through the infernal Saturday evening traffic and finally reach Beale's Wharf, Southwark, you and I shall go into the alehouse there, to buy you a meal and then share a bowl of punch. On the way, we shall drop Jamie at Mr Dilly's, my publisher, in Poultry and I shall collect the lad on my return, for I have a *personal* matter to discuss with you.'

Her heart thumped and her cheeks were really burning now.

'Ooh, sir. Whatever can you mean?'

* * *

The fisherman's daughter had a huge, delicious meal of roast beef, roast potatoes, Yorkshire pudding, gravy, peas and real cabbage in the alehouse kitchen at eight o'clock. A strange time of day to have dinner, she'd thought. Then she and Boswell found a quiet alcove in the crowded taproom, where the landlord and Job Moyse, master of the

Ann and Elizabeth, joined them for a glass of rum punch, bringing back painful memories of Will.

That had been twenty minutes ago and now 'The Girl from Botany Bay' and her 'lawyer man' were alone in the alcove. Starting this second large glassful, Mary realized that it was making her temperature even higher but her spirits even lower.

'Cheer yourself, Mary Broad! My stars, anyone would think that you were back in the days of Tyburn Tree and tomorrow morning you were going to be swaying about in Jack Ketch's cart not Job Moyse's ship!'

'I'm usually full of Cornish cheer nowadays, as you know, sir, but so many bad things have happened to me that I can't believe that any good ones can possibly happen. Whenever things look bright, then something truly terrible happens. I'm *sure* my relations won't treat me well when I get back to Fowey. Mr and Mrs Puckey have always behaved rather grand towards me. Just because they can read 'n' write words! I don't trust 'em and that's the honest truth. And how do I know that they ain't poisoned my father's mind against me?'

'Oh, you *are* getting maudlin with the punch, lass! For goodness' sake, it is your duty to go and see your aged father in the evening of his life, and your other kin. And, indeed, it *may* be in your best interests: in case it should be true that a considerable sum of money has been left to your father.'

'But –'

'Irrespective of that, Mary, I wish to assure you of ten pounds yearly, which you will continue to receive as long as you behave well.'

'But, sir! You've already paid for my passage and my food 'n' drink aboard ship and my lovely clothes and my food an' rent at Little Titchfield Street – and my roast beef and –'

'Quiet, woman!' He slapped his fat hand on the table, shaking the punch bowl. 'Hear me out! As a pitifully inadequate payment for all your suffering, I shall pay you a gratuity of ten pounds yearly, *from The Mary Broad Fund*, which you will continue to receive as long as you behave well. No more Miss Pondmans and ducklakes.'

'*Your* brain's more addled than mine, beggin' yer pardon, sir. You mean, no more Miss Lakemans an' duckponds.'

'Saucy wench!' He pretended to scowl. 'How dare you mock a member of both the English and Scottish Bars because he muddies – *muddles* his lakes and his ponds!'

'Well, you told me to cheer myself, your Noble Lordshipness. 'Tweren't *my* fault if you got in a puddle wi' yer lakes an' yer ponds!' She poked him in his fat side and they both roared.

Taking out a clean yellow silk handkerchief, he wiped the tears from her eyes and then his own.

'Seriously, though, Mary dear. If future subscriptions to the fund should fail – as sadly seems likely – *I* shall make up the money, or even pay the whole amount myself, even though I am not a wealthy man. And I shall continue to do so. Being, therefore, independent, you can quit your relations whenever you please.'

She clasped his plump, warm hands. 'But I can't take no more from *you*! Why should you do that for me?'

'I have told you before: because of the terrible injustices that you have suffered.'

He opened his purse and took out the shiniest coins that she had ever seen.

'Now, here are five golden guineas, five shillings of which are for your use until the first of November, and the other five pounds for the half year beginning on that day. I shall send you another five pounds on the first of May next year. And so it will continue: the first of November and the first of May. You must, of course, personally acknowledge receipt of these future payments.'

'What does that mean: personally ack– acknowledge receipt?'

'Write to tell me that you have received the money.'

She looked at him in astonishment.

'But, sir, you know I can't write!'

'I have thought of that. Now, as you see, mine host has put a quill and a sheet of paper on the table. You have in your pocket that piece of cloth you always carry with you, with your mark on it: "M.B.". Take it out and copy it for me. This is so that I can test the copy against the mark that you will put at the bottom of all the letters which somebody else will write for you.'

While she performed this ink-splashing task, Boswell murmured, 'Apart from the letters of receipt, I hope that you will write to this old fogy now and then to let him know how you are faring down in Cornwall. Knowing you as I do, I am sure that you have a bright future, if God grants you continued good health.'

She handed him the paper and he placed it before him to dry.

'Sir?'

'Yes?'

'What about my poor friends in Newgate? Dear life, they could *die* there!'

'Trust me, my dear, trust me.'

'Thank 'ee, sir,' she sniffed. 'It's just that they mean so very much to me, after all we've been through together.'

'I know, Mary, I know… I see Job Moyse is waiting patiently by the door, to take you aboard. I shall conduct you to your cabin.'

Five minutes later, Job Moyse having left the pair of them at the cabin door, James Boswell hugged Mary Broad and kissed her lips. A gentle affair after Will's rough love-making.

Goodness, if Dolly could see me now! Ha, she's probably looking in one of Mr Morgan's big shiny silver bowls at this very moment and seeing everything, the little witch. Pray God, Mr Boswell gets her out of that slaves' kitchen soon.

James Boswell released her reluctantly as usual. 'Well, I shall bid you *adieu*, Mary Broad, brave fishergirl. Safe passage tomorrow morn and through the rest of your *long* life.'

'Thank you most kindly, sir,' she said and grinned. 'May *your* life be a long'un, too Oh, sir?'

'Yes?'

'… *I've* got a present for *you*.' With trembling fingers she took an envelope from her pocket.

'What on earth...'

'Open your hands, sir.'

He laid out his sweating palms and she emptied the envelope. Seventeen dry, tripled-veined leaves lay here, each nearly as big as his thumb.

'What are these?'

'Leaves from the sweet tea vine, Mr Boswell. All that's left of those that helped keep us alive from Sydney Cove to Coupang.'

The sad dark-brown eyes filled with tears and he swallowed hard.

'Oh, Mary Broad. *Dear* Mary Broad. This is the best present anyone has ever given me.'

CHAPTER 74

St Fimbarrus's! There it was, outlined against the hillside trees: the tower of the dear old parish church, overlooking those tiny grey stone houses huddled at the waterside. There it was, waiting for the fishergirl as it had always done, those countless occasions she'd been out here in the harbour with the returning fishing boats. The trees had lost many of their leaves and it was a time of year in Cornwall that had always filled her with foreboding. There were low black clouds over those trees and it would surely rain at any moment.

The sou'wester was doing its devil best to get her home quickly, and the closer the Town Quay, the tighter the knot in her stomach. Lord, by the look of things, every one of Fowey's one thousand inhabitants was either on or around the quay! But it was still too far away to make out her little old father.

As the *Ann and Elizabeth* drew near, the bells rang round this beautiful, hill-flanked harbour to welcome 'The Girl from Botany Bay'. She remembered so well the set of ringers' rules which the bellringers had once shown her, up there inside that tall, square, bluish-grey, four-pointed tower. Painted on a board hanging there was a picture of the ringers themselves, beneath which were the rules, called 'Ringer's Rhyme', which those sturdy Cornish fellows had recited to her.

Hark how the Chirping Treble sings most clear
And Covering Tom comes rolling in the rear.
We ring the Quick to Church, the Dead to Grave...

And Mary Broad back from the Grave!

The ringing was a signal for the crowd to cheer wildly and a small dog to leap into the dark-grey whitecaps and start swimming against wind and tide towards the ship. Could it be–?

'Pincher!' she shrieked. 'Aw, my Pincher! You *ain't* forgotten me! You *ain't* forgotten your mistress, my lovely boy! Aw, just look at you swimming, just look at you.'

Avast! This devilish sou'wester was driving the *Ann and Elizabeth* too fast, far too fast. It was sweeping the ship towards the little dog; already she was nearly upon him!

'Aw, no! Not after all this time. Don't let her kill my Pincher! don't let her kill my little ol' dog!'

He'd vanished.

Frantically she stretched over the larboard rail…

Nothing.

She hurtled to the starboard…

Nothing.

She slumped to the salty deck. The hard, uncaring deck.

'Not Pincher, too! O Lord, how much more must I take?'

She closed her eyes.

CHAPTER 75

The next thing she knew was that the vessel was bumping the quay and the gangplank was out. But Mary Broad couldn't move. How long she had lain thus, she didn't know. Blurred faces peering down at her. Distant voices mumbling meaningless words. The front of her green woollen frock wet. Chin, too.

Rain? No, 'Pincher!' Her darling dog was wriggling in her arms and licking the tears from her face. If 'The Girl from Botany Bay' had had any doubts about whether she'd been right to return, they'd been washed away by this deliriously happy little terrier. What better homecoming could any mortal have?

'Aw, my beauty! Pincher, my beauty! Aw, just to look into your lovely brown eyes…'

The quicker he licked the tears, the more they flowed.

Somebody else was all over her now and was struggling to sit her up.

'Mary, my darlin' daughter. Hi, wake up! Wake up! Aw, my sweet'art.' His voice broke. 'Aw, my darlin' gal, you've come back to your old father.'

'Aw, Father,' she choked, 'I love you. I love you so very, very much. Forgive me for bringing so much misery to the evening of your life. I should never have suggested to Catherine Prior and Mary Shepherd that we should sport upon poor ol' Miss Lakeman, for *she* loves pretty pink roses, too. 'Twas all my fault that I landed at the stinking bottom of the world.'

Furiously he wiped the tears from his own grey eyes.

''Twere no fault o' yourn, Mary Broad. 'Twere the system of justice in this dang country. 'Tis a system of *in*justice for poor fisherfolk like us.

'You've aged, daughter,' he sighed, pulling her to her shaky feet, while she cradled Pincher. 'Lord save us, you've aged a mighty deal.

But 'tis no wonder, after all you've been through, you poor suffering child. Still, there's more flesh on you; that's something.'

'Mr Boswell's good food did that, Father,' she said, sniffing violently. But the tears kept coming. She studied him closely and her heart missed a beat. *Lord, how old he is! Like a skellinton!* 'How – how have *you* been keeping?'

'Aw, mustn't grumble. Pretty good for an old'un,' he grinned, showing his black, broken teeth. 'I'll be a dang sight betterer now, I'm telling you, now that my sunny gal's home.

'Mary… Mr Castel told you about the money that might be left to me, didn't he? Folk tell me that that means I could be getting *sixty thousand pound*, or even more! There's still what they call "legal problems" to sort out, but if all goes well, then we'll be rich, daughter!'

'I'll believe it when it happens, Father,' she murmured, squeezing his cold, shaking hands. 'At the moment, I've got all the riches I need right here in my arms: you and Pincher. Well, almost all…'

'Yes, 'tis a pity Dolly couldn't share this moment.'

'Yes, Dolly, of course; and – and… I – I… There's someone I'm mighty fond of, who's still in Newgate Gaol. J-Jimmy Martin. He was very good to me and my poor darlings. Very good indeed.'

CHAPTER 76

'Merry Christmas, Father,' sighed Mary, forcing a smile, as they and Pincher sat on the rush mat and gazed into the turf fire.

'Dang me, daughter! At least say it like you mean it!'

'I can't help myself. Of course I'm pleased to be home with you; there was a time when I thought I'd never *see* another Christmas Eve.'

'Well then. *I'm* sad, too, that our Dolly's still slaving her poor little insides out at Mr Morgan's at Christmas. But at least we've been given this beautiful saffern cake this evening by Mrs Austen at Place. And we've just swallowed these lovely pasties and rabbit pie that you made yourself, bless you. 'Tis a dang sight betterer than that Christmas Eve when we were starving and had to go a-sheep-stealin', ain't it?'

'Of course it is, and I thank the good Lord for it.'

'Well then, gal.'

'Well, Father, 'tis mortal sad I feel because Mother ain't here, nor my little Emanuel; nor poor Charlotte, who I'd told so much about Lord Jesus's birthday,' she choked.

'And,' she said, 'I thought Jimmy would have come to see me. 'Twas more than a month ago when Mr Boswell wrote to me, saying as how he'd at last got my dear friends out of Newgate and that they'd called at his house to thank him. But I ain't had no word from Jimmy at all. Aw, Jimmy Martin, you with eyes of forget-me-not blue, have you forgotten *me*?

'Dear life!' she cried, 'd'you think he's *dead*, Father? Being as how it's such cold weather and he's so skinny and he's suffered so much?'

The old man patted her arm, which was covered by the plaid shawl that James Boswell had given her in London. This lovely and warm green woollen frock was another reminder of his kindness.

'Only the Almighty knows, gal. But I tell you: *I* thought for a brave long time that *you* were, didn't I? And *my* prayers were answered in the Lord's good time, weren't they?'

Fighting back the tears, she fondled Pincher's ears.

'Aw, I do hope you're right. I do hope so.'

''Tas been heavy seas for days, Mary; no skipper in his right mind would have ventured from port. And as there's been snowstorms for near a week, the wagons can't get to and from London neither… 'Tain't often we get snow at all in Cornwall, leave alone plaguy blizzards! Oh, 'tis a foul night out there tonight. Just hark at that howling wind!'

She bit her lip. 'Aw, Father, wouldn't it be terrible if, after sailing round the world and surviving, he drownded in the four hundred mile of water from London to Fowey?'

'Dang me, gal, you've certainly got the mullygrubs these days. You've turned into a proper ol' fretter. You used to be so easy-going.'

'I've never been in love before, Father.'

He put another tab on the fire, then his tired eyes peered at hers in the resulting glow.

'Gor, you *do* love him, don't you, Mary Broad?'

'I *do*, Father,' she sobbed. 'I *do*! Aw, I miss him so very much!'

'Quiet, Pincher!' he shouted, for the terrier was barking madly. 'Quiet! That's only snow falling off the roof. There's no one stupid enough to be out there on a night like this.'

The door flew open and a shower of snow was blown into the turf fire, causing a sizzling – like Father's spit did.

'Stupid, ye call me, Mr Broad?' laughed the snow-covered wretch, slamming the door behind him.

'Jimmy!' Rot the snow, Mary Broad didn't care. Flinging her arms round him, she kissed his frozen lips, melting them with her own fire of desire.

'Jeez, get this fanged fiend away from me ankles, woman! Me shackle wounds are healing grand, I don't want them opened agin. And don't let him tear these sheets of paper in me bag. They were written by me and the three lads while we were in Newgate and are entitled: *Memorandums by James Martin.* I want our great-great-great-great-great-grandchilder to read them one day so they'll know all about The Girl from Botany Bay: The Convict Girl.'

HISTORICAL NOTES

* Jimmy Martin's *Memorandums* did escape Pincher's teeth and are among the Jeremy Bentham Papers, at University College, London.
* Will Bryant had left his *Journal* with Wanjon who showed it to Captain Bligh on his return to Coupang in October 1792. Bligh managed to have part of it copied but the original seems to have gone for ever. Most of the Coupang archive was used by the British during the occupation of Timor, 1811-17, for making cartridges.
* Peter Heywood was sentenced to be hanged for mutiny. With only five days to go he received a royal pardon, thanks to his sister Nessy's efforts.
* Four of the Rose Hill escapers were recaptured, naked and wretched, in 1795, just a hundred miles up the coast from Port Jackson. The fifth man had died.
* John Butcher finally had his wish and returned, in 1795, but as a private in the New South Wales Corps. He was granted twenty-five acres.
* Sarah Young had moved in with a marine lieutenant and returned to England at the end of her sentence. She had probably paid for the passage with money left her by the officer when his tour of duty ended.
* James Boswell died in 1795, by which time he was paying Mary the full sum himself. Whether the payments continued posthumously is not known. The Boswell Papers, at Yale University, contain a letter that he wrote from his Ayrshire estate on 13 October 1794, to his brother David, which included this request: 'Be as good as to... put into the banking shop of Mr Devaynes & Co. five pounds from me to the account of the Rev.

Mr Baron at Lestwithiel [sic], Cornwall, and write to him that you have done so. He takes charge of paying the gratuity to Mary Broad.' The payment was acknowledged on 1 November 1794 by the Revd John Baron and marked 'M.B.'.

* Mary Broad disappears from history after this. It has been impossible to determine whether she received a share of any legacy, or to trace a record of any remarriage, or of her burial. A Mary Bryant did marry a Richard Thomas in St Breage parish, Cornwall, on 13 October 1807. They were destined to have two children, Mary Ann and Richard. If that was our Mary, she had given birth at the ages of 42 and 44. However, there is no evidence that the two Marys were the same person.
* 'The best present anyone has ever given me' has survived. In 1956, Yale University Library presented ten of the brittle brown leaves to the Mitchell Library, Sydney, New South Wales.

I have used author's licence both to clear the mist surrounding the circumstances of Charlotte's conception and to develop relationships between Mary and Jimmy and between Jane Langley and James Cox. James did leave that note for Sarah Young.

Cover Design: The Digital Canvas Company
Forres
Scotland
bookcovers@digican.co.uk

Layout: Stephen M.L. Young
latouveilhe@mac.com

Font: Adobe Garamond (11pt)

Copies of this book can be ordered via the Internet:

www.librario.com

or from:

Librario Publishing Ltd
Brough House
Milton Brodie
Kinloss
Moray IV36 2UA
Tel /Fax No 01343 850 617